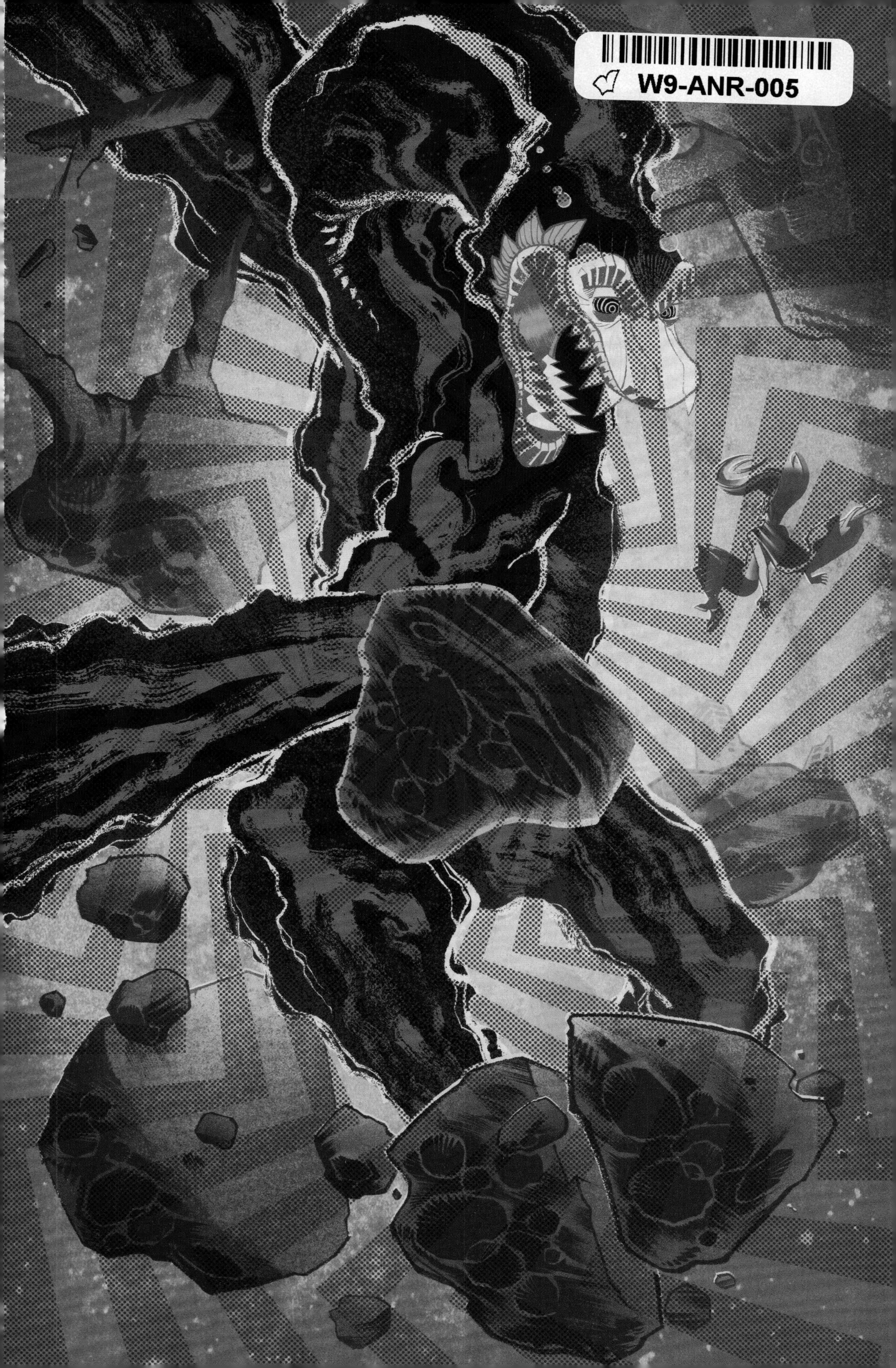

WANDA MAXIMOFF is building a new life for herself. In a desire to atone for her past wrongs, she's using her abilities to help people by solving magical crimes.

But Wanda has discovered something: WITCHCRAFT is broken. Now, the SCARLET WITCH is on a mission to find the source of the ailment and fix it.

Recently, Wanda encountered a woman along the WITCHES' ROAD who also called herself the Scarlet Witch. It turns out that this woman, NATALYA MAXIMOFF, was Wanda's biological mother.

Now, Wanda seeks more answers.

Scarlet Witch

The Final Hex

James Robinson
writer

Leila Del Duca (#11), **Annapaola Martello** (#12), **Jonathan Marks-Barravecchia** (#13), **Shawn Crystal** (#14) & **Vanesa Del Rey** (#15)
artists

Felipe Sobreiro (#11), **Matt Yackey** (#12), **Rachelle Rosenberg** (#13), **Chris Brunner** (#14) & **Jordie Bellaire** (#15)
color artists

VC's Cory Petit
letterer

David Aja
cover artist

Emily Shaw & Christina Harrington
editor

Mark Paniccia
senior editor

Scarlet Witch created by Stan Lee & Jack Kirby

Jennifer Grünwald
collection editor

Caitlin O'Connell
assistant editor

Kateri Woody
associate managing editor

Mark D. Beazley
editor, special projects

Jeff Youngquist
vp production & special projects

David Gabriel
svp print, sales & marketing

Adam Del Re
book designer

Axel Alonso
editor in chief

Joe Quesada
chief creative officer

Dan Buckley
president

Alan Fine
executive producer

SCARLET WITCH VOL. 3: THE FINAL HEX. Contains material originally published in magazine form as SCARLET WITCH #11-15. First printing 2017. ISBN# 978-1-302-90266-7. Published by MARVEL WORLDWIDE, INC., a subsidiary of MARVEL ENTERTAINMENT, LLC. OFFICE OF PUBLICATION: 135 West 50th Street, New York, NY 10020.

Printed in Canada. DAN BUCKLEY, President, Marvel Entertainment; JOE QUESADA, Chief Creative Officer; TOM BREVOORT, SVP of Publishing; DAVID BOGART, SVP of Business Affairs & Operations, Publishing & Partnership; C.B. CEBULSKI, VP of Brand Management & Development, Asia; DAVID GABRIEL, SVP of Sales & Marketing, Publishing; JEFF YOUNGQUIST, VP of Production & Special Projects; DAN CARR, Executive Director of Publishing Technology; ALEX MORALES, Director of Publishing Operations; SUSAN CRESPI, Production Manager; STAN LEE, Chairman Emeritus. For information regarding advertising in Marvel Comics or on Marvel.com, please contact Vit DeBellis, Integrated Sales Manager, at vdebellis@marvel.com. For Marvel subscription inquiries, please call 888-511-5480. **Manufactured between 2/24/2017 and 3/28/2017 by SOLISCO PRINTERS, SCOTT, QC, CANADA.**

10 9 8 7 6 5 4 3 2 1

Scarlet Witch

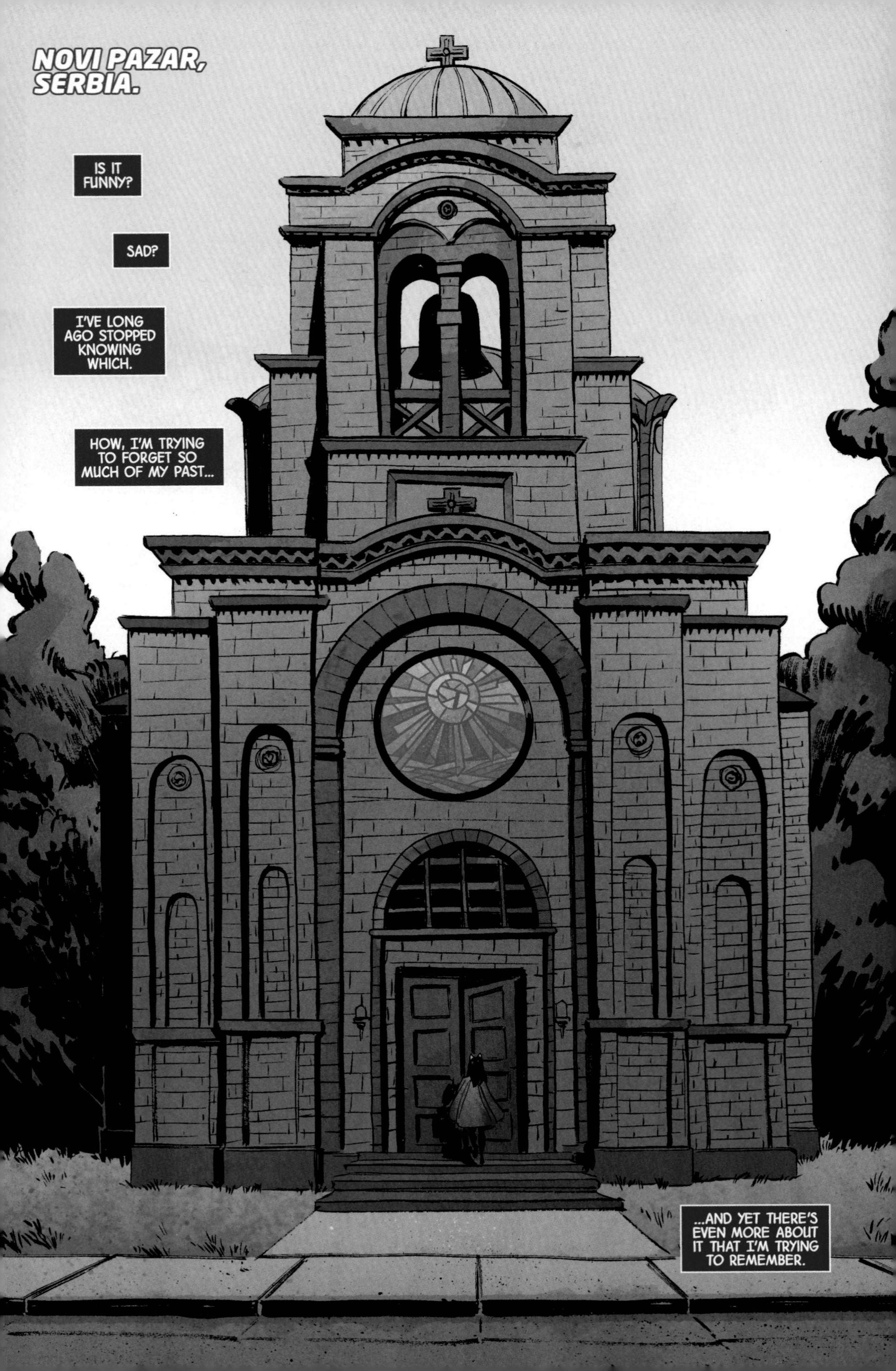
NOVI PAZAR, SERBIA.
IS IT FUNNY?
SAD?
I'VE LONG AGO STOPPED KNOWING WHICH.
HOW, I'M TRYING TO FORGET SO MUCH OF MY PAST...
...AND YET THERE'S EVEN MORE ABOUT IT THAT I'M TRYING TO REMEMBER.

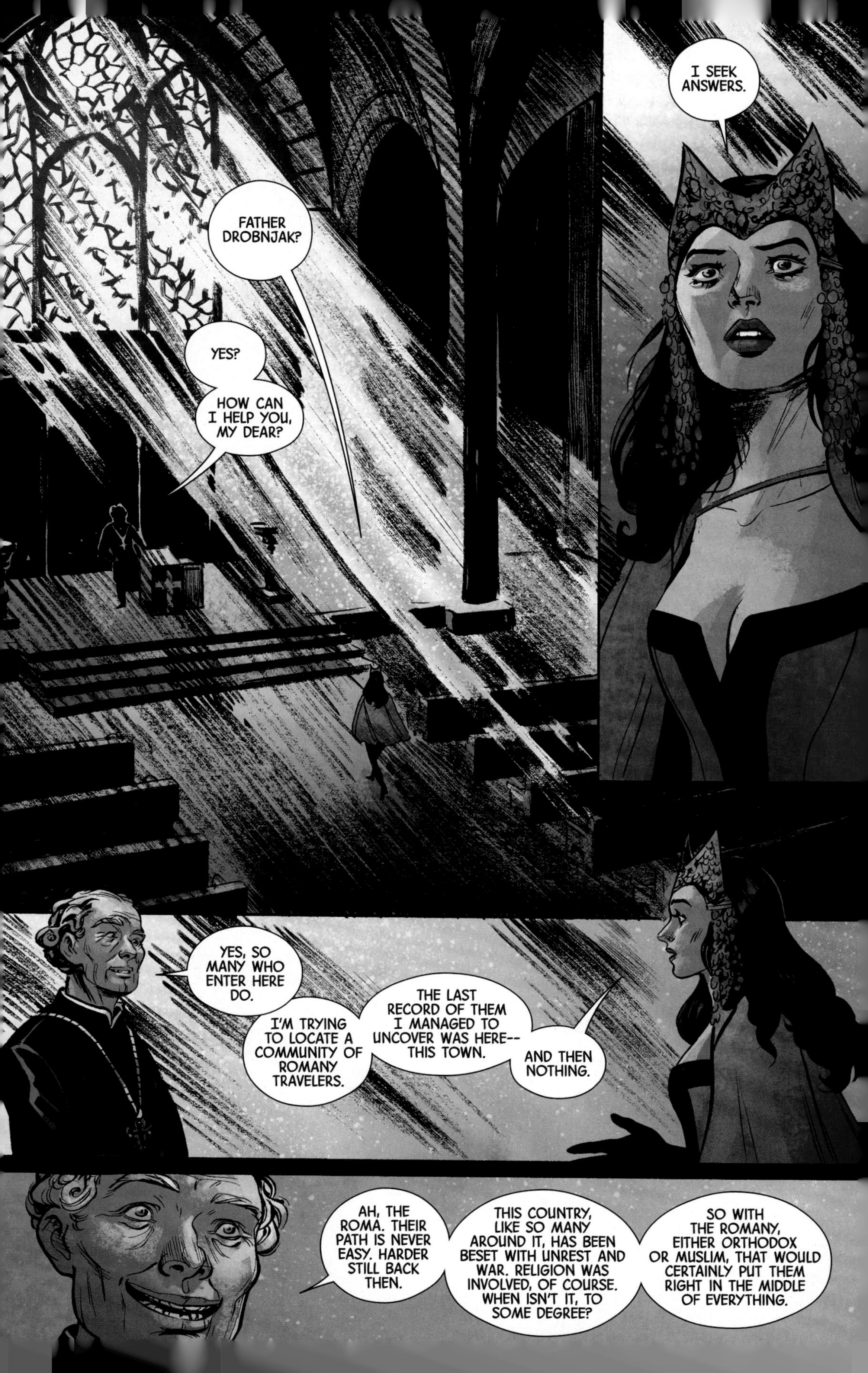
FATHER DROBNJAK?
YES?
HOW CAN I HELP YOU, MY DEAR?
I SEEK ANSWERS.
YES, SO MANY WHO ENTER HERE DO.
I'M TRYING TO LOCATE A COMMUNITY OF ROMANY TRAVELERS.
THE LAST RECORD OF THEM I MANAGED TO UNCOVER WAS HERE-- THIS TOWN.
AND THEN NOTHING.
AH, THE ROMA. THEIR PATH IS NEVER EASY. HARDER STILL BACK THEN.
THIS COUNTRY, LIKE SO MANY AROUND IT, HAS BEEN BESET WITH UNREST AND WAR. RELIGION WAS INVOLVED, OF COURSE. WHEN ISN'T IT, TO SOME DEGREE?
SO WITH THE ROMANY, EITHER ORTHODOX OR MUSLIM, THAT WOULD CERTAINLY PUT THEM RIGHT IN THE MIDDLE OF EVERYTHING.

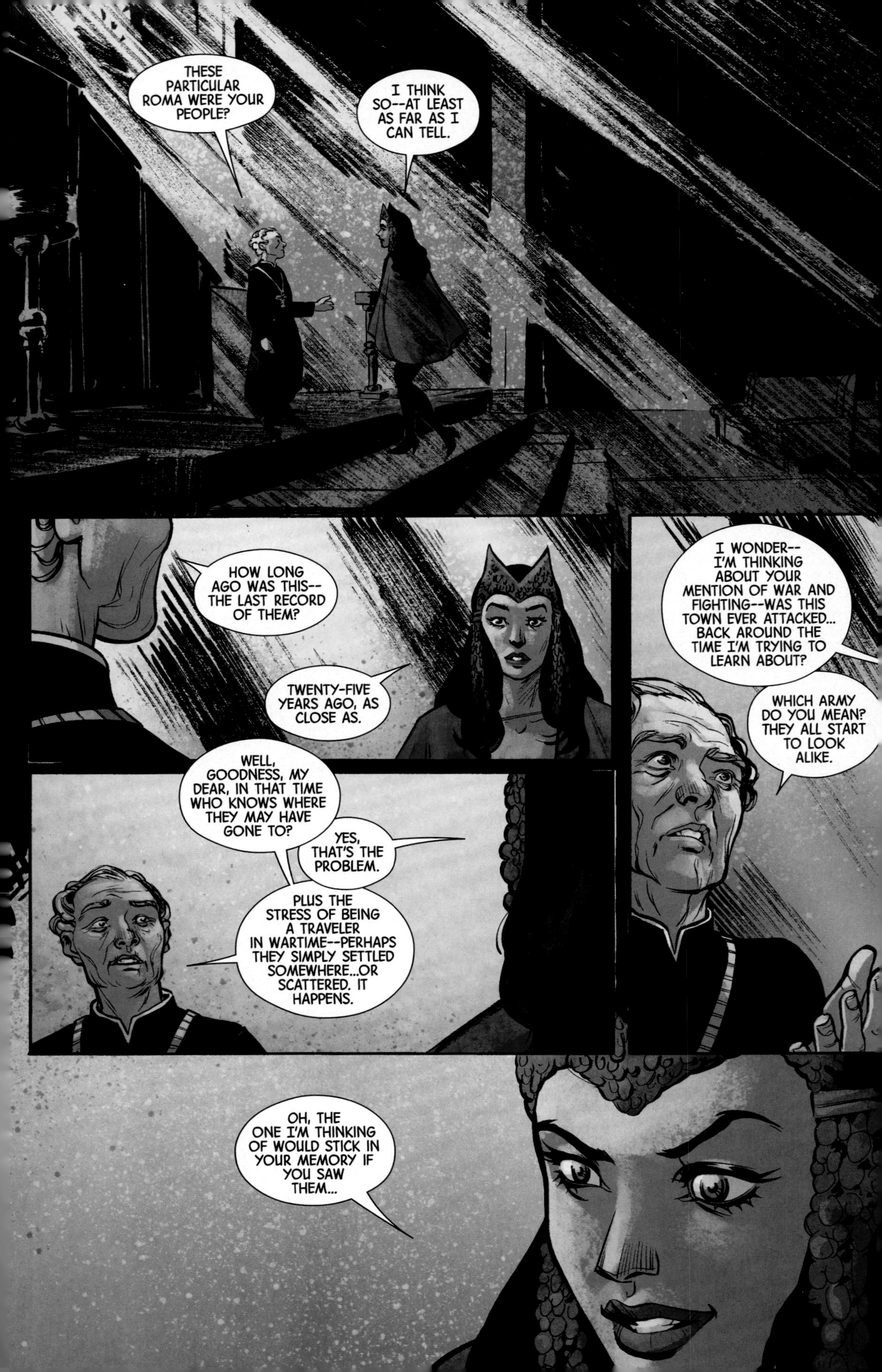
THESE PARTICULAR ROMA WERE YOUR PEOPLE?
I THINK SO--AT LEAST AS FAR AS I CAN TELL.
HOW LONG AGO WAS THIS--THE LAST RECORD OF THEM?
TWENTY-FIVE YEARS AGO, AS CLOSE AS.
I WONDER--I'M THINKING ABOUT YOUR MENTION OF WAR AND FIGHTING--WAS THIS TOWN EVER ATTACKED... BACK AROUND THE TIME I'M TRYING TO LEARN ABOUT?
WHICH ARMY DO YOU MEAN? THEY ALL START TO LOOK ALIKE.
WELL, GOODNESS, MY DEAR, IN THAT TIME WHO KNOWS WHERE THEY MAY HAVE GONE TO?
YES, THAT'S THE PROBLEM.
PLUS THE STRESS OF BEING A TRAVELER IN WARTIME--PERHAPS THEY SIMPLY SETTLED SOMEWHERE...OR SCATTERED. IT HAPPENS.
OH, THE ONE I'M THINKING OF WOULD STICK IN YOUR MEMORY IF YOU SAW THEM...

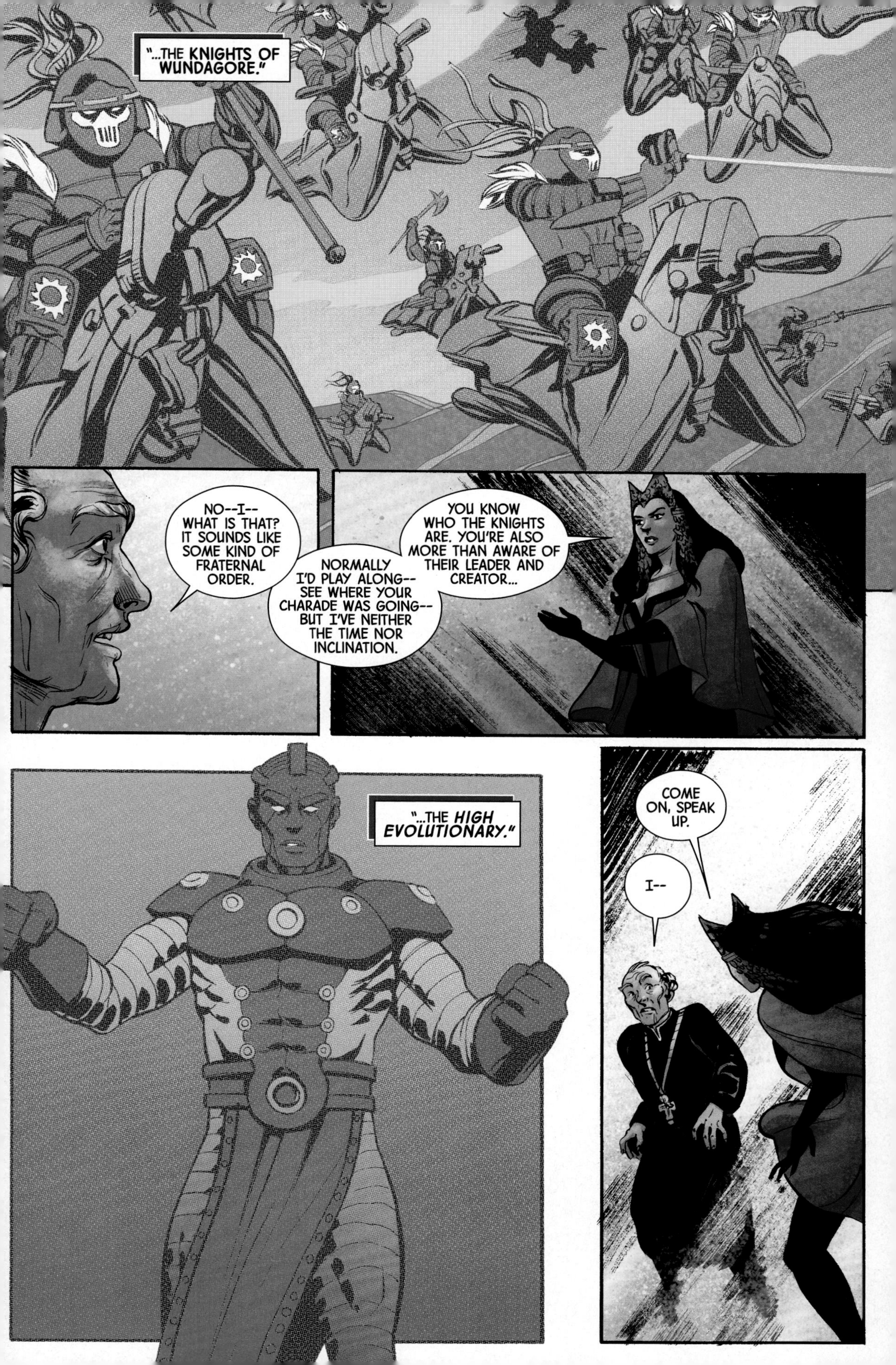
"...THE KNIGHTS OF WUNDAGORE."
NO--I-- WHAT IS THAT? IT SOUNDS LIKE SOME KIND OF FRATERNAL ORDER.
NORMALLY I'D PLAY ALONG-- SEE WHERE YOUR CHARADE WAS GOING-- BUT I'VE NEITHER THE TIME NOR INCLINATION.
YOU KNOW WHO THE KNIGHTS ARE. YOU'RE ALSO MORE THAN AWARE OF THEIR LEADER AND CREATOR...
"...THE HIGH EVOLUTIONARY."
COME ON, SPEAK UP.
I--

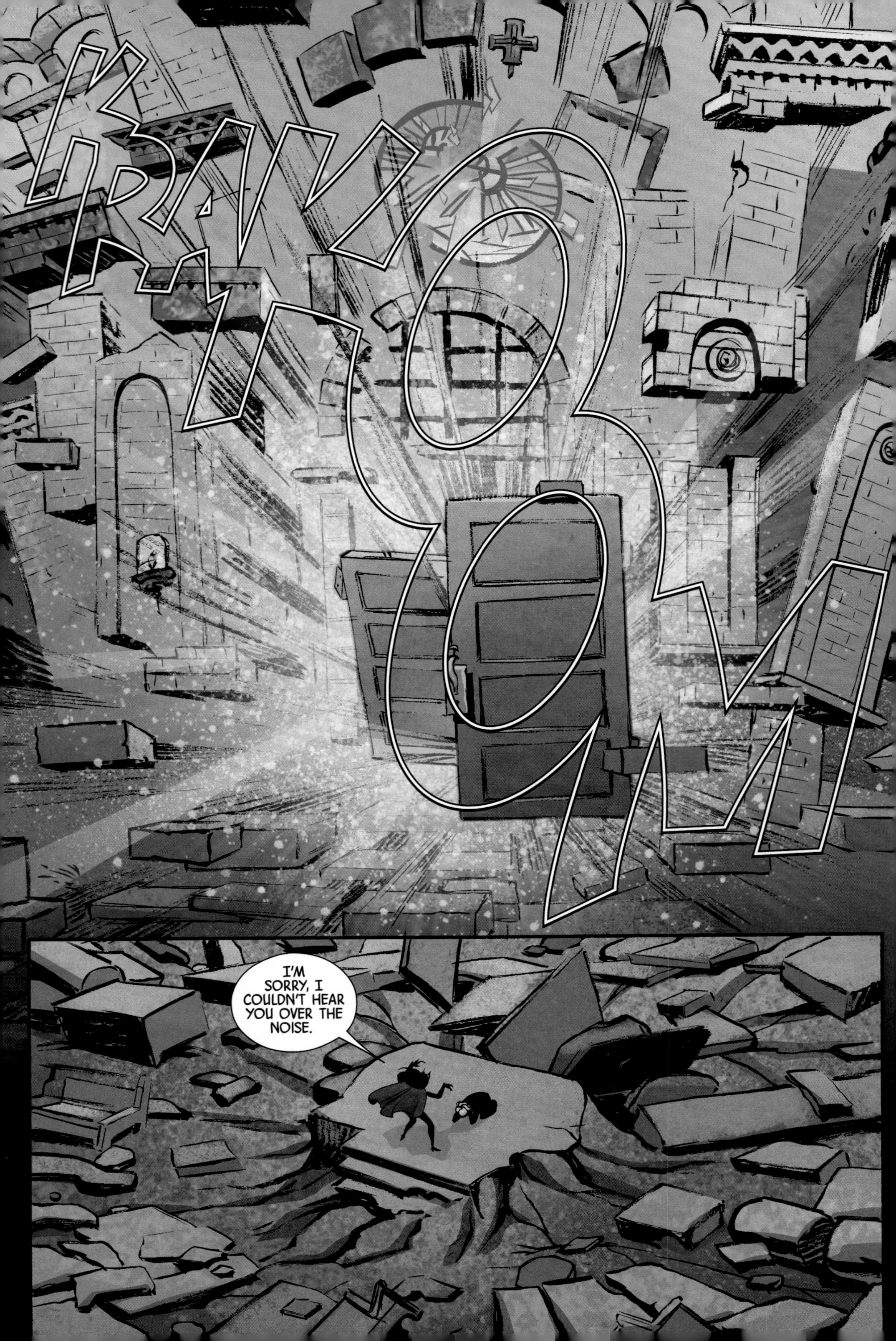
I'M SORRY, I COULDN'T HEAR YOU OVER THE NOISE.

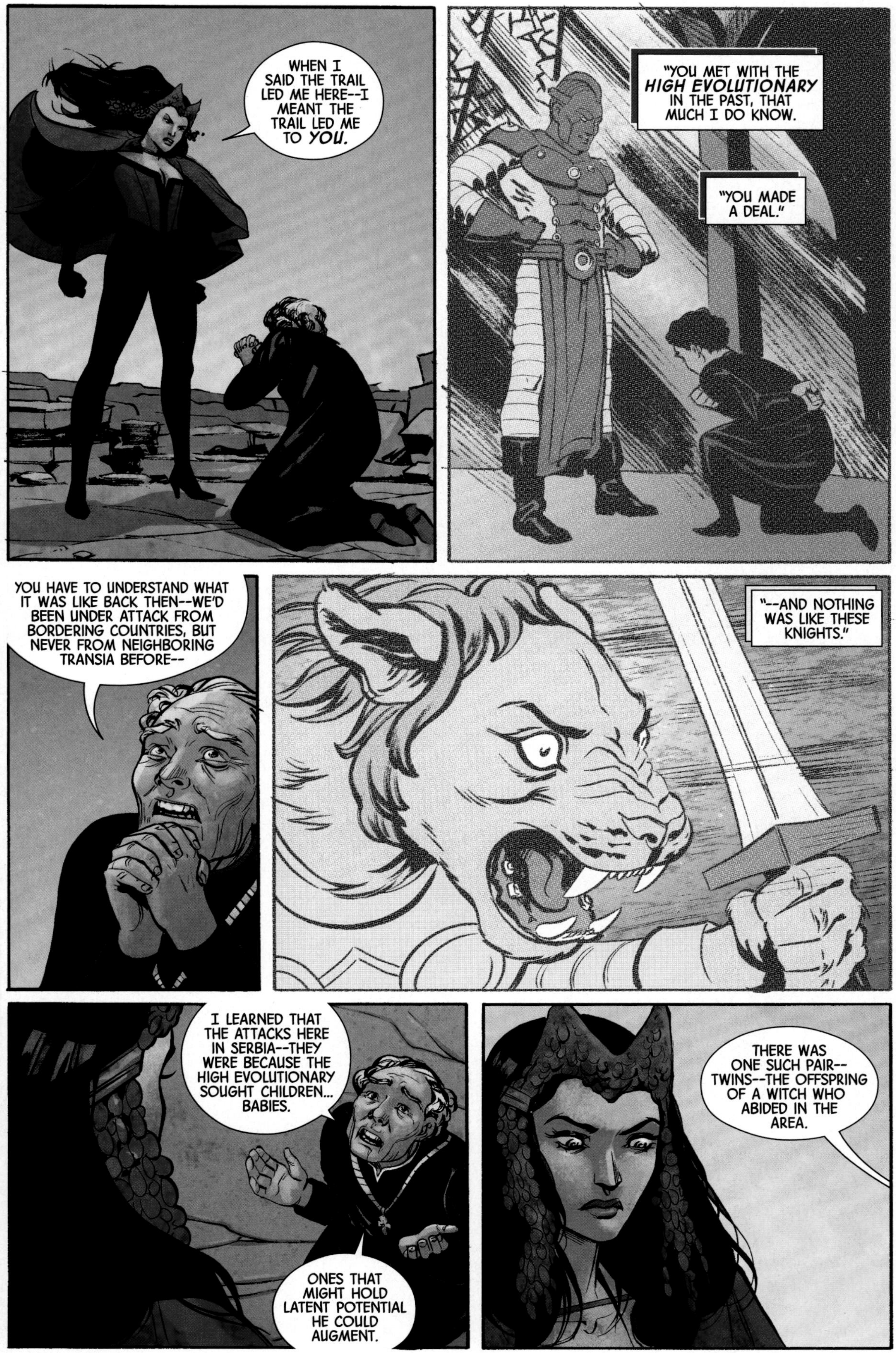
WHEN I SAID THE TRAIL LED ME HERE--I MEANT THE TRAIL LED ME TO YOU.
"YOU MET WITH THE HIGH EVOLUTIONARY IN THE PAST, THAT MUCH I DO KNOW.
"YOU MADE A DEAL."
YOU HAVE TO UNDERSTAND WHAT IT WAS LIKE BACK THEN--WE'D BEEN UNDER ATTACK FROM BORDERING COUNTRIES, BUT NEVER FROM NEIGHBORING TRANSIA BEFORE--
"--AND NOTHING WAS LIKE THESE KNIGHTS."
I LEARNED THAT THE ATTACKS HERE IN SERBIA--THEY WERE BECAUSE THE HIGH EVOLUTIONARY SOUGHT CHILDREN... BABIES.
ONES THAT MIGHT HOLD LATENT POTENTIAL HE COULD AUGMENT.
THERE WAS ONE SUCH PAIR--TWINS--THE OFFSPRING OF A WITCH WHO ABIDED IN THE AREA.

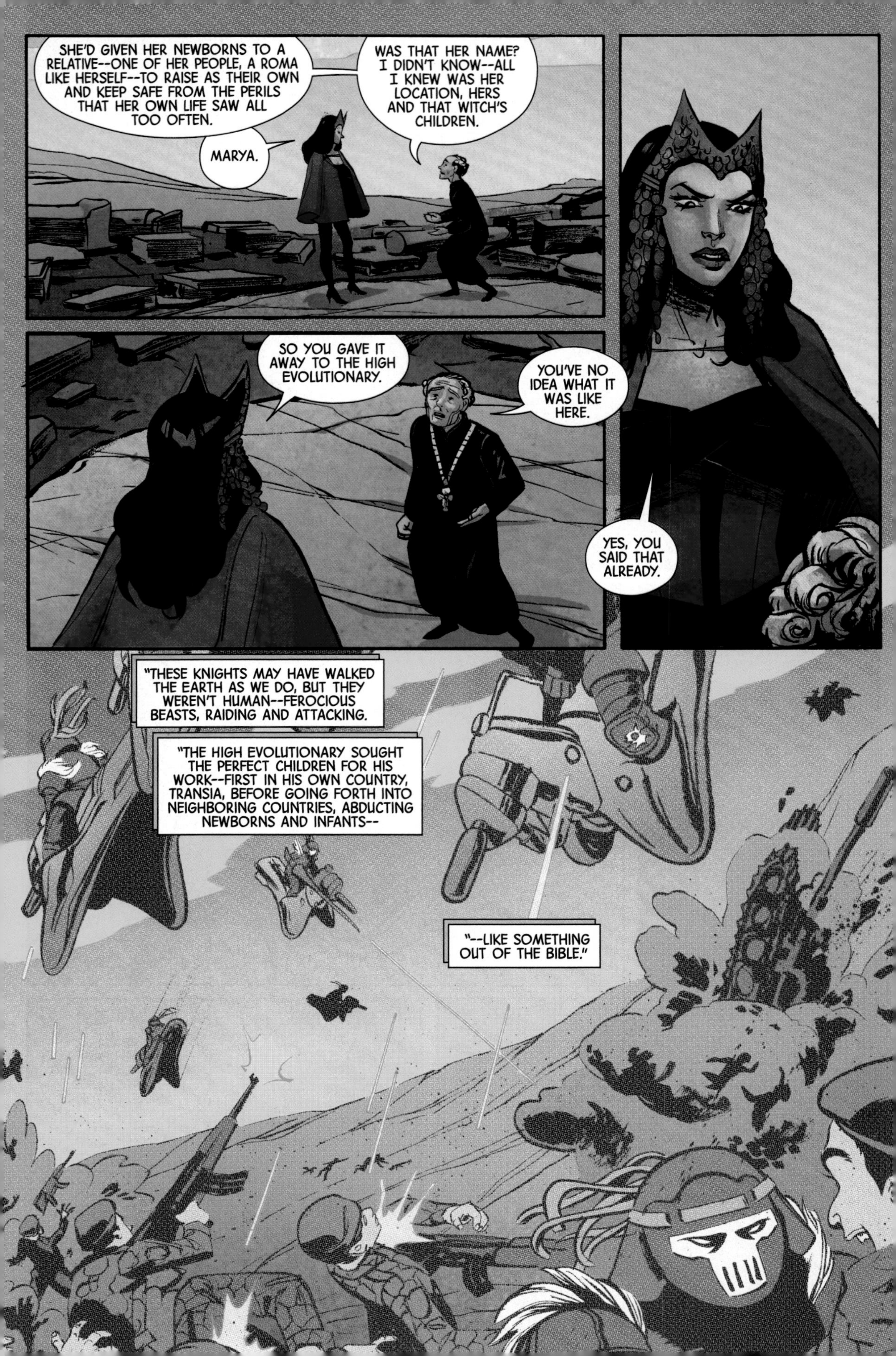
SHE'D GIVEN HER NEWBORNS TO A RELATIVE--ONE OF HER PEOPLE, A ROMA LIKE HERSELF--TO RAISE AS THEIR OWN AND KEEP SAFE FROM THE PERILS THAT HER OWN LIFE SAW ALL TOO OFTEN.
MARYA.
WAS THAT HER NAME? I DIDN'T KNOW--ALL I KNEW WAS HER LOCATION, HERS AND THAT WITCH'S CHILDREN.
SO YOU GAVE IT AWAY TO THE HIGH EVOLUTIONARY.
YOU'VE NO IDEA WHAT IT WAS LIKE HERE.
YES, YOU SAID THAT ALREADY.
"THESE KNIGHTS MAY HAVE WALKED THE EARTH AS WE DO, BUT THEY WEREN'T HUMAN--FEROCIOUS BEASTS, RAIDING AND ATTACKING.
"THE HIGH EVOLUTIONARY SOUGHT THE PERFECT CHILDREN FOR HIS WORK--FIRST IN HIS OWN COUNTRY, TRANSIA, BEFORE GOING FORTH INTO NEIGHBORING COUNTRIES, ABDUCTING NEWBORNS AND INFANTS--
"--LIKE SOMETHING OUT OF THE BIBLE."

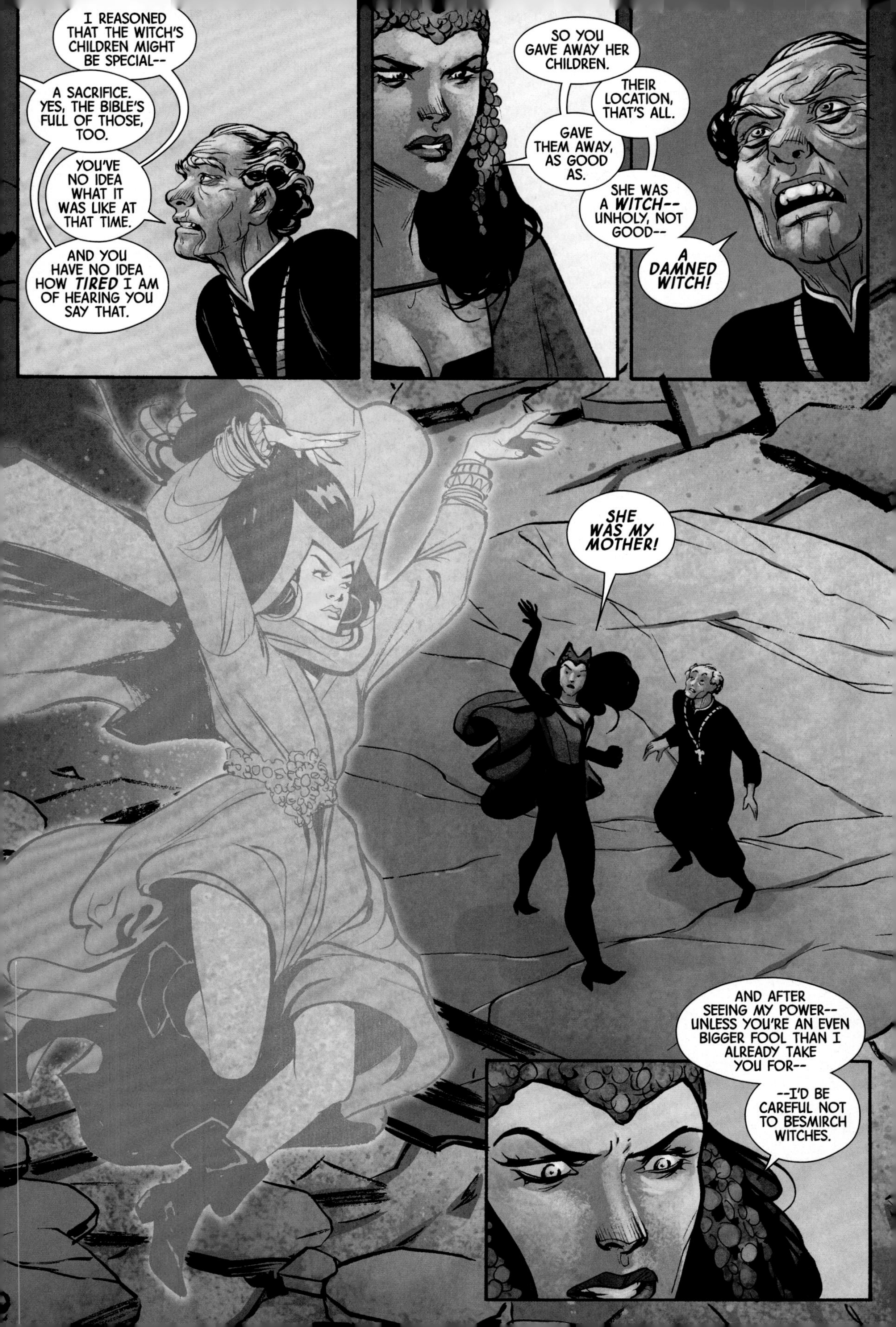
I REASONED THAT THE WITCH'S CHILDREN MIGHT BE SPECIAL--
A SACRIFICE. YES, THE BIBLE'S FULL OF THOSE, TOO.
YOU'VE NO IDEA WHAT IT WAS LIKE AT THAT TIME.
AND YOU HAVE NO IDEA HOW *TIRED* I AM OF HEARING YOU SAY THAT.
SO YOU GAVE AWAY HER CHILDREN.
THEIR LOCATION, THAT'S ALL.
GAVE THEM AWAY, AS GOOD AS.
SHE WAS A *WITCH*-- UNHOLY, NOT GOOD--
A DAMNED WITCH!
SHE WAS MY MOTHER!
AND AFTER SEEING MY POWER-- UNLESS YOU'RE AN EVEN BIGGER FOOL THAN I ALREADY TAKE YOU FOR--
--I'D BE CAREFUL NOT TO BESMIRCH WITCHES.

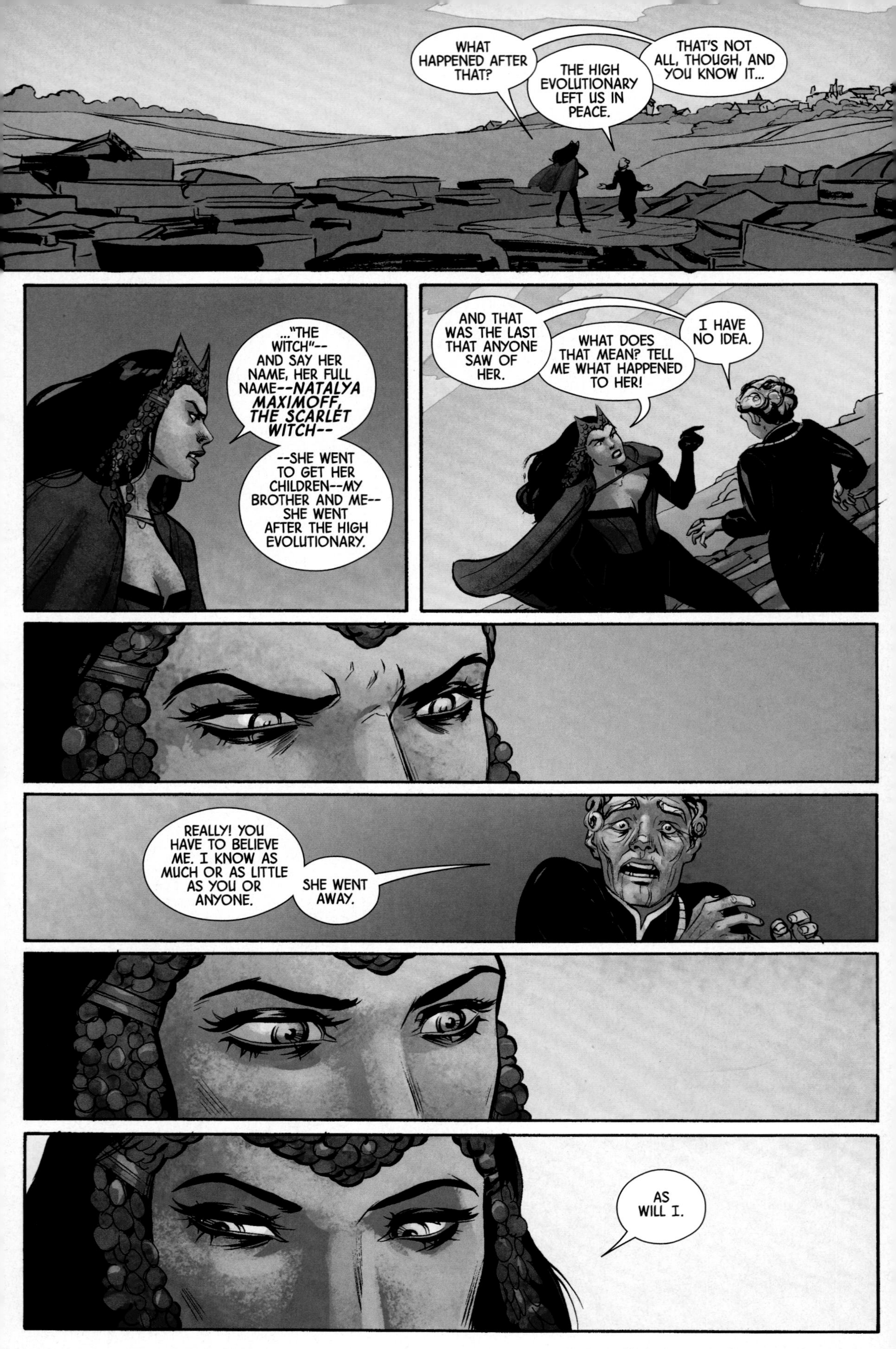
WHAT HAPPENED AFTER THAT?
THE HIGH EVOLUTIONARY LEFT US IN PEACE.
THAT'S NOT ALL, THOUGH, AND YOU KNOW IT...
..."THE WITCH"-- AND SAY HER NAME, HER FULL NAME--*NATALYA MAXIMOFF, THE SCARLET WITCH*--
--SHE WENT TO GET HER CHILDREN--MY BROTHER AND ME--SHE WENT AFTER THE HIGH EVOLUTIONARY.
AND THAT WAS THE LAST THAT ANYONE SAW OF HER.
WHAT DOES THAT MEAN? TELL ME WHAT HAPPENED TO HER!
I HAVE NO IDEA.
REALLY! YOU HAVE TO BELIEVE ME. I KNOW AS MUCH OR AS LITTLE AS YOU OR ANYONE.
SHE WENT AWAY.
AS WILL I.

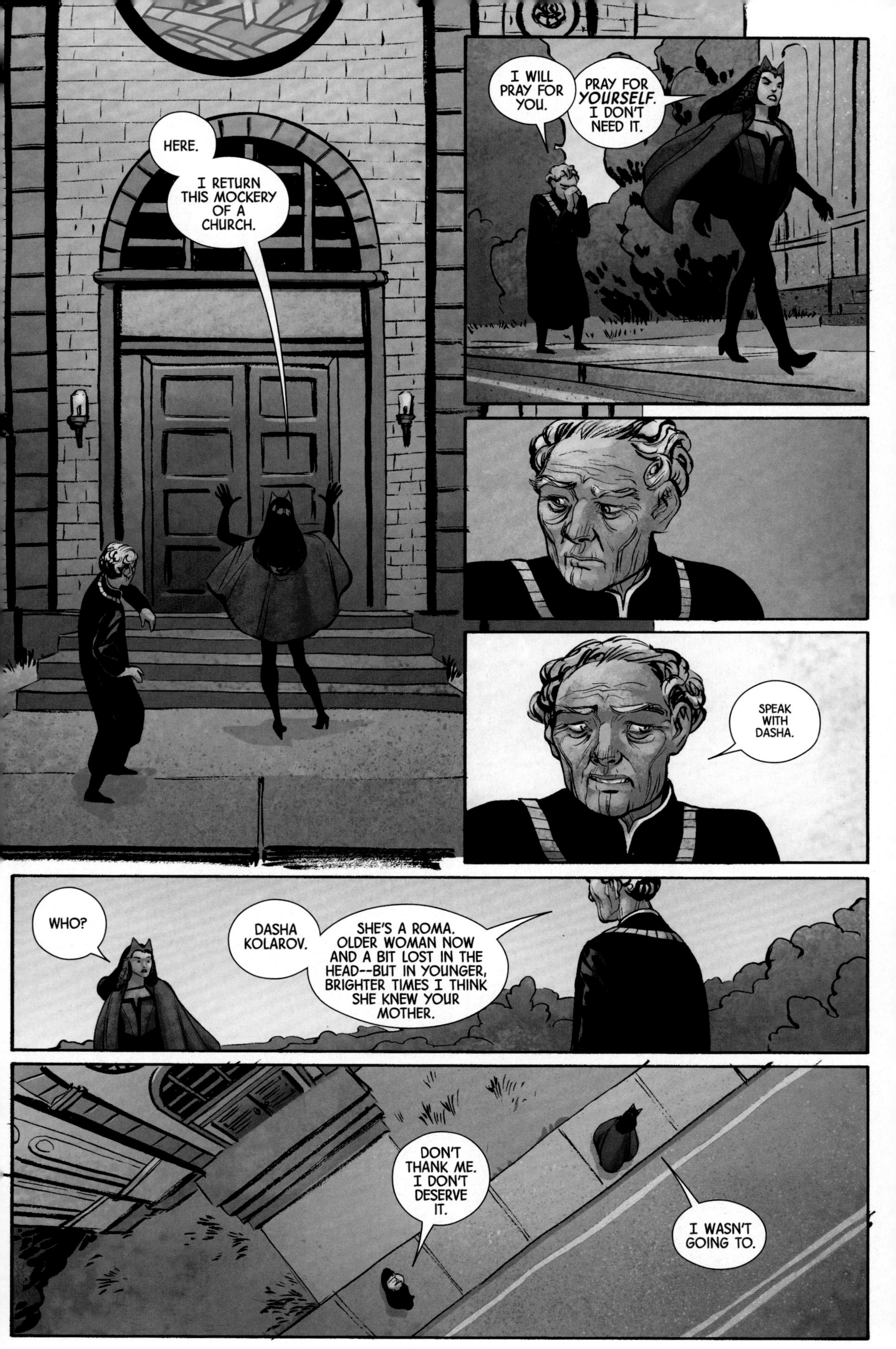
HERE.
I RETURN THIS MOCKERY OF A CHURCH.
I WILL PRAY FOR YOU.
PRAY FOR *YOURSELF*. I DON'T NEED IT.
SPEAK WITH DASHA.
WHO?
DASHA KOLAROV.
SHE'S A ROMA. OLDER WOMAN NOW AND A BIT LOST IN THE HEAD--BUT IN YOUNGER, BRIGHTER TIMES I THINK SHE KNEW YOUR MOTHER.
DON'T THANK ME. I DON'T DESERVE IT.
I WASN'T GOING TO.

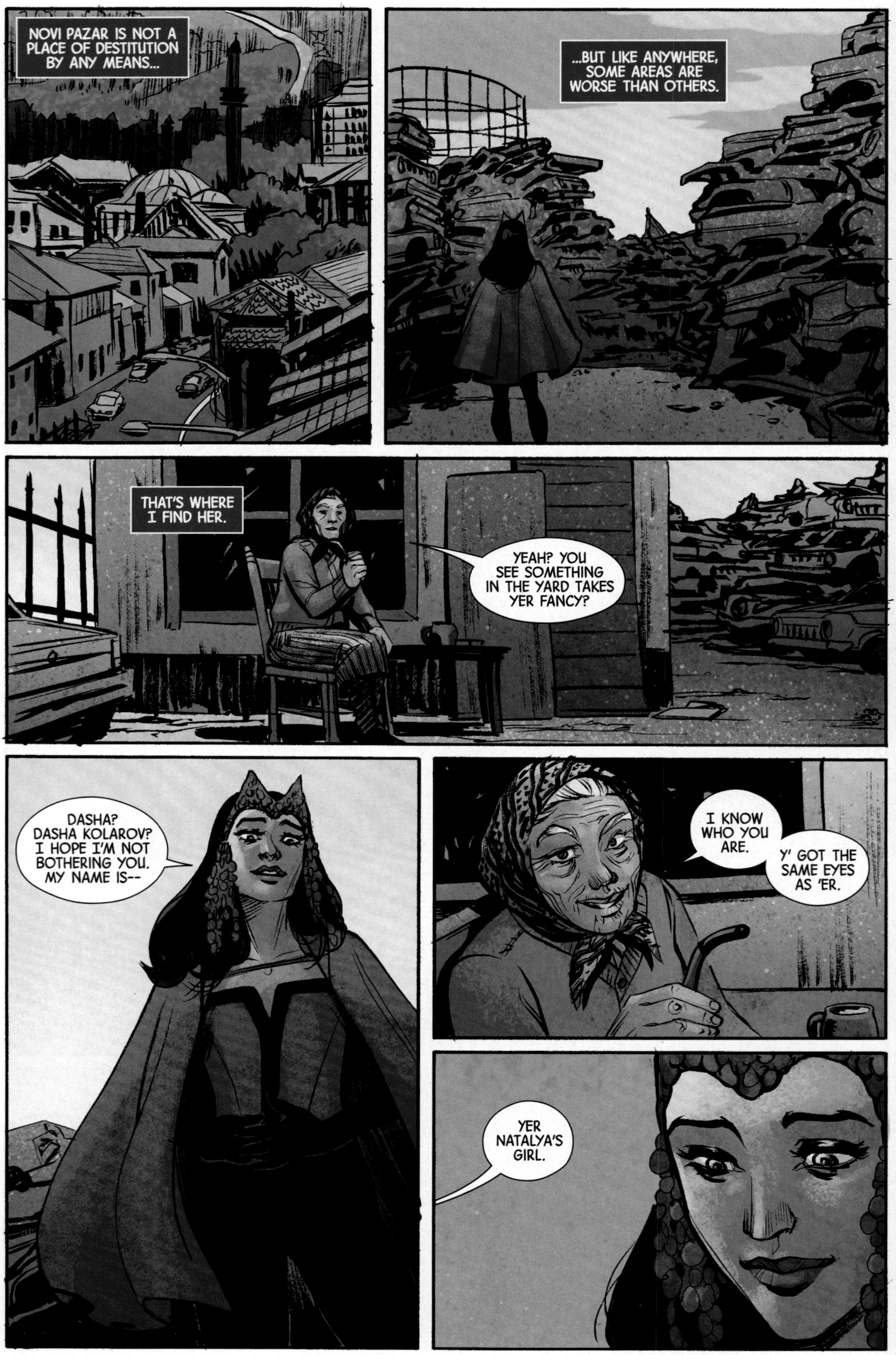
NOVI PAZAR IS NOT A PLACE OF DESTITUTION BY ANY MEANS...
...BUT LIKE ANYWHERE, SOME AREAS ARE WORSE THAN OTHERS.
THAT'S WHERE I FIND HER.
YEAH? YOU SEE SOMETHING IN THE YARD TAKES YER FANCY?
DASHA? DASHA KOLAROV? I HOPE I'M NOT BOTHERING YOU. MY NAME IS--
I KNOW WHO YOU ARE.
Y' GOT THE SAME EYES AS 'ER.
YER NATALYA'S GIRL.

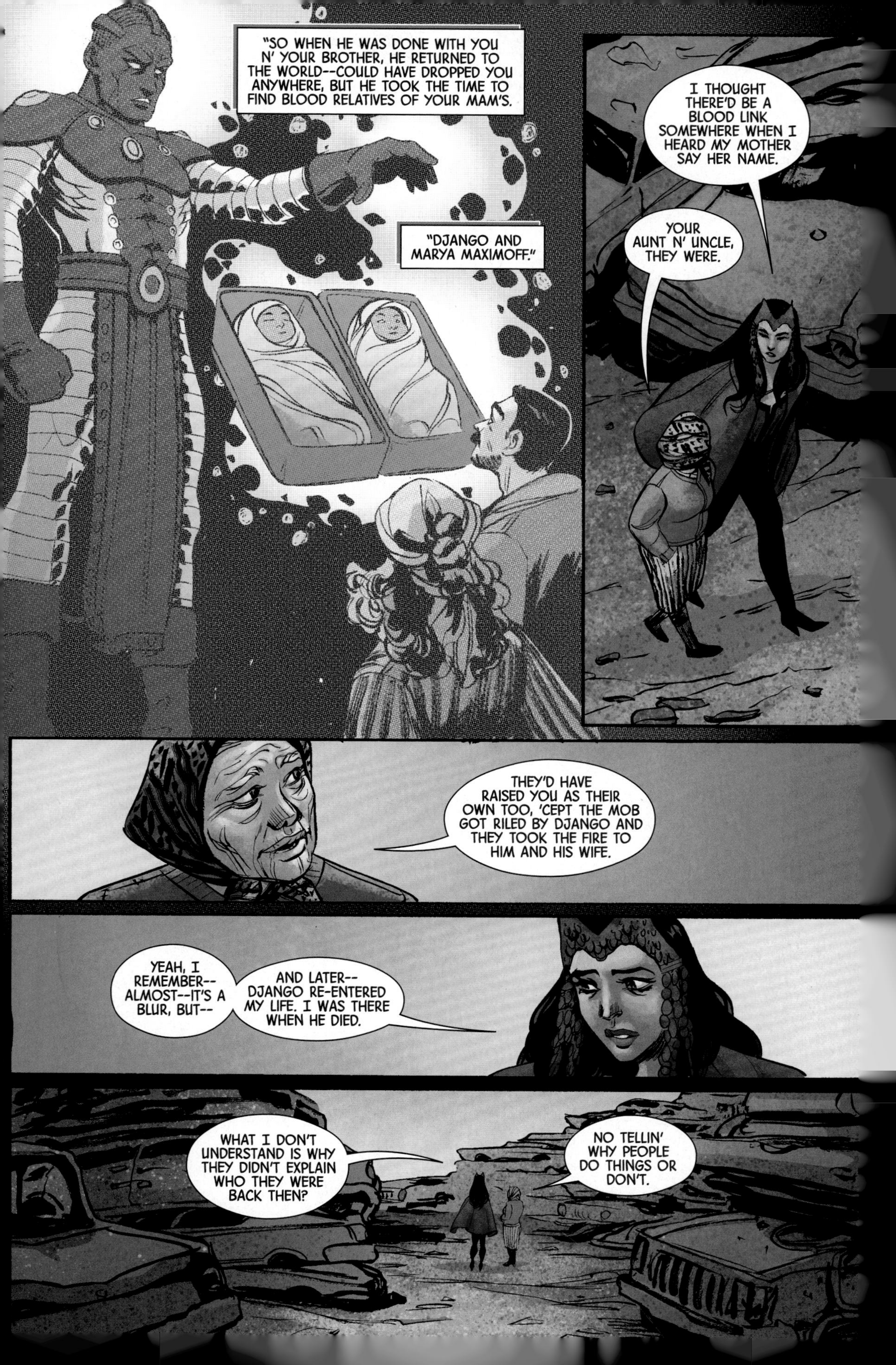
"SO WHEN HE WAS DONE WITH YOU N' YOUR BROTHER, HE RETURNED TO THE WORLD--COULD HAVE DROPPED YOU ANYWHERE, BUT HE TOOK THE TIME TO FIND BLOOD RELATIVES OF YOUR MAM'S.
"DJANGO AND MARYA MAXIMOFF."
I THOUGHT THERE'D BE A BLOOD LINK SOMEWHERE WHEN I HEARD MY MOTHER SAY HER NAME.
YOUR AUNT N' UNCLE, THEY WERE.
THEY'D HAVE RAISED YOU AS THEIR OWN TOO, 'CEPT THE MOB GOT RILED BY DJANGO AND THEY TOOK THE FIRE TO HIM AND HIS WIFE.
YEAH, I REMEMBER-- ALMOST--IT'S A BLUR, BUT--
AND LATER-- DJANGO RE-ENTERED MY LIFE. I WAS THERE WHEN HE DIED.
WHAT I DON'T UNDERSTAND IS WHY THEY DIDN'T EXPLAIN WHO THEY WERE BACK THEN?
NO TELLIN' WHY PEOPLE DO THINGS OR DON'T.

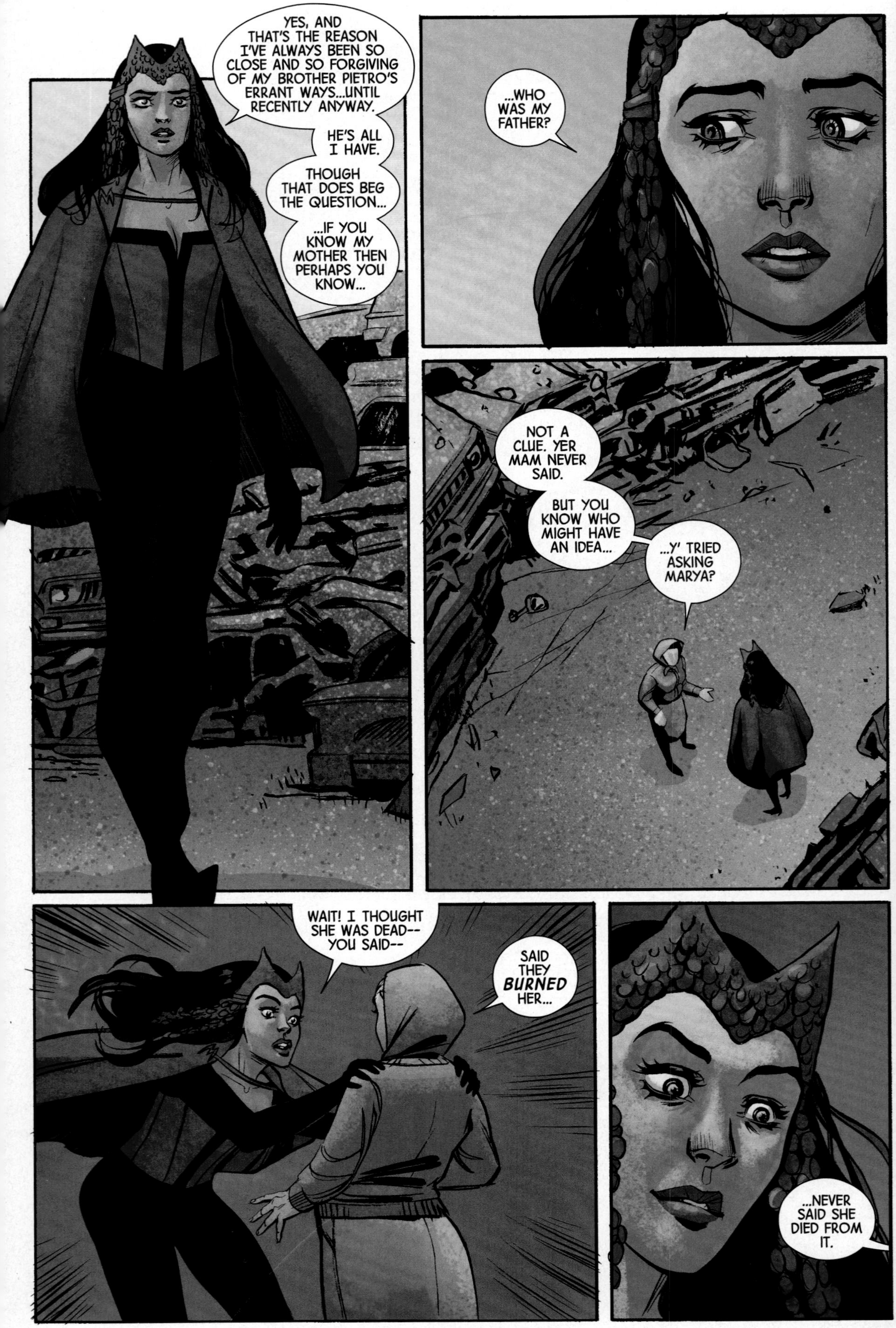
YES, AND THAT'S THE REASON I'VE ALWAYS BEEN SO CLOSE AND SO FORGIVING OF MY BROTHER PIETRO'S ERRANT WAYS...UNTIL RECENTLY ANYWAY.
HE'S ALL I HAVE.
THOUGH THAT DOES BEG THE QUESTION...
...IF YOU KNOW MY MOTHER THEN PERHAPS YOU KNOW...
...WHO WAS MY FATHER?
NOT A CLUE. YER MAM NEVER SAID.
BUT YOU KNOW WHO MIGHT HAVE AN IDEA...
...Y' TRIED ASKING MARYA?
WAIT! I THOUGHT SHE WAS DEAD-- YOU SAID--
SAID THEY BURNED HER...
...NEVER SAID SHE DIED FROM IT.

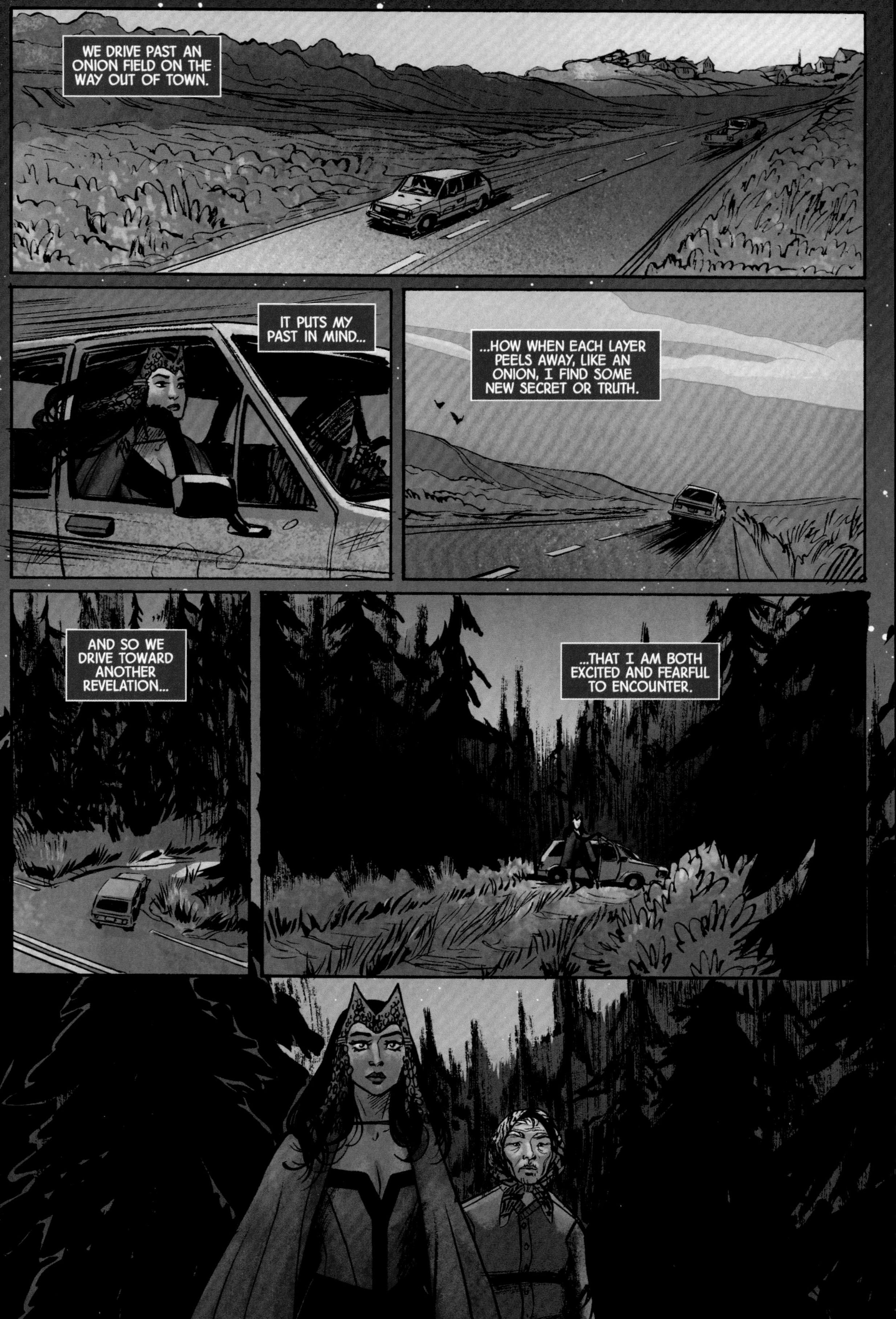
WE DRIVE PAST AN ONION FIELD ON THE WAY OUT OF TOWN.
IT PUTS MY PAST IN MIND...
...HOW WHEN EACH LAYER PEELS AWAY, LIKE AN ONION, I FIND SOME NEW SECRET OR TRUTH.
AND SO WE DRIVE TOWARD ANOTHER REVELATION...
...THAT I AM BOTH EXCITED AND FEARFUL TO ENCOUNTER.

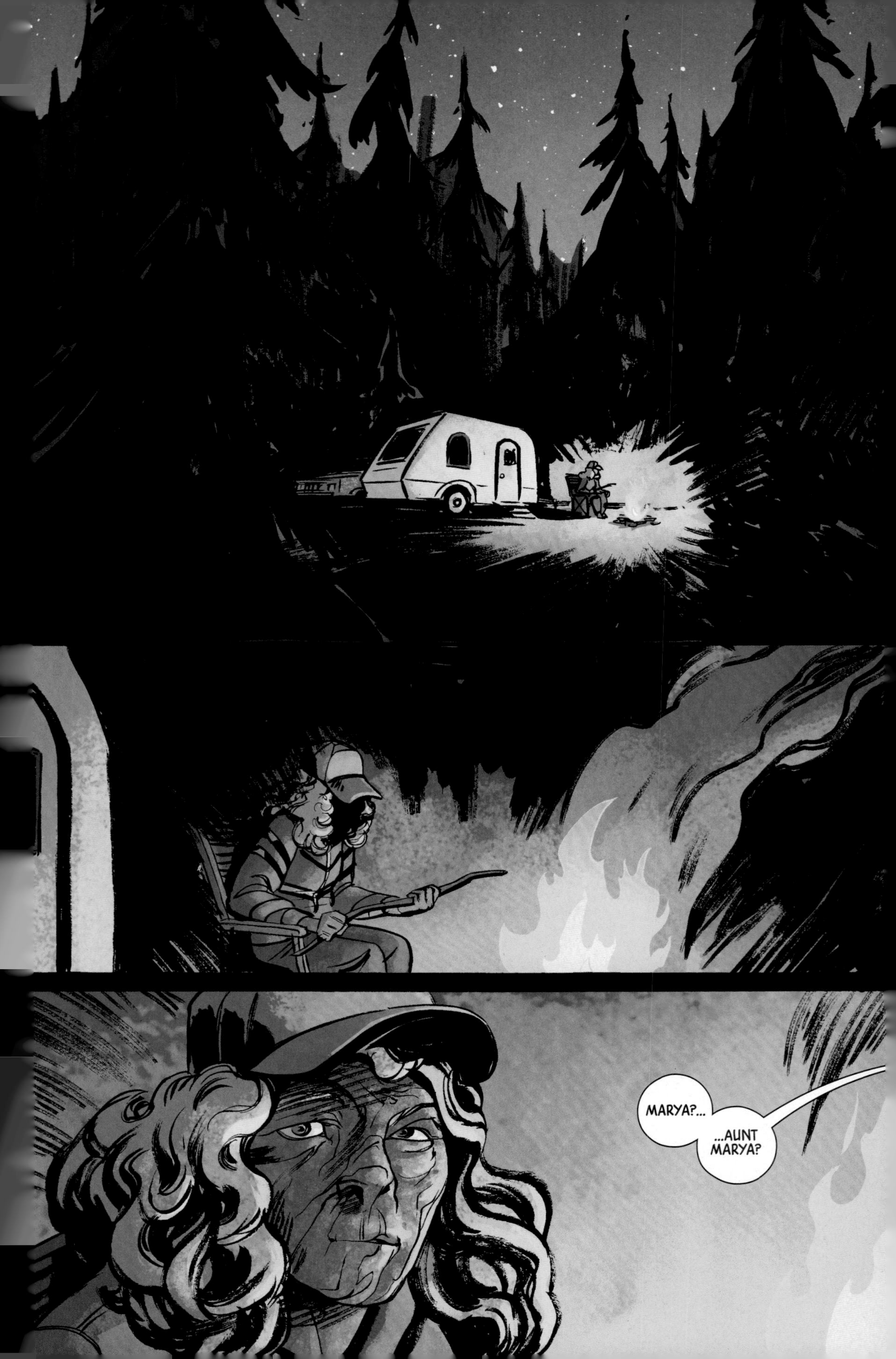
MARYA?...
...AUNT MARYA?

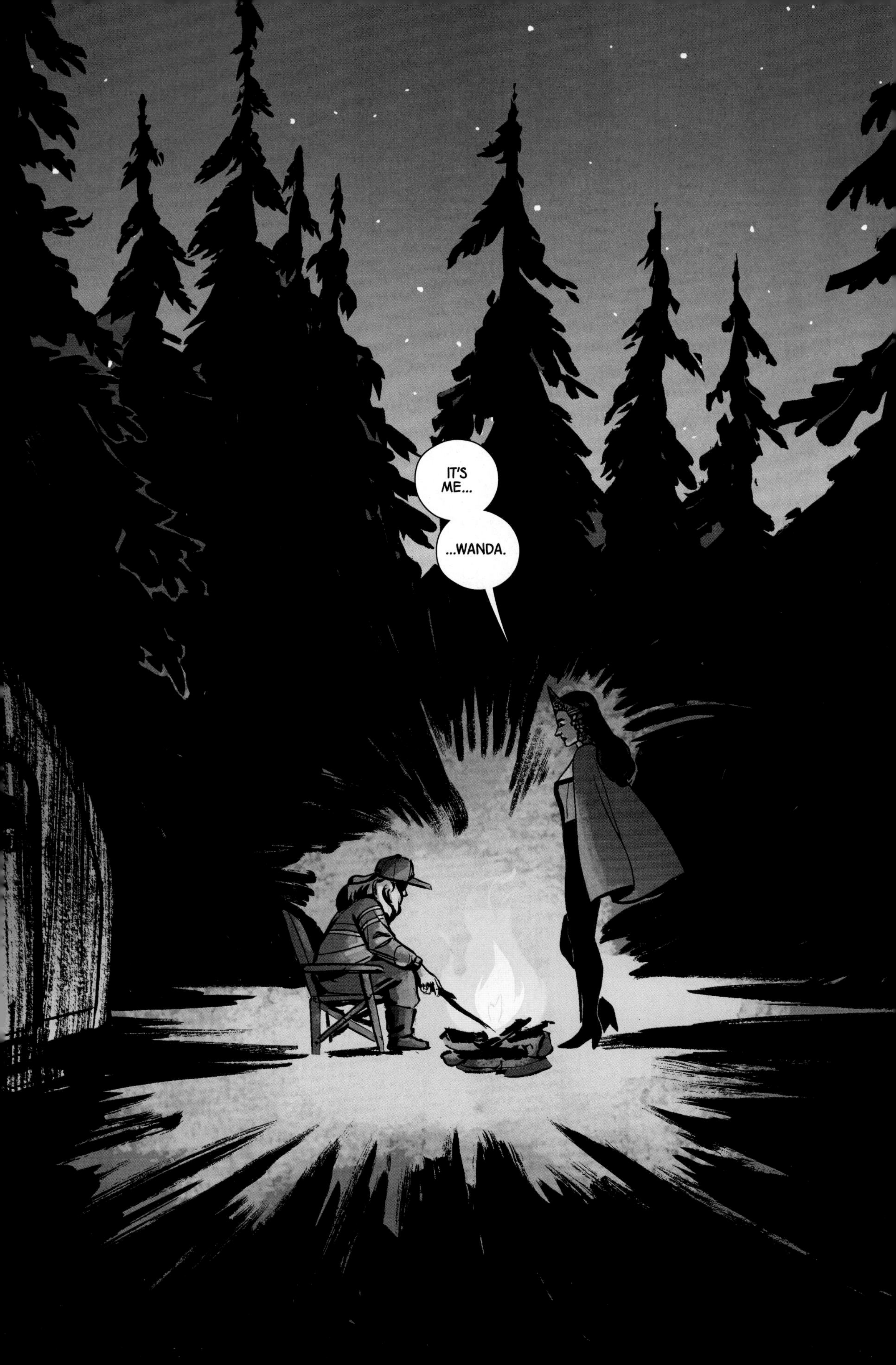
IT'S ME...
...WANDA.

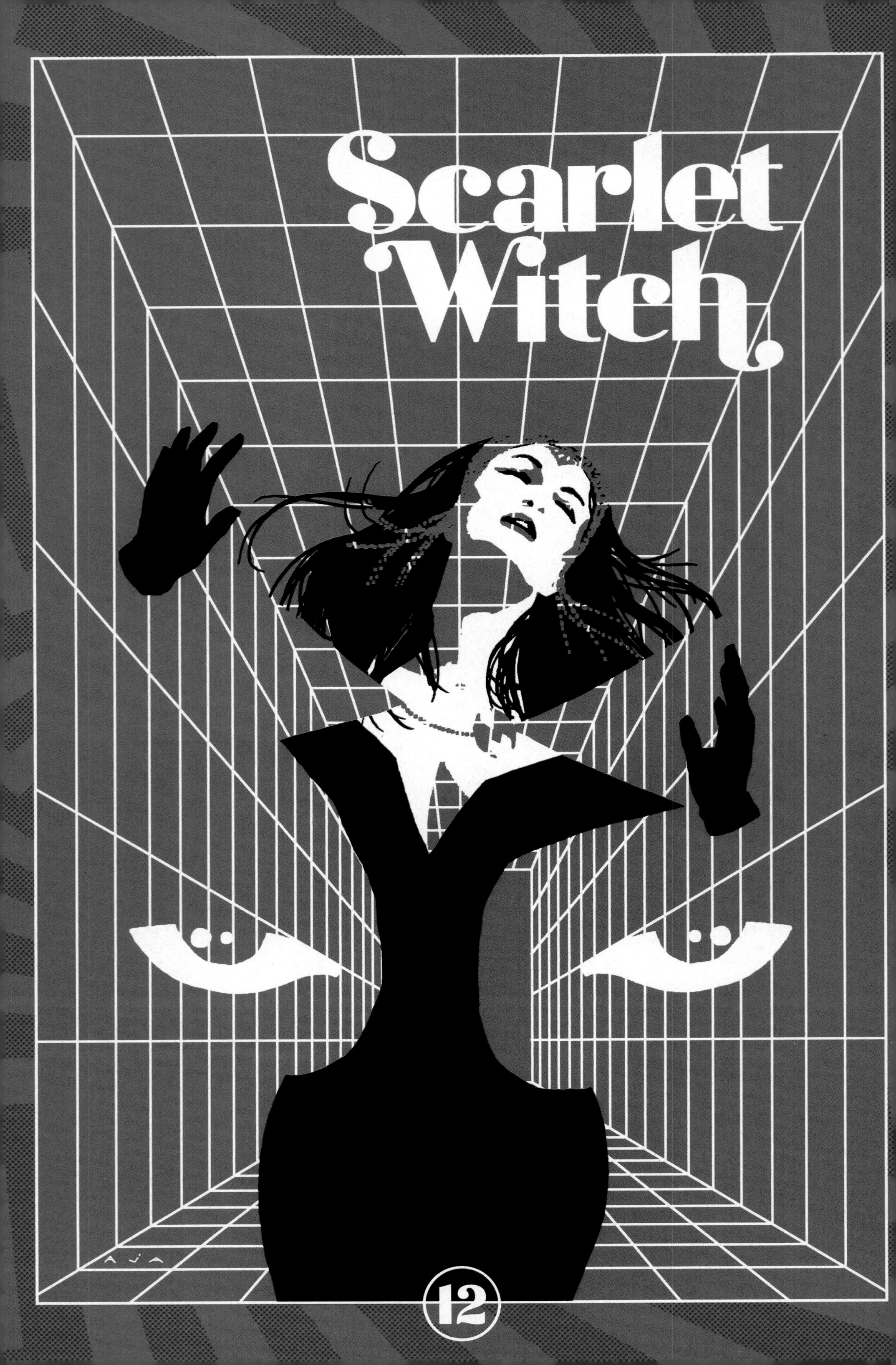
Scarlet Witch
AJA
12

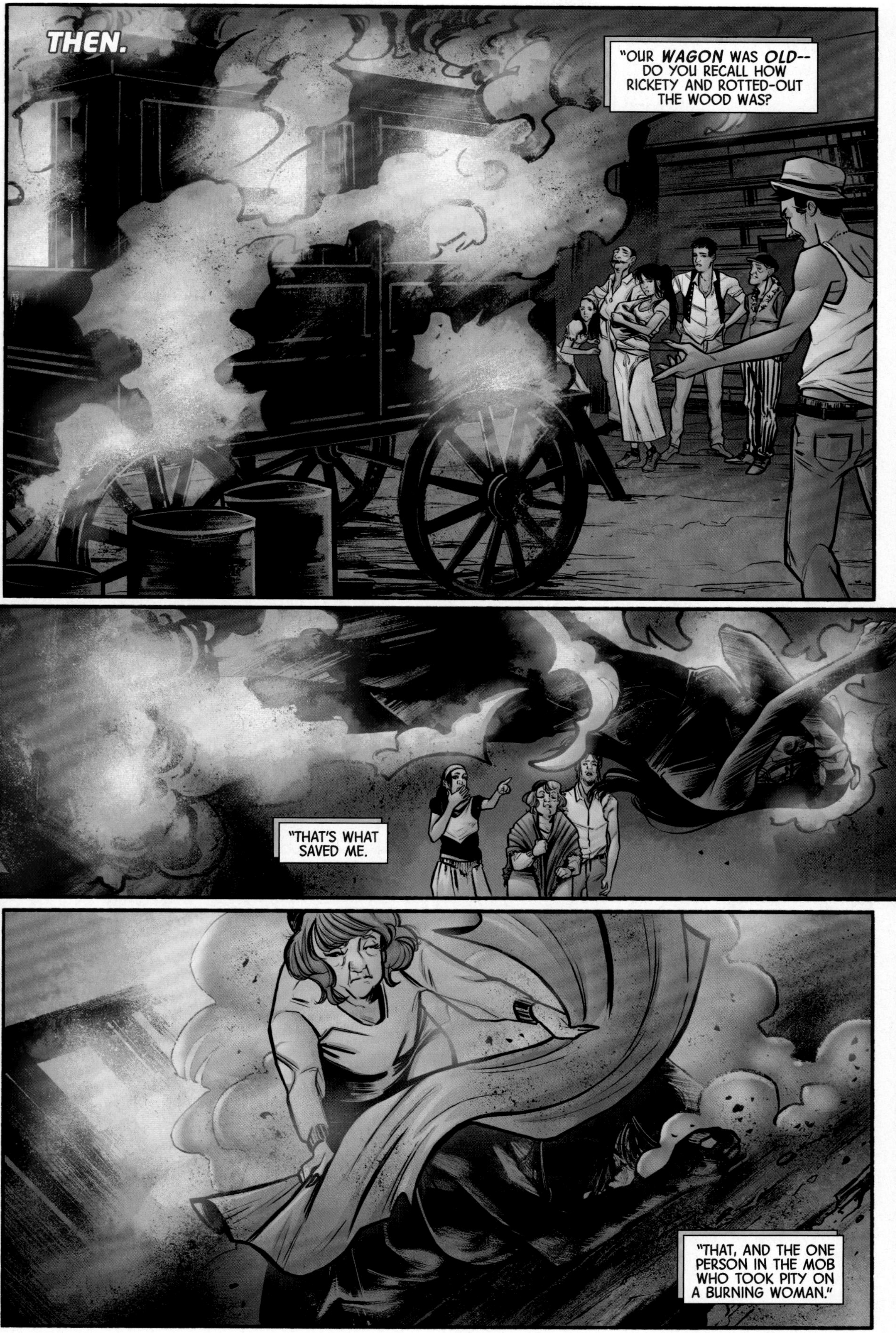
THEN.
"OUR WAGON WAS OLD-- DO YOU RECALL HOW RICKETY AND ROTTED-OUT THE WOOD WAS?
"THAT'S WHAT SAVED ME.
"THAT, AND THE ONE PERSON IN THE MOB WHO TOOK PITY ON A BURNING WOMAN."

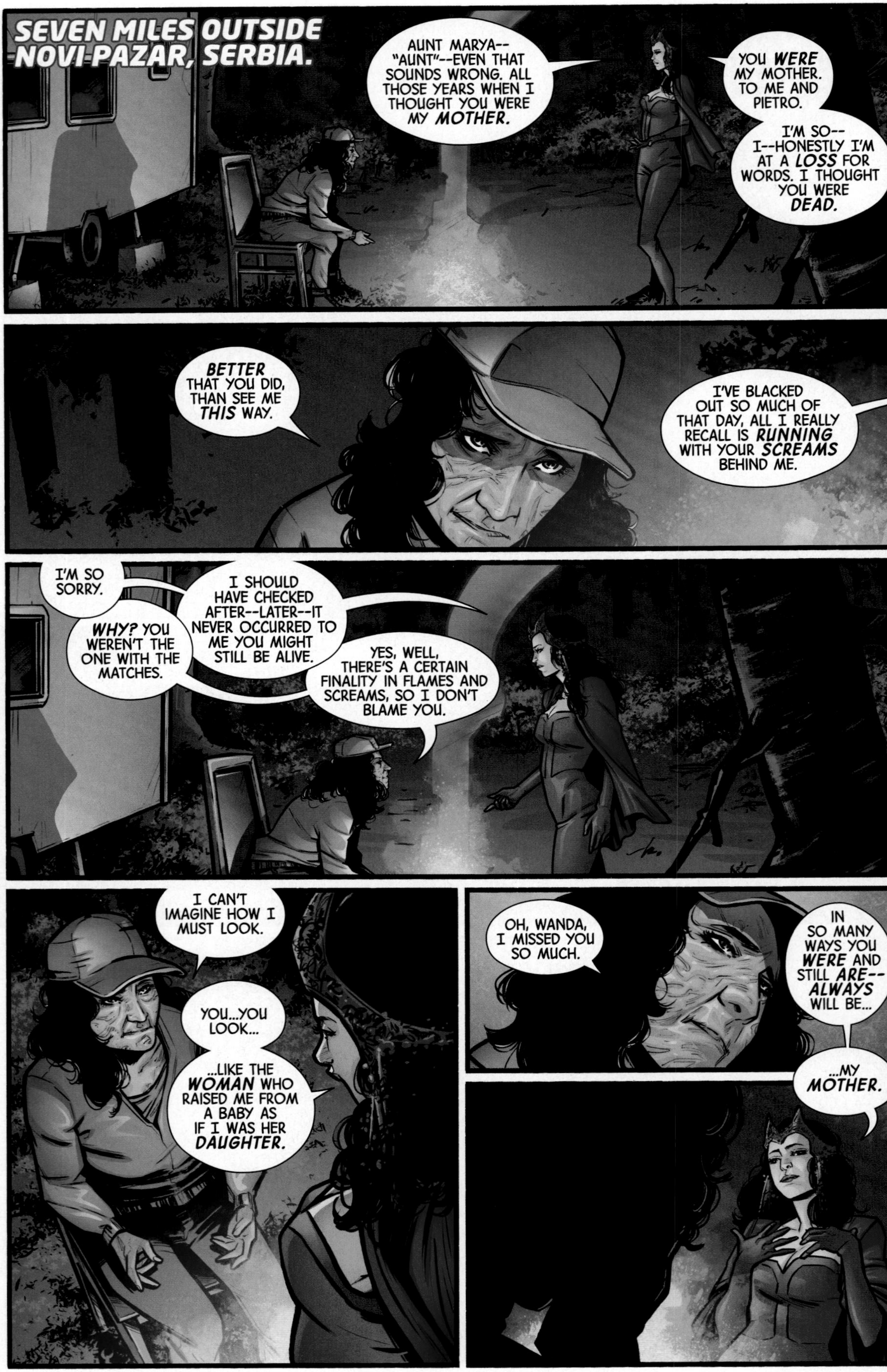
SEVEN MILES OUTSIDE NOVI-PAZAR, SERBIA.
AUNT MARYA-- "AUNT"--EVEN THAT SOUNDS WRONG. ALL THOSE YEARS WHEN I THOUGHT YOU WERE MY MOTHER.
YOU WERE MY MOTHER. TO ME AND PIETRO.
I'M SO-- I--HONESTLY I'M AT A LOSS FOR WORDS. I THOUGHT YOU WERE DEAD.
BETTER THAT YOU DID, THAN SEE ME THIS WAY.
I'VE BLACKED OUT SO MUCH OF THAT DAY, ALL I REALLY RECALL IS RUNNING WITH YOUR SCREAMS BEHIND ME.
I'M SO SORRY.
WHY? YOU WEREN'T THE ONE WITH THE MATCHES.
I SHOULD HAVE CHECKED AFTER--LATER--IT NEVER OCCURRED TO ME YOU MIGHT STILL BE ALIVE.
YES, WELL, THERE'S A CERTAIN FINALITY IN FLAMES AND SCREAMS, SO I DON'T BLAME YOU.
I CAN'T IMAGINE HOW I MUST LOOK.
YOU...YOU LOOK...
...LIKE THE WOMAN WHO RAISED ME FROM A BABY AS IF I WAS HER DAUGHTER.
OH, WANDA, I MISSED YOU SO MUCH.
IN SO MANY WAYS YOU WERE AND STILL ARE-- ALWAYS WILL BE...
...MY MOTHER.

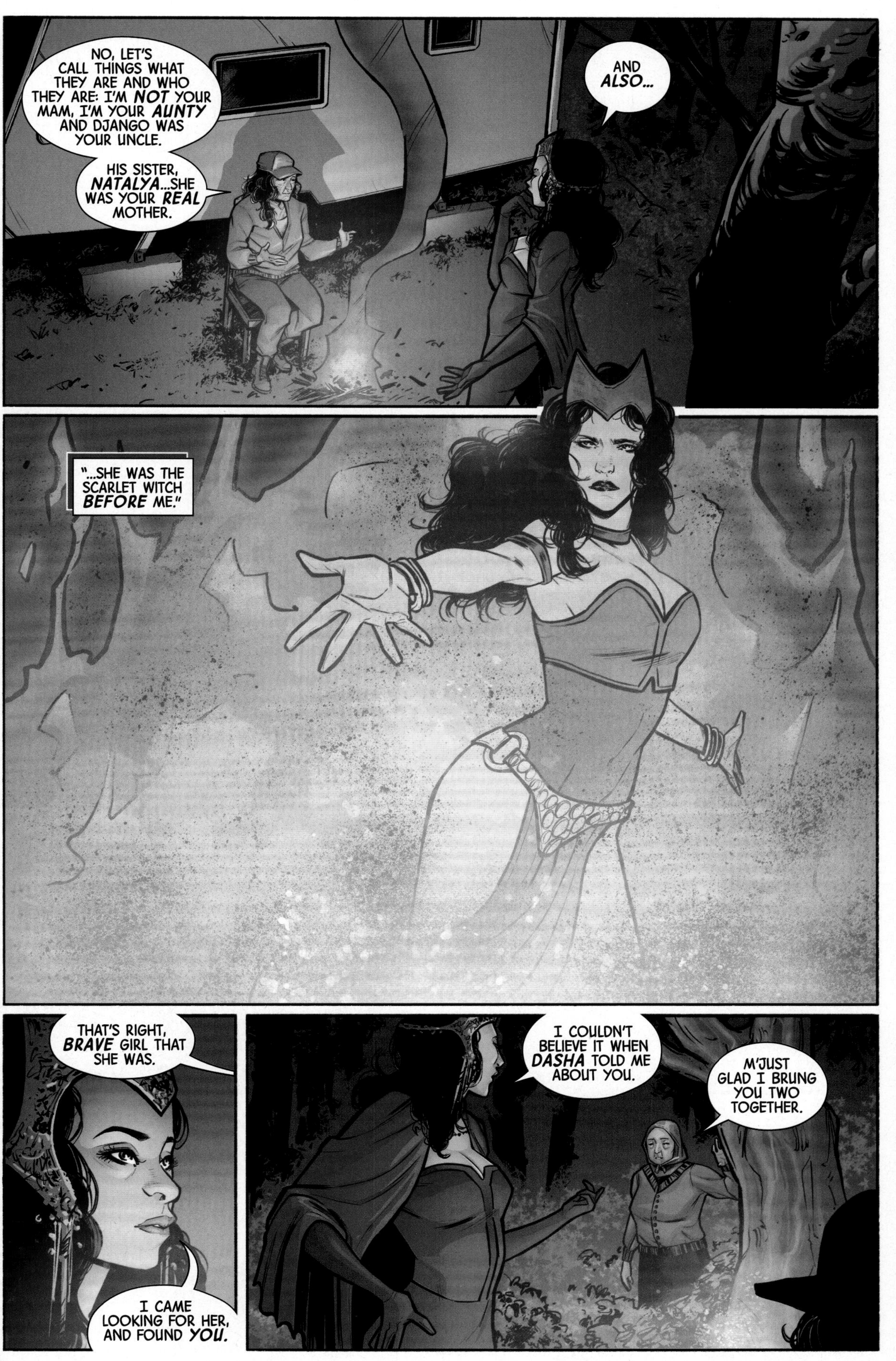
NO, LET'S CALL THINGS WHAT THEY ARE AND WHO THEY ARE: I'M NOT YOUR MAM, I'M YOUR AUNTY AND DJANGO WAS YOUR UNCLE.
HIS SISTER, NATALYA...SHE WAS YOUR REAL MOTHER.
AND ALSO...
"...SHE WAS THE SCARLET WITCH BEFORE ME."
THAT'S RIGHT, BRAVE GIRL THAT SHE WAS.
I CAME LOOKING FOR HER, AND FOUND YOU.
I COULDN'T BELIEVE IT WHEN DASHA TOLD ME ABOUT YOU.
M'JUST GLAD I BRUNG YOU TWO TOGETHER.

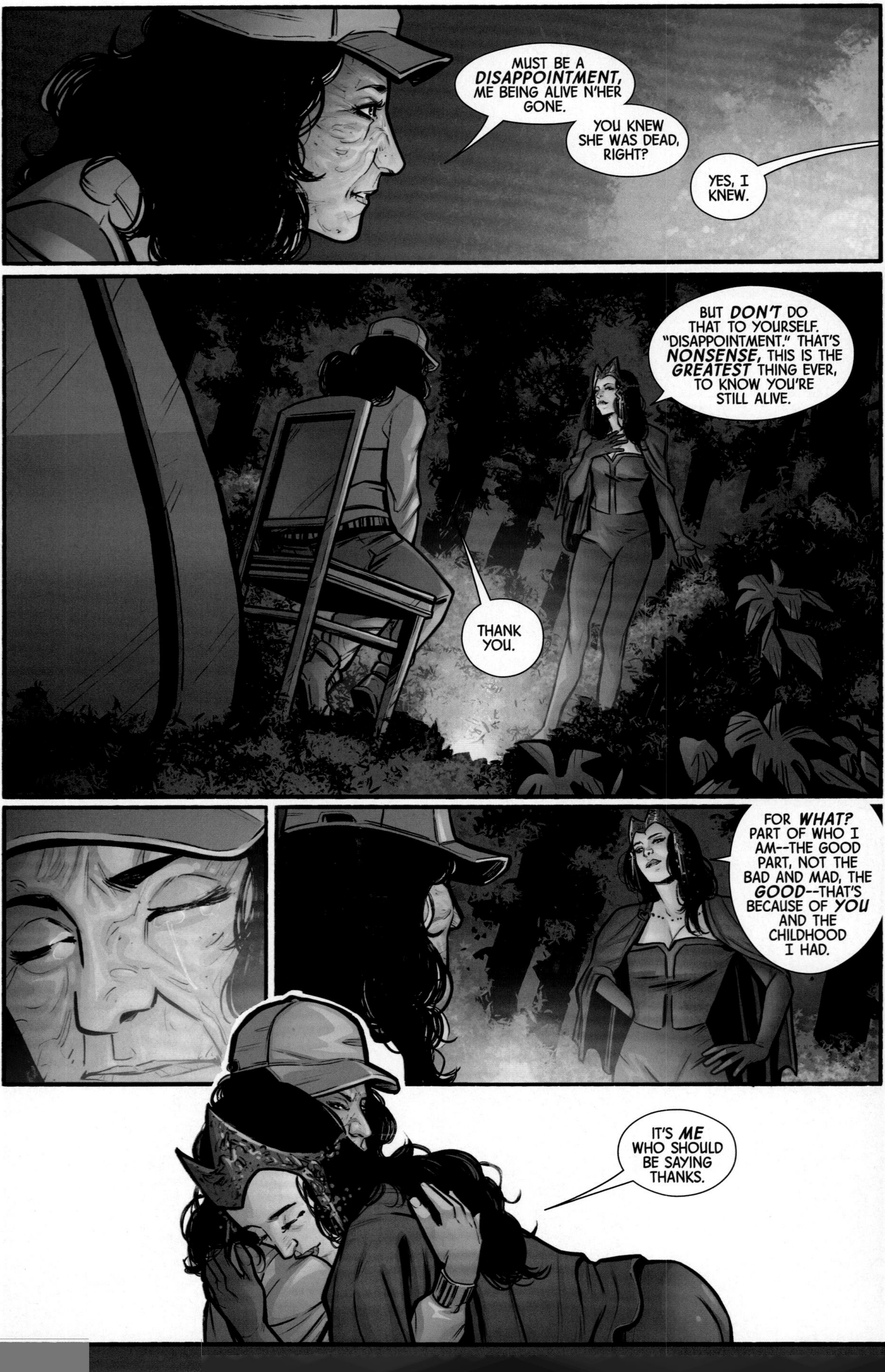
MUST BE A *DISAPPOINTMENT,* ME BEING ALIVE N'HER GONE.
YOU KNEW SHE WAS DEAD, RIGHT?
YES, I KNEW.
BUT *DON'T* DO THAT TO YOURSELF. "DISAPPOINTMENT." THAT'S *NONSENSE,* THIS IS THE *GREATEST* THING EVER, TO KNOW YOU'RE STILL ALIVE.
THANK YOU.
FOR *WHAT?* PART OF WHO I AM--THE GOOD PART, NOT THE BAD AND MAD, THE *GOOD*--THAT'S BECAUSE OF *YOU* AND THE CHILDHOOD I HAD.
IT'S *ME* WHO SHOULD BE SAYING THANKS.

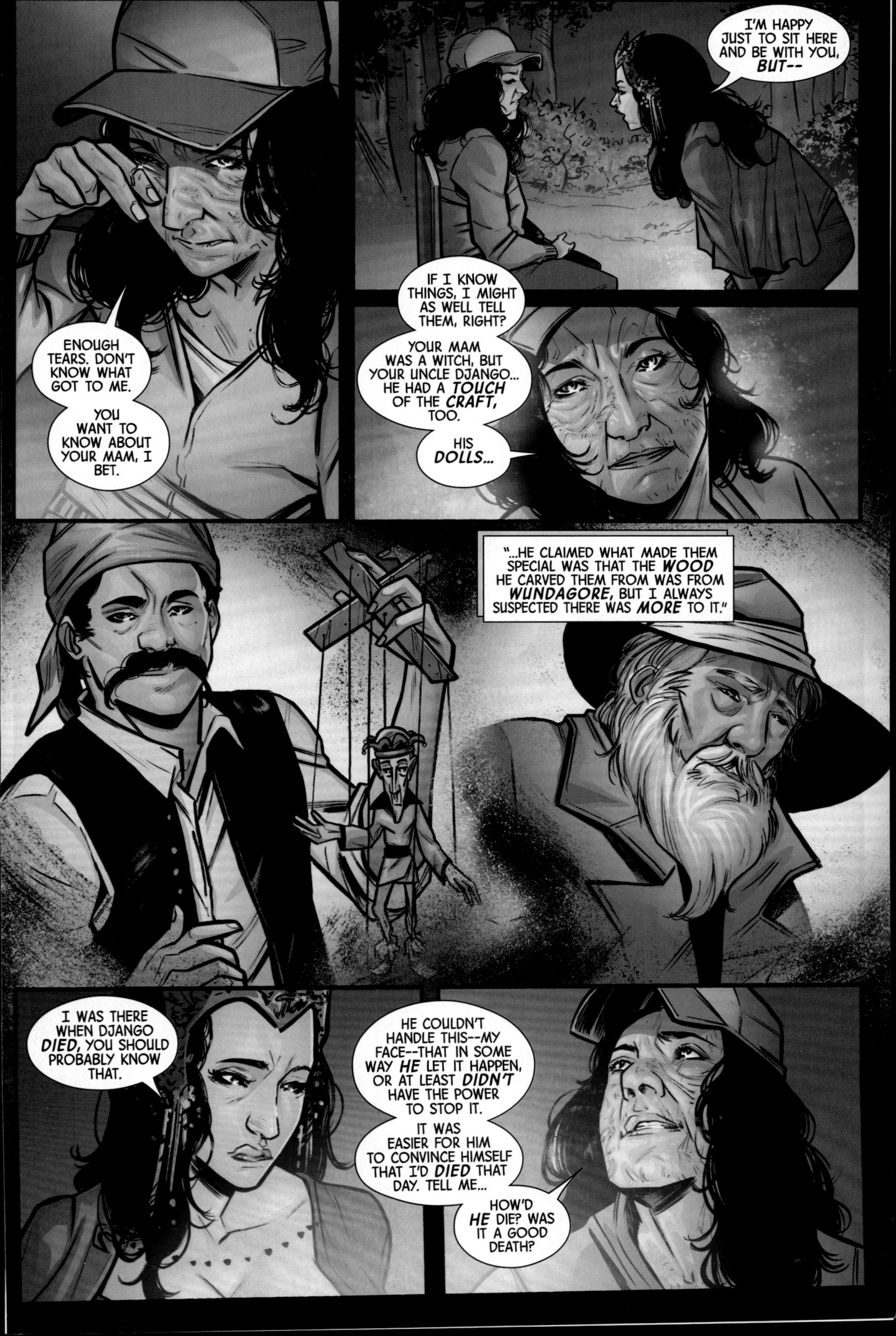
ENOUGH TEARS. DON'T KNOW WHAT GOT TO ME.
YOU WANT TO KNOW ABOUT YOUR MAM, I BET.
I'M HAPPY JUST TO SIT HERE AND BE WITH YOU, BUT--
IF I KNOW THINGS, I MIGHT AS WELL TELL THEM, RIGHT?
YOUR MAM WAS A WITCH, BUT YOUR UNCLE DJANGO... HE HAD A TOUCH OF THE CRAFT, TOO.
HIS DOLLS...
"...HE CLAIMED WHAT MADE THEM SPECIAL WAS THAT THE WOOD HE CARVED THEM FROM WAS FROM WUNDAGORE, BUT I ALWAYS SUSPECTED THERE WAS MORE TO IT."
I WAS THERE WHEN DJANGO DIED, YOU SHOULD PROBABLY KNOW THAT.
HE COULDN'T HANDLE THIS--MY FACE--THAT IN SOME WAY HE LET IT HAPPEN, OR AT LEAST DIDN'T HAVE THE POWER TO STOP IT.
IT WAS EASIER FOR HIM TO CONVINCE HIMSELF THAT I'D DIED THAT DAY. TELL ME...
HOW'D HE DIE? WAS IT A GOOD DEATH?

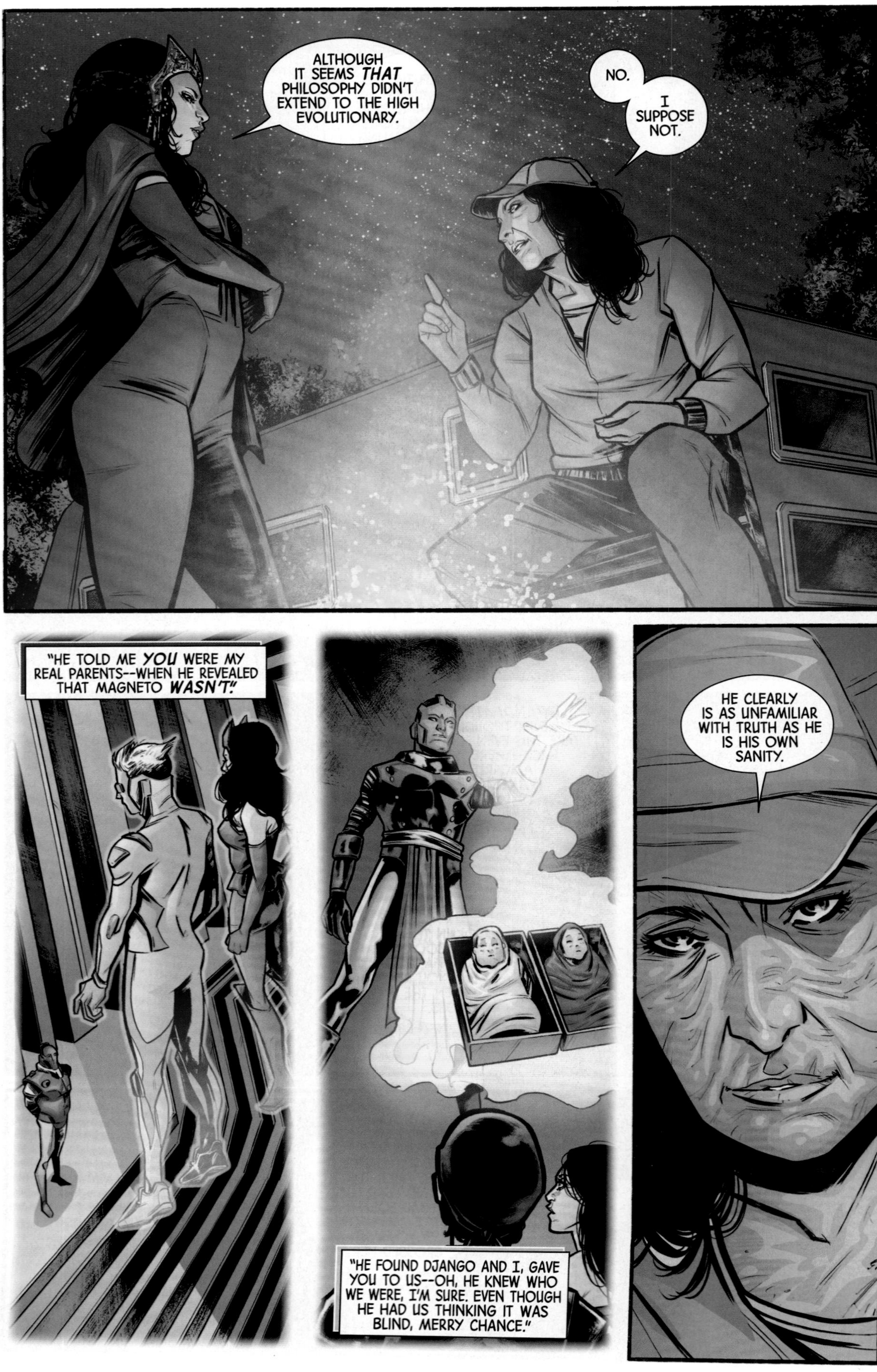

ALTHOUGH IT SEEMS THAT PHILOSOPHY DIDN'T EXTEND TO THE HIGH EVOLUTIONARY.
NO.
I SUPPOSE NOT.
"HE TOLD ME YOU WERE MY REAL PARENTS--WHEN HE REVEALED THAT MAGNETO WASN'T!"
"HE FOUND DJANGO AND I, GAVE YOU TO US--OH, HE KNEW WHO WE WERE, I'M SURE. EVEN THOUGH HE HAD US THINKING IT WAS BLIND, MERRY CHANCE."
HE CLEARLY IS AS UNFAMILIAR WITH TRUTH AS HE IS HIS OWN SANITY.

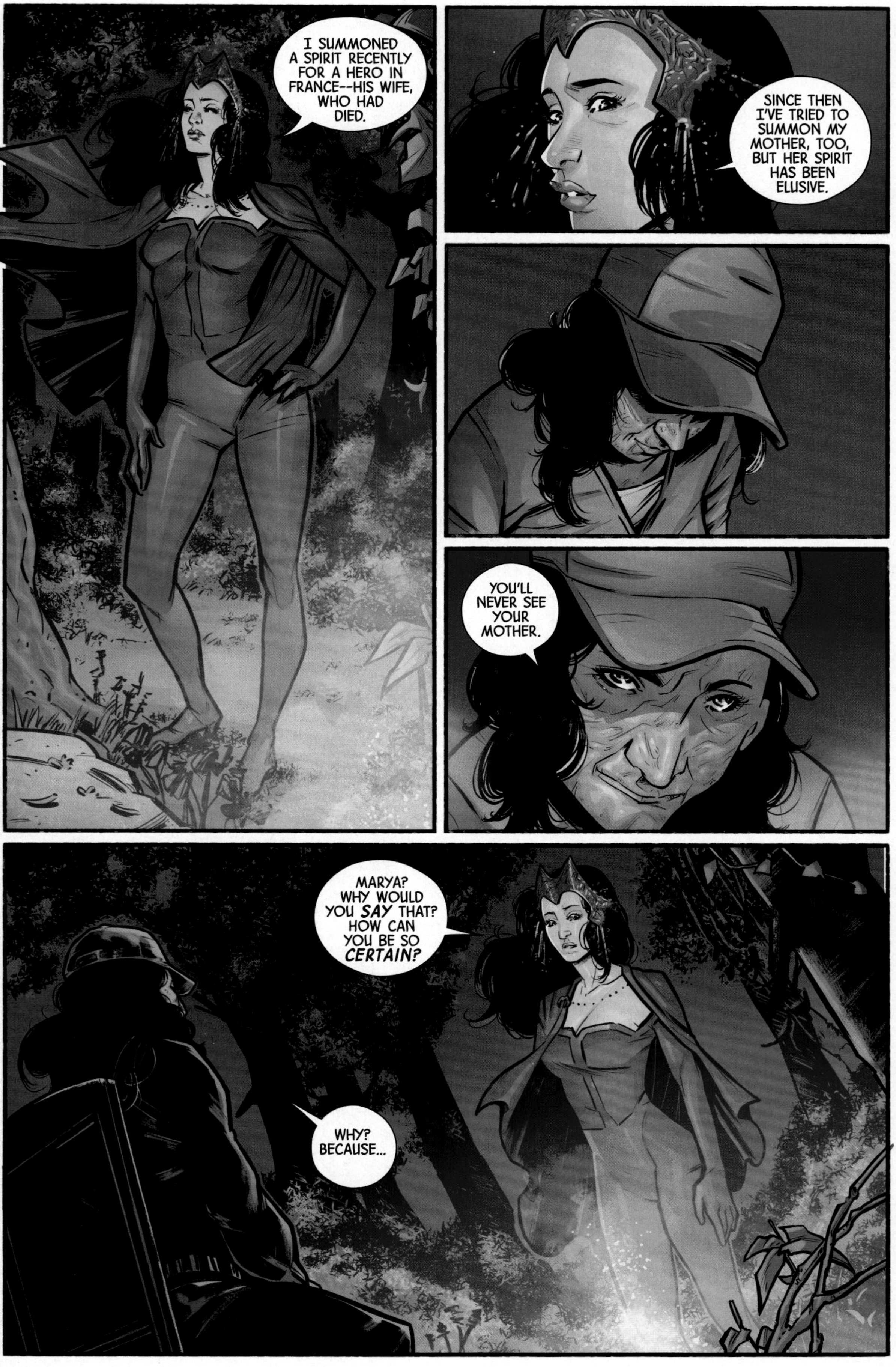
I SUMMONED A SPIRIT RECENTLY FOR A HERO IN FRANCE--HIS WIFE, WHO HAD DIED.
SINCE THEN I'VE TRIED TO SUMMON MY MOTHER, TOO, BUT HER SPIRIT HAS BEEN ELUSIVE.
YOU'LL NEVER SEE YOUR MOTHER.
MARYA? WHY WOULD YOU SAY THAT? HOW CAN YOU BE SO CERTAIN?
WHY? BECAUSE...

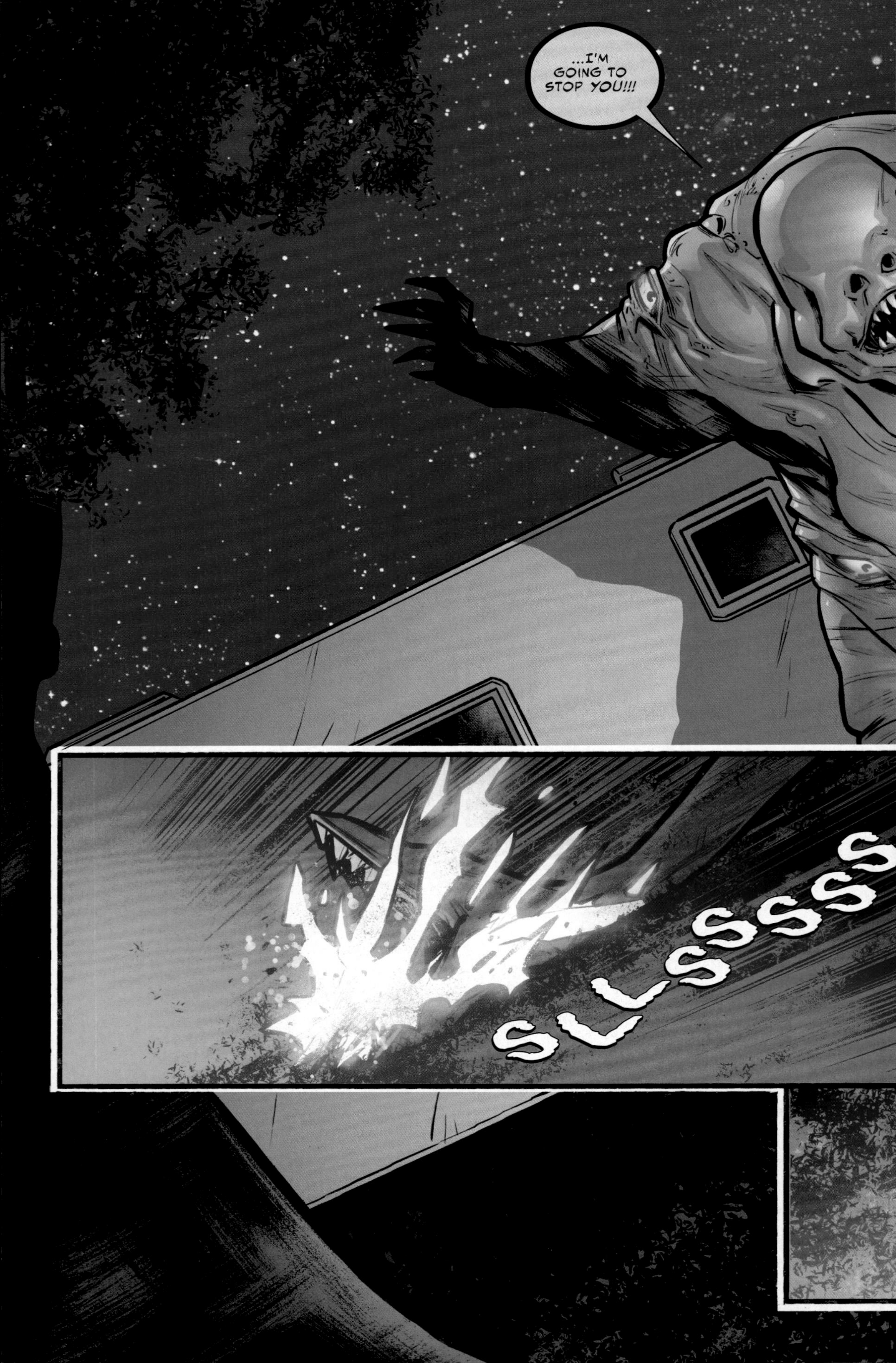
...I'M GOING TO STOP YOU!!!
SLUSSSSSS

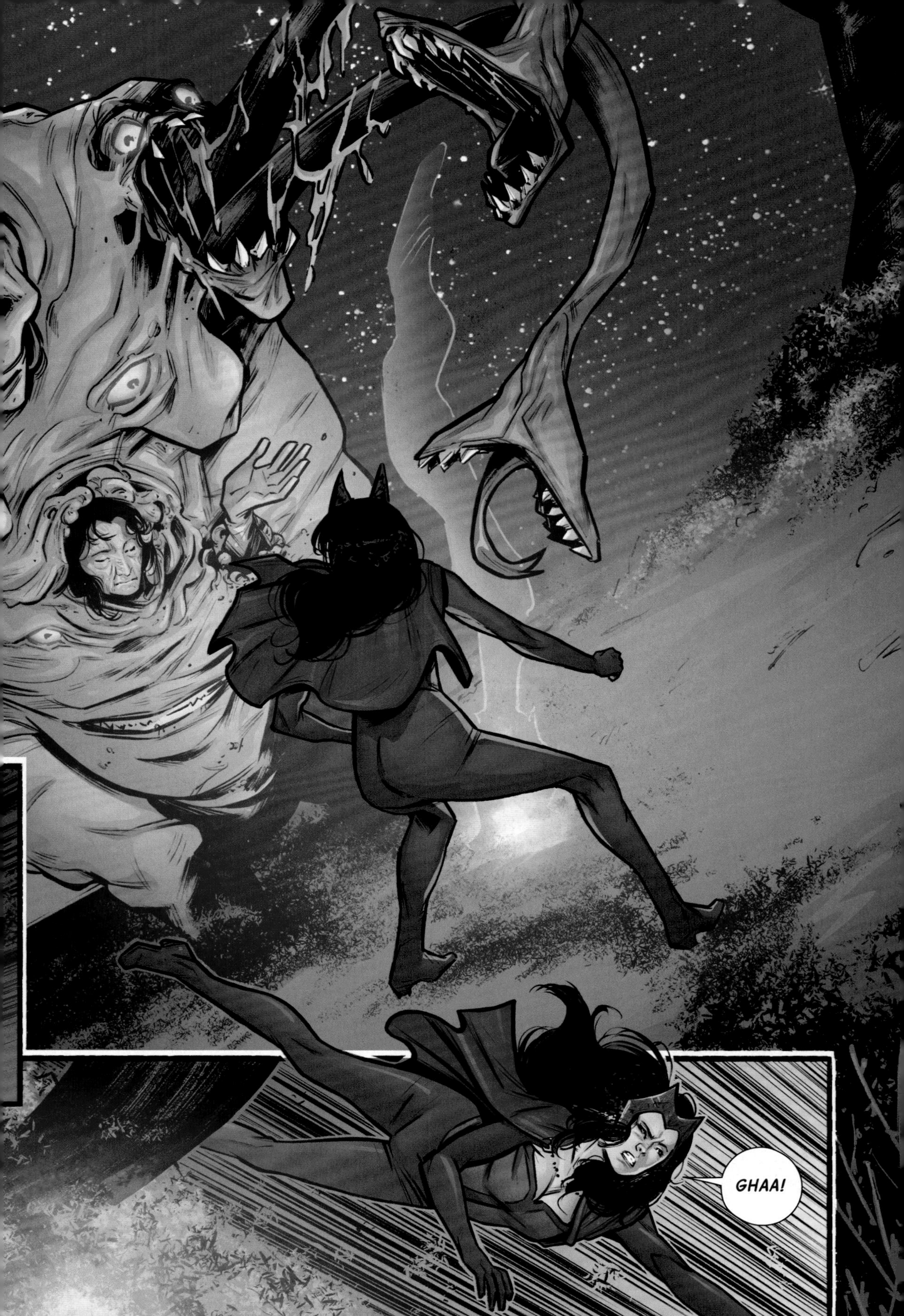
GHAA!

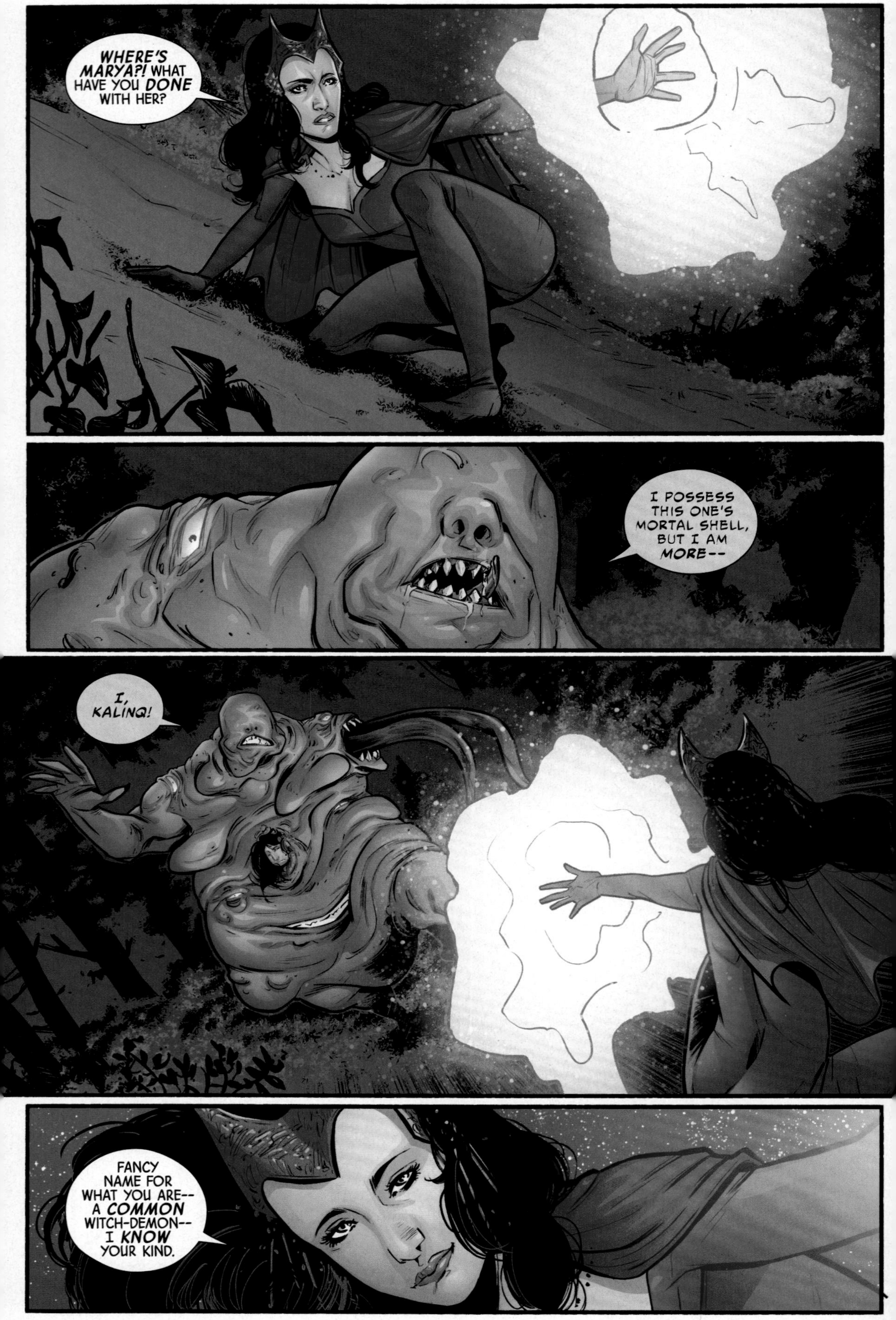
WHERE'S MARYA?! WHAT HAVE YOU DONE WITH HER?
I POSSESS THIS ONE'S MORTAL SHELL, BUT I AM MORE--
I, KALINQ!
FANCY NAME FOR WHAT YOU ARE-- A COMMON WITCH-DEMON-- I KNOW YOUR KIND.

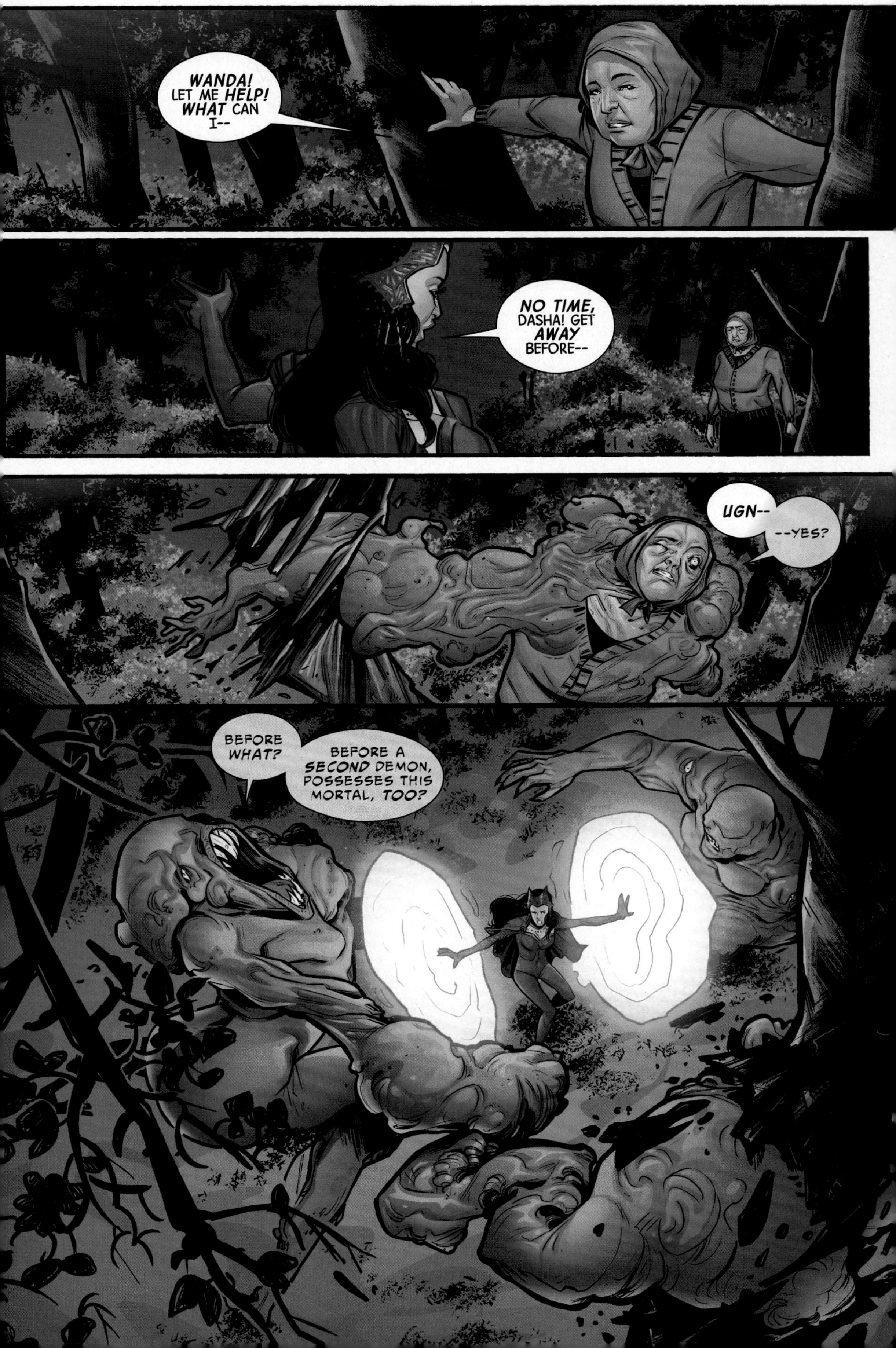
WANDA! LET ME HELP! WHAT CAN I--
NO TIME, DASHA! GET AWAY BEFORE--
UGN--
--YES?
BEFORE WHAT?
BEFORE A SECOND DEMON, POSSESSES THIS MORTAL, TOO?

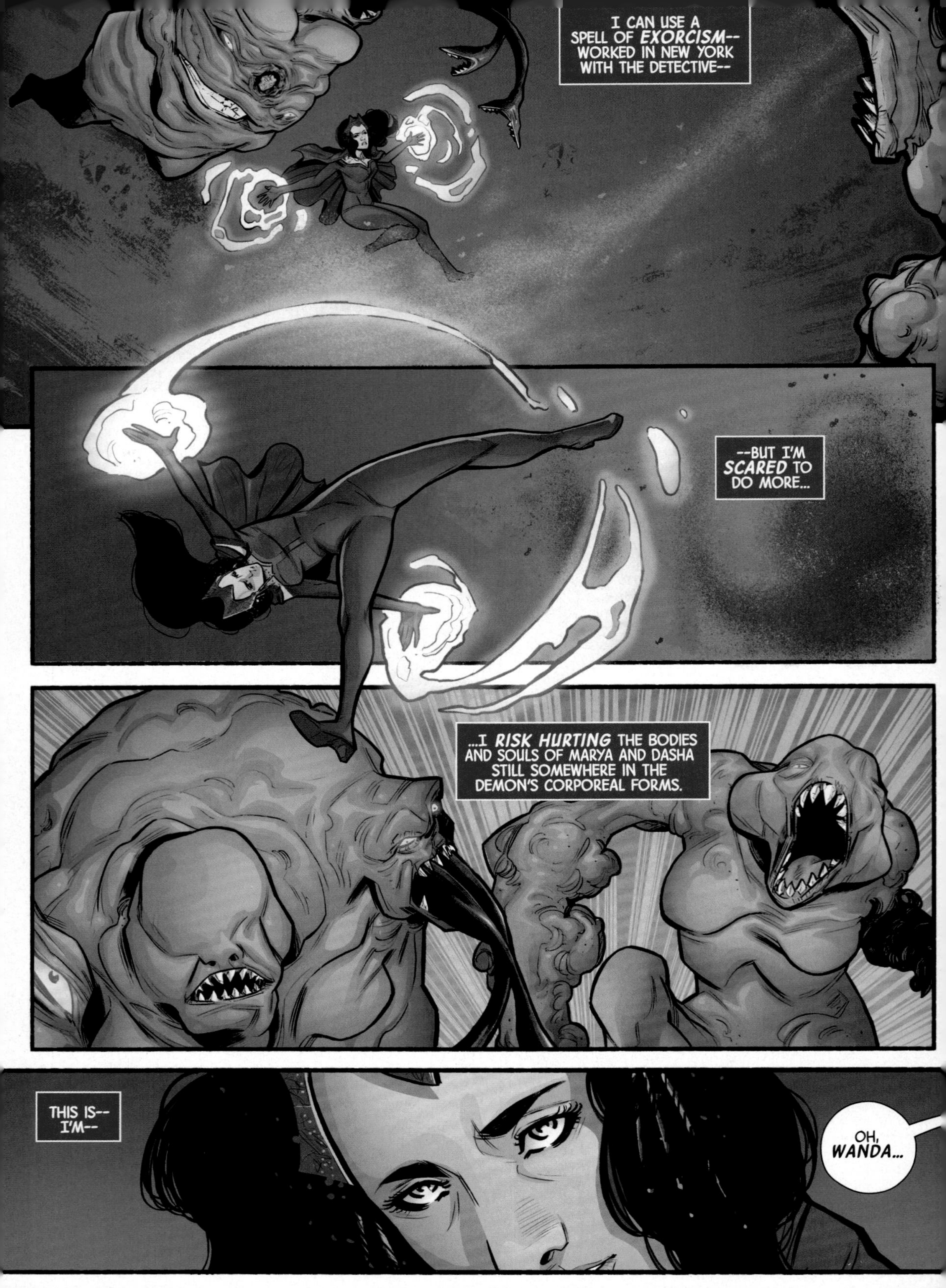
I CAN USE A SPELL OF *EXORCISM*-- WORKED IN NEW YORK WITH THE DETECTIVE--
--BUT I'M *SCARED* TO DO MORE...
...I *RISK HURTING* THE BODIES AND SOULS OF MARYA AND DASHA STILL SOMEWHERE IN THE DEMON'S CORPOREAL FORMS.
THIS IS-- I'M--
OH, *WANDA*...

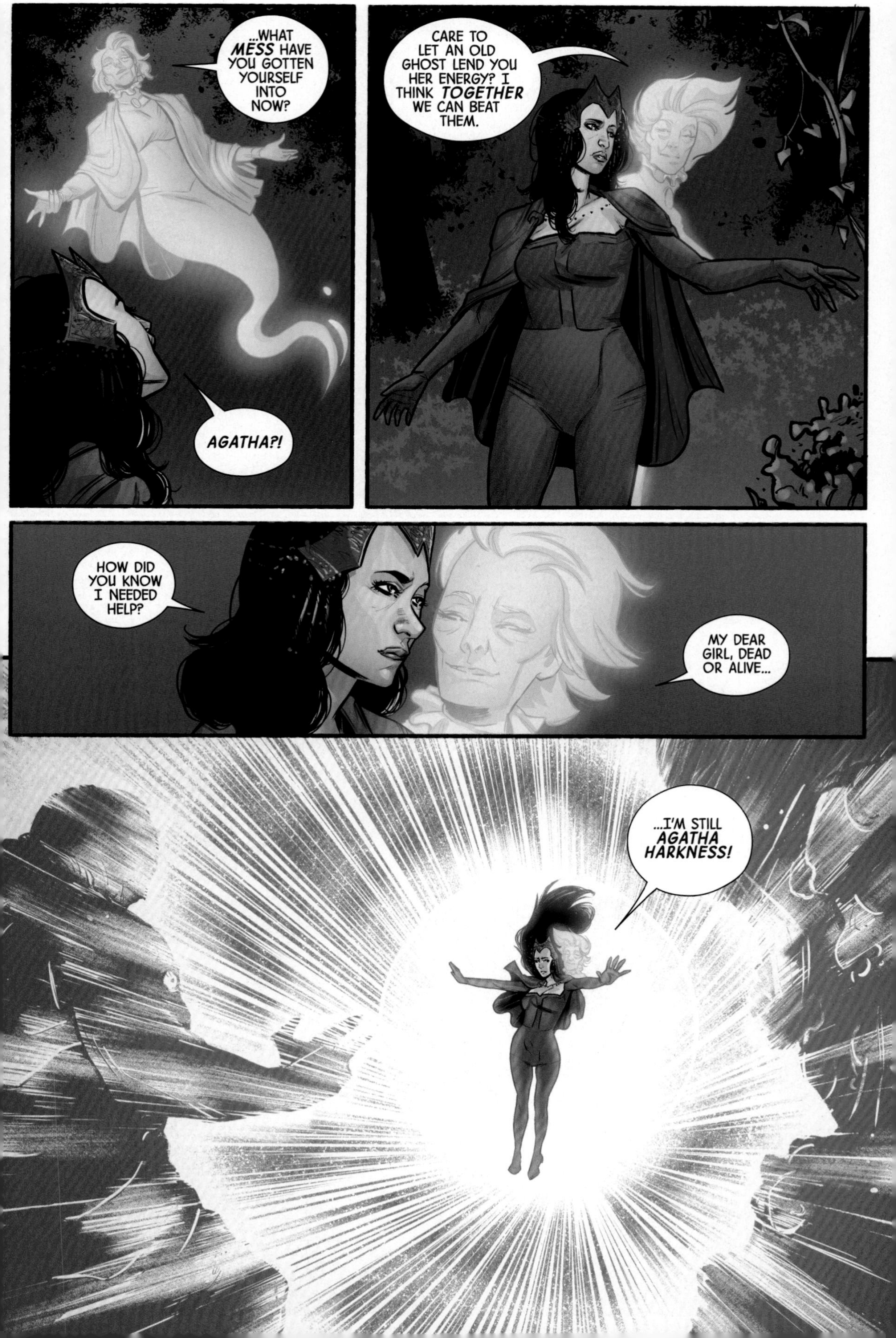
...WHAT MESS HAVE YOU GOTTEN YOURSELF INTO NOW?
AGATHA?!
CARE TO LET AN OLD GHOST LEND YOU HER ENERGY? I THINK TOGETHER WE CAN BEAT THEM.
HOW DID YOU KNOW I NEEDED HELP?
MY DEAR GIRL, DEAD OR ALIVE...
...I'M STILL AGATHA HARKNESS!

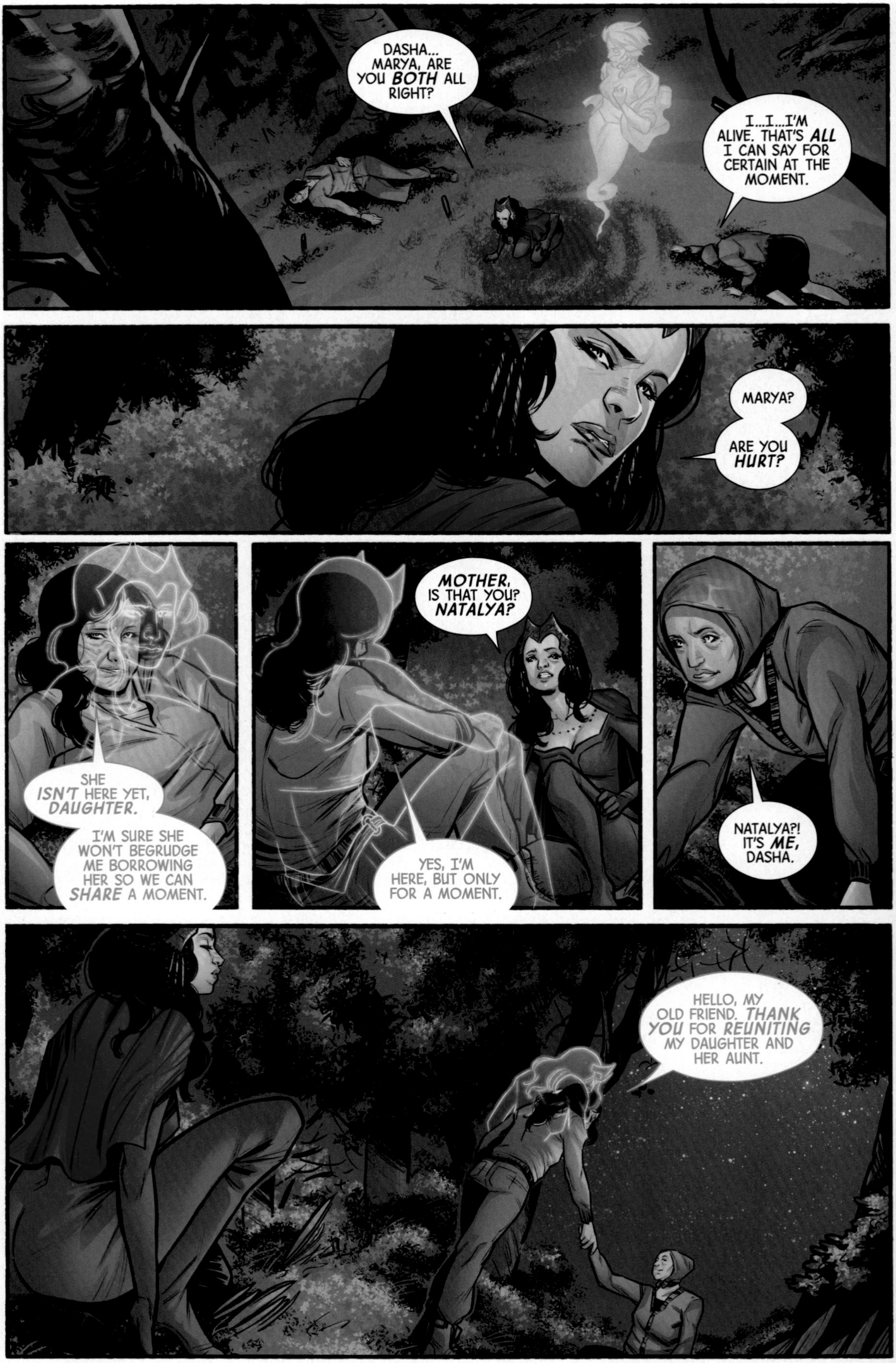

DASHA... MARYA, ARE YOU BOTH ALL RIGHT?
I...I...I'M ALIVE. THAT'S ALL I CAN SAY FOR CERTAIN AT THE MOMENT.
MARYA?
ARE YOU HURT?
SHE ISN'T HERE YET, DAUGHTER.
I'M SURE SHE WON'T BEGRUDGE ME BORROWING HER SO WE CAN SHARE A MOMENT.
MOTHER, IS THAT YOU? NATALYA?
YES, I'M HERE, BUT ONLY FOR A MOMENT.
NATALYA?! IT'S ME, DASHA.
HELLO, MY OLD FRIEND. THANK YOU FOR REUNITING MY DAUGHTER AND HER AUNT.

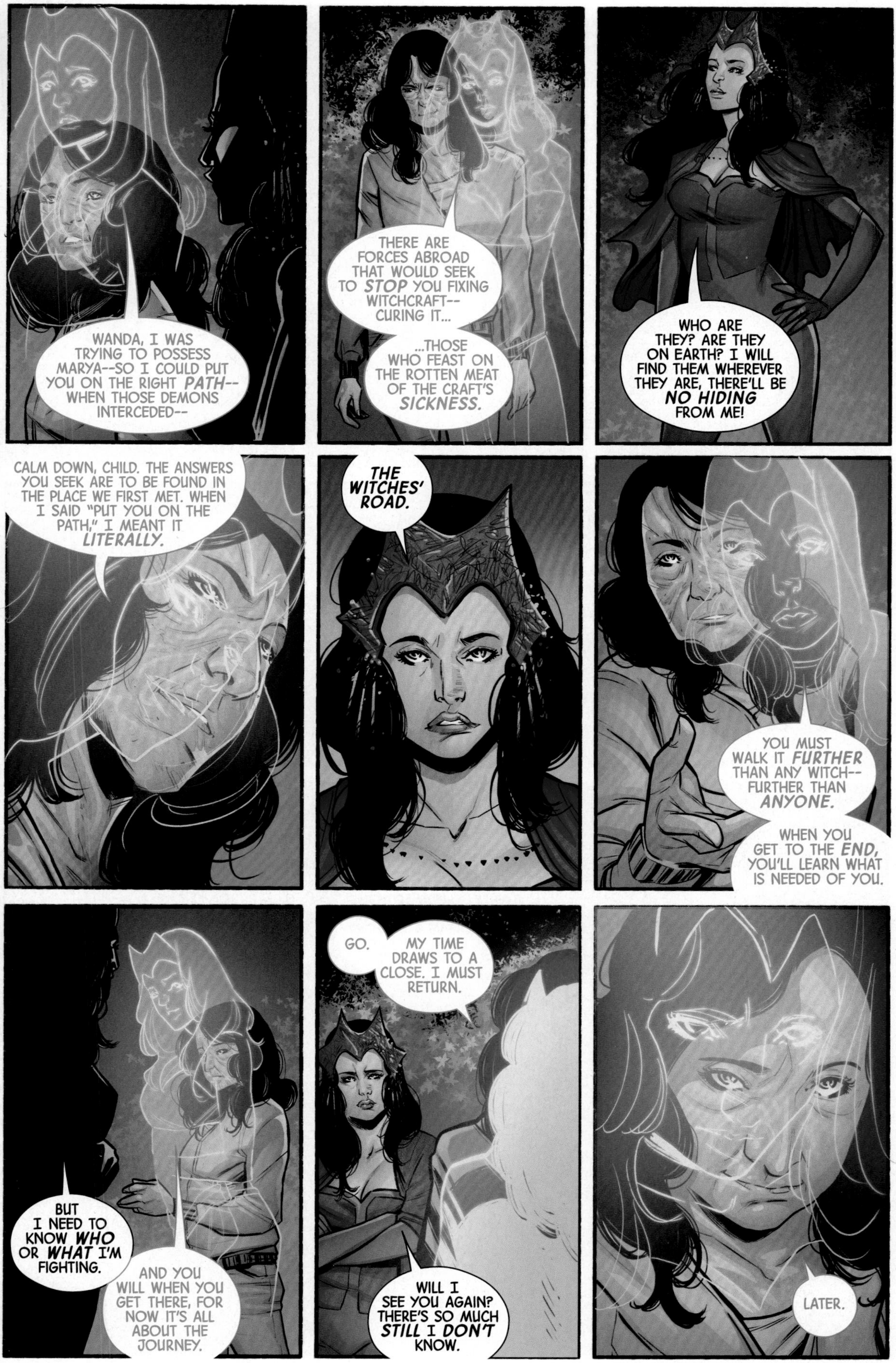
WANDA, I WAS TRYING TO POSSESS MARYA--SO I COULD PUT YOU ON THE RIGHT PATH--WHEN THOSE DEMONS INTERCEDED--
THERE ARE FORCES ABROAD THAT WOULD SEEK TO STOP YOU FIXING WITCHCRAFT--CURING IT...
...THOSE WHO FEAST ON THE ROTTEN MEAT OF THE CRAFT'S SICKNESS.
WHO ARE THEY? ARE THEY ON EARTH? I WILL FIND THEM WHEREVER THEY ARE, THERE'LL BE NO HIDING FROM ME!
CALM DOWN, CHILD. THE ANSWERS YOU SEEK ARE TO BE FOUND IN THE PLACE WE FIRST MET. WHEN I SAID "PUT YOU ON THE PATH," I MEANT IT LITERALLY.
THE WITCHES' ROAD.
YOU MUST WALK IT FURTHER THAN ANY WITCH--FURTHER THAN ANYONE.
WHEN YOU GET TO THE END, YOU'LL LEARN WHAT IS NEEDED OF YOU.
BUT I NEED TO KNOW WHO OR WHAT I'M FIGHTING.
AND YOU WILL WHEN YOU GET THERE, FOR NOW IT'S ALL ABOUT THE JOURNEY.
GO.
MY TIME DRAWS TO A CLOSE. I MUST RETURN.
WILL I SEE YOU AGAIN? THERE'S SO MUCH STILL I DON'T KNOW.
LATER.

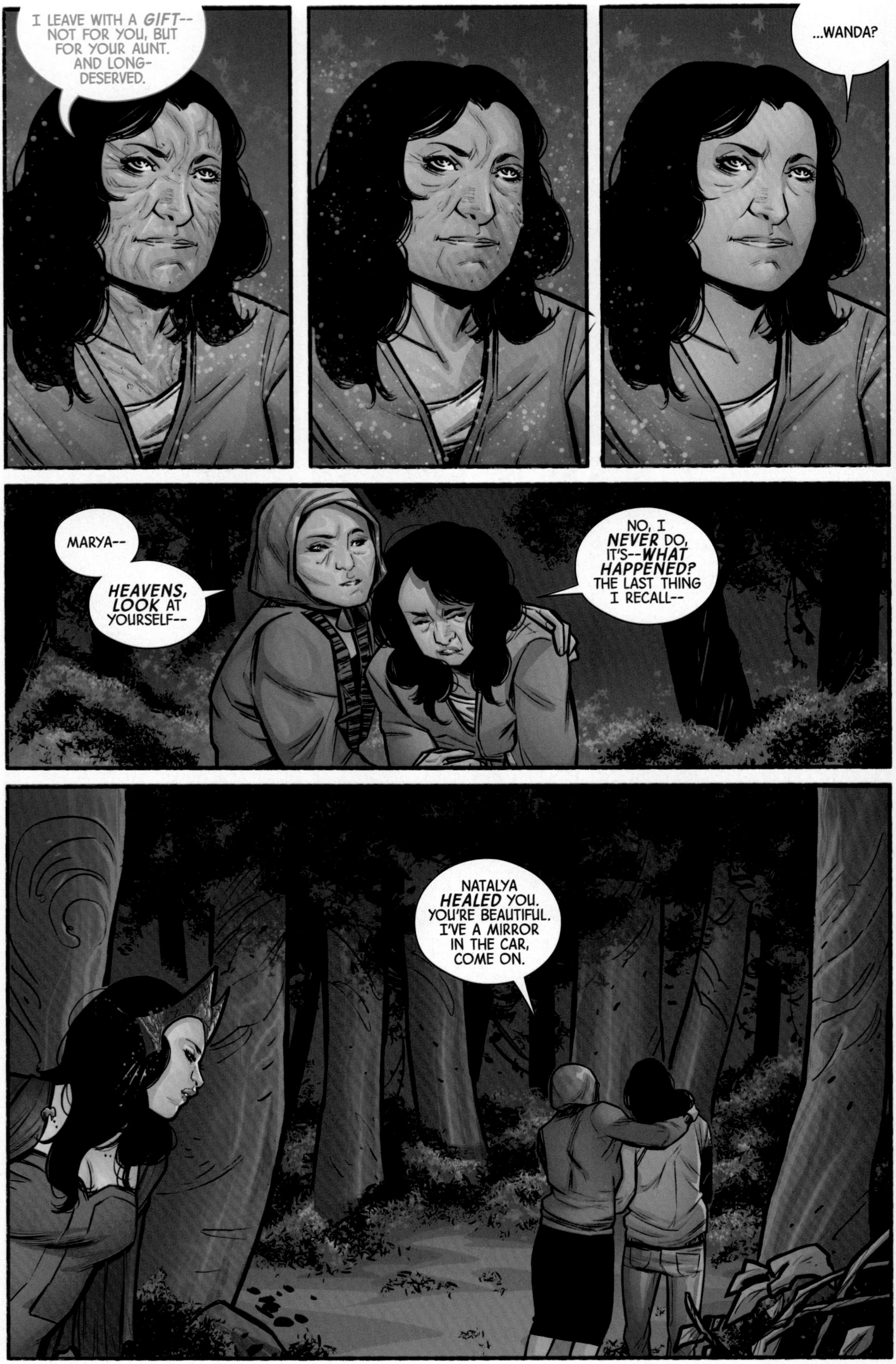
I LEAVE WITH A GIFT-- NOT FOR YOU, BUT FOR YOUR AUNT. AND LONG-DESERVED.
...WANDA?
MARYA--
HEAVENS, LOOK AT YOURSELF--
NO, I NEVER DO, IT'S--WHAT HAPPENED? THE LAST THING I RECALL--
NATALYA HEALED YOU. YOU'RE BEAUTIFUL. I'VE A MIRROR IN THE CAR, COME ON.

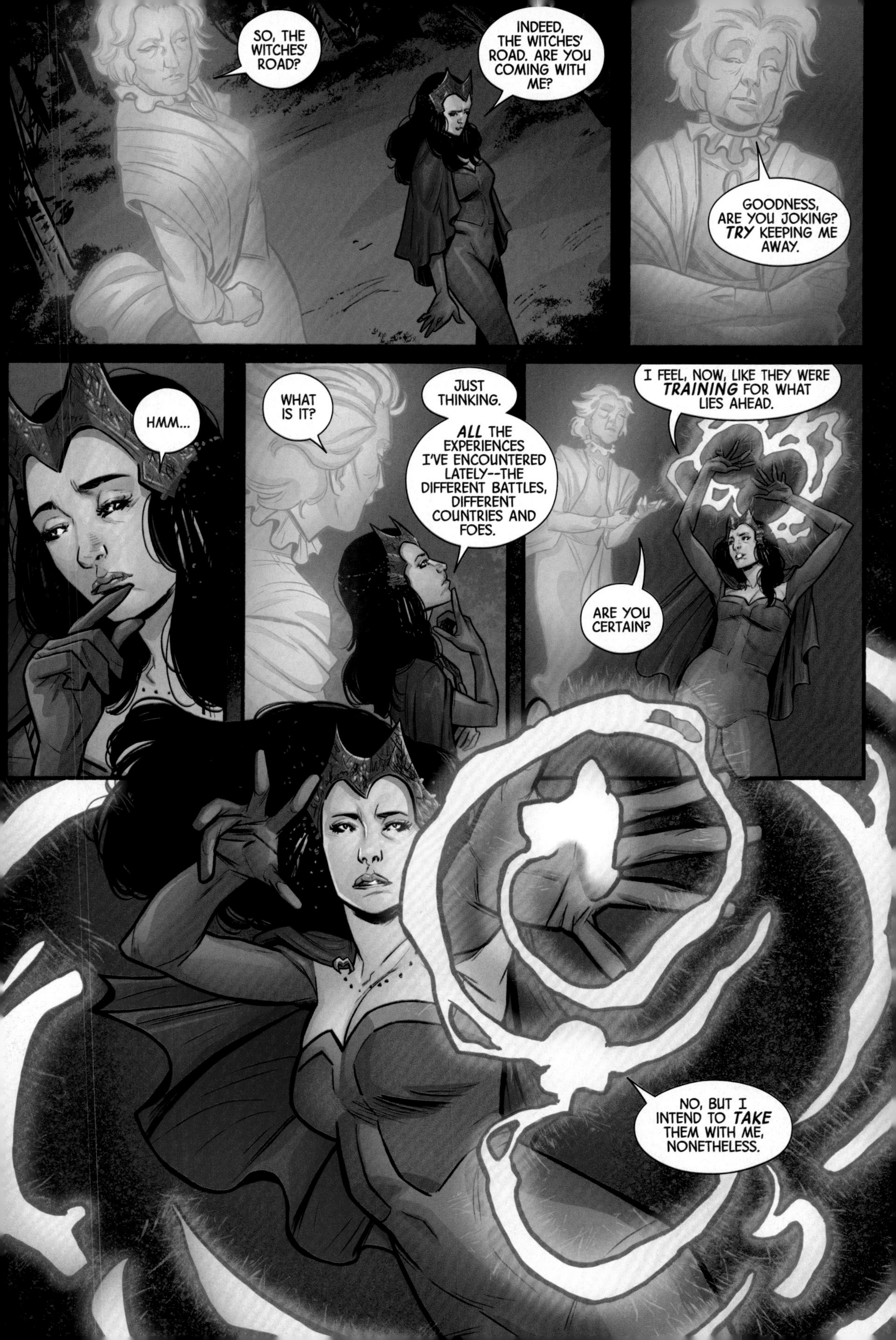
SO, THE WITCHES' ROAD?
INDEED, THE WITCHES' ROAD. ARE YOU COMING WITH ME?
GOODNESS, ARE YOU JOKING? TRY KEEPING ME AWAY.
HMM...
WHAT IS IT?
JUST THINKING.
ALL THE EXPERIENCES I'VE ENCOUNTERED LATELY--THE DIFFERENT BATTLES, DIFFERENT COUNTRIES AND FOES.
I FEEL, NOW, LIKE THEY WERE TRAINING FOR WHAT LIES AHEAD.
ARE YOU CERTAIN?
NO, BUT I INTEND TO TAKE THEM WITH ME, NONETHELESS.

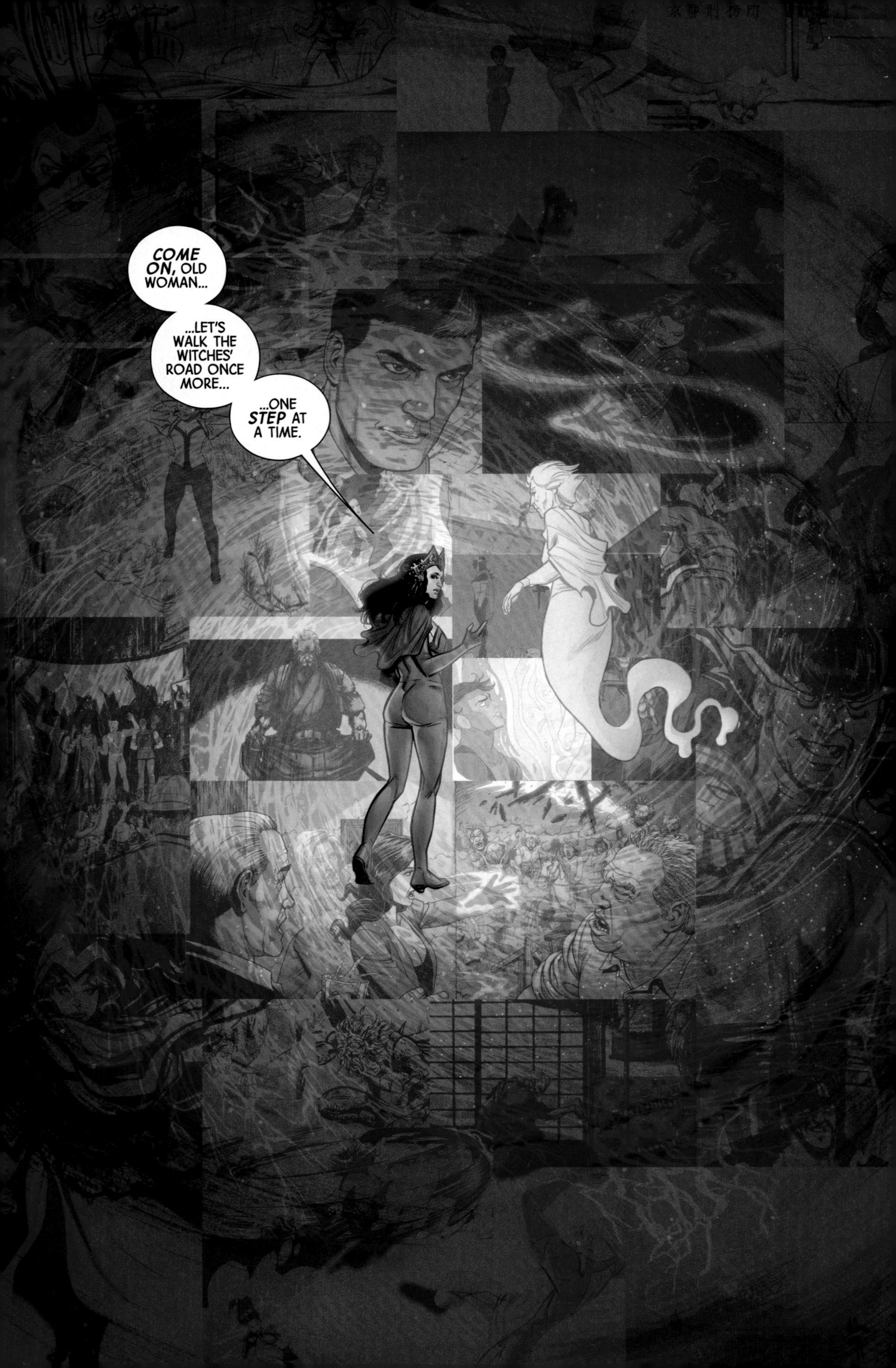

COME ON, OLD WOMAN...
...LET'S WALK THE WITCHES' ROAD ONCE MORE...
...ONE STEP AT A TIME.

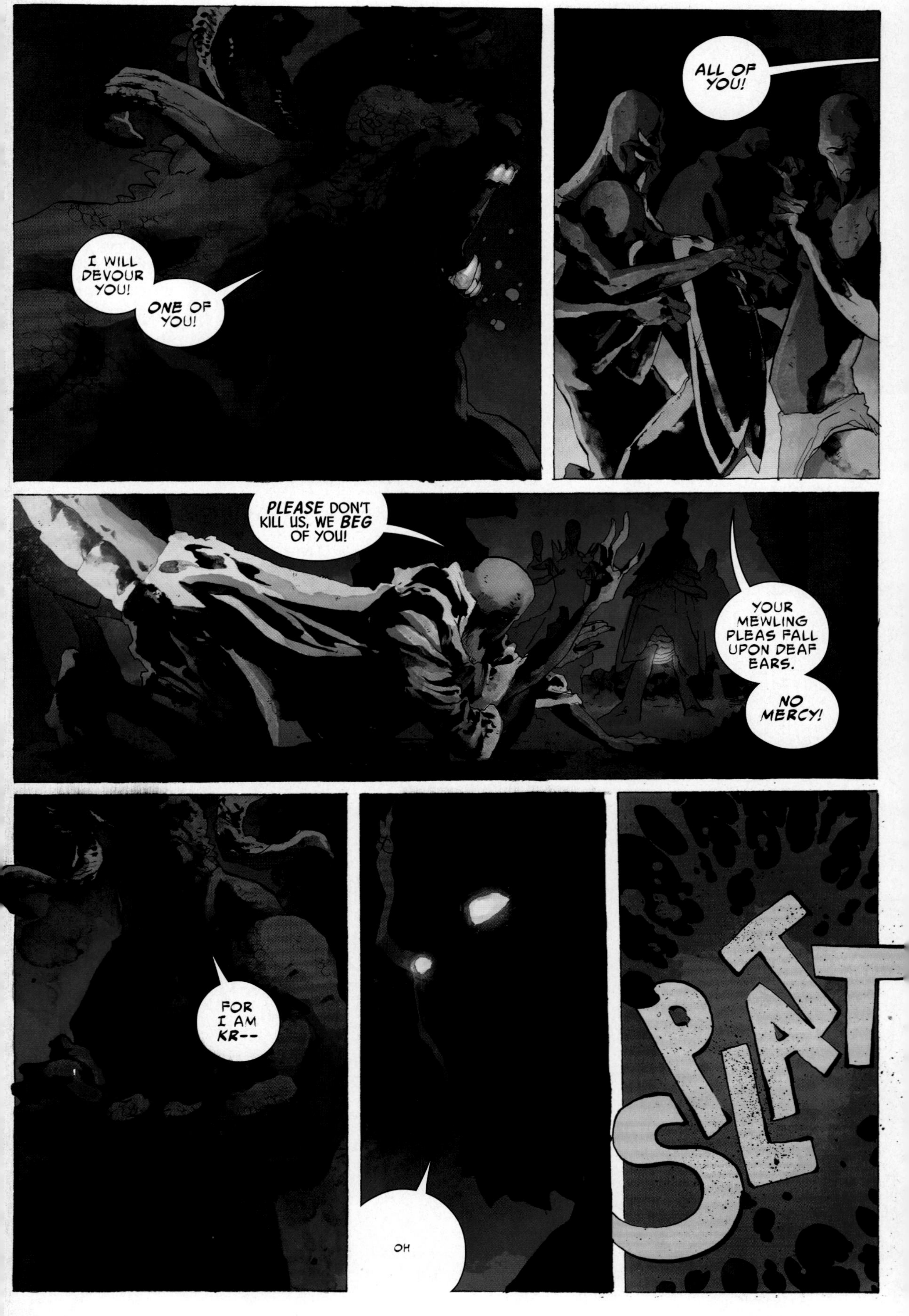
I WILL DEVOUR YOU!
ONE OF YOU!
ALL OF YOU!
PLEASE DON'T KILL US, WE BEG OF YOU!
YOUR MEWLING PLEAS FALL UPON DEAF EARS.
NO MERCY!
FOR I AM KR--
OH
SPLAT

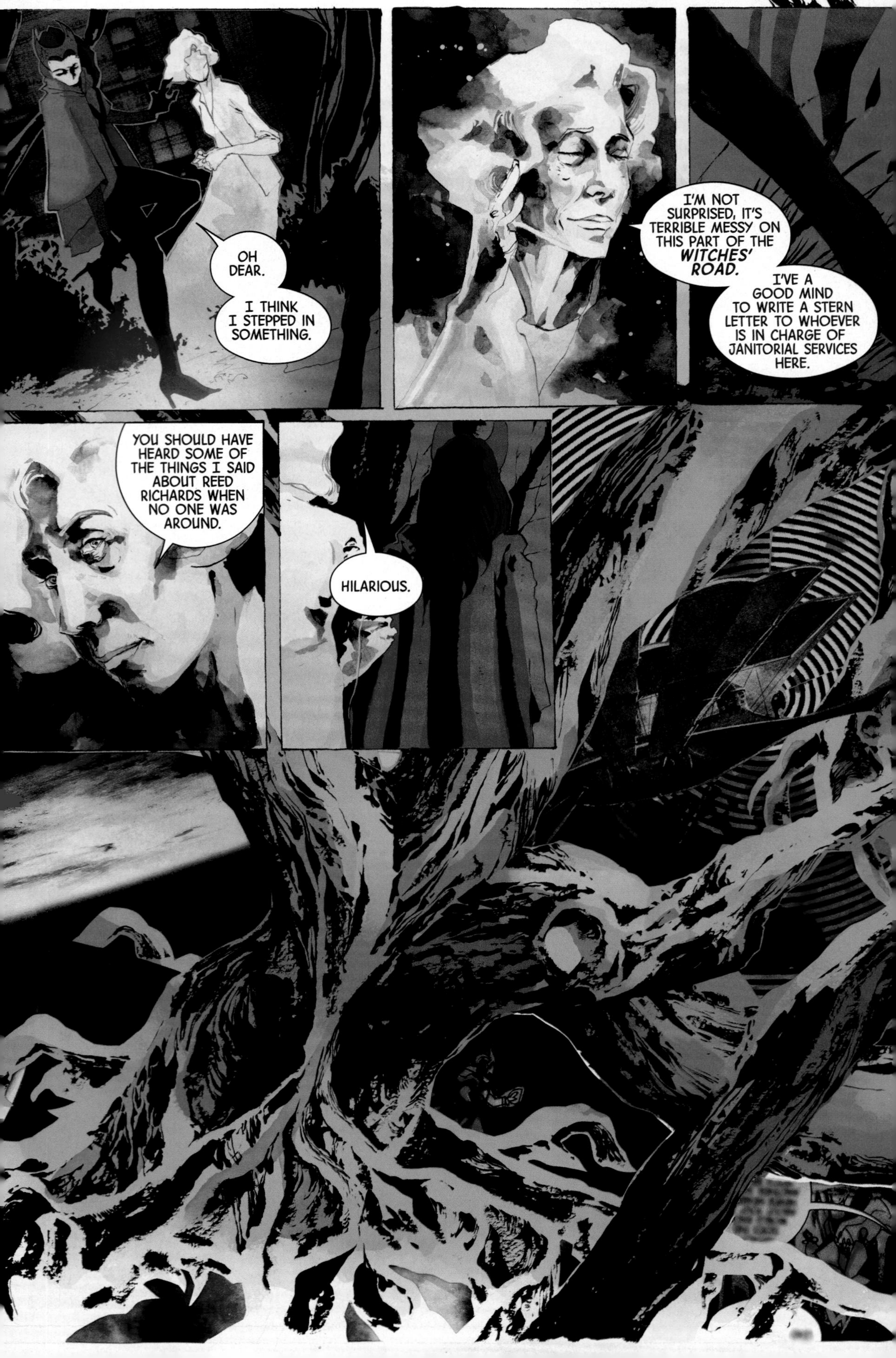
OH DEAR.
I THINK I STEPPED IN SOMETHING.
I'M NOT SURPRISED, IT'S TERRIBLE MESSY ON THIS PART OF THE WITCHES' ROAD.
I'VE A GOOD MIND TO WRITE A STERN LETTER TO WHOEVER IS IN CHARGE OF JANITORIAL SERVICES HERE.
YOU SHOULD HAVE HEARD SOME OF THE THINGS I SAID ABOUT REED RICHARDS WHEN NO ONE WAS AROUND.
HILARIOUS.

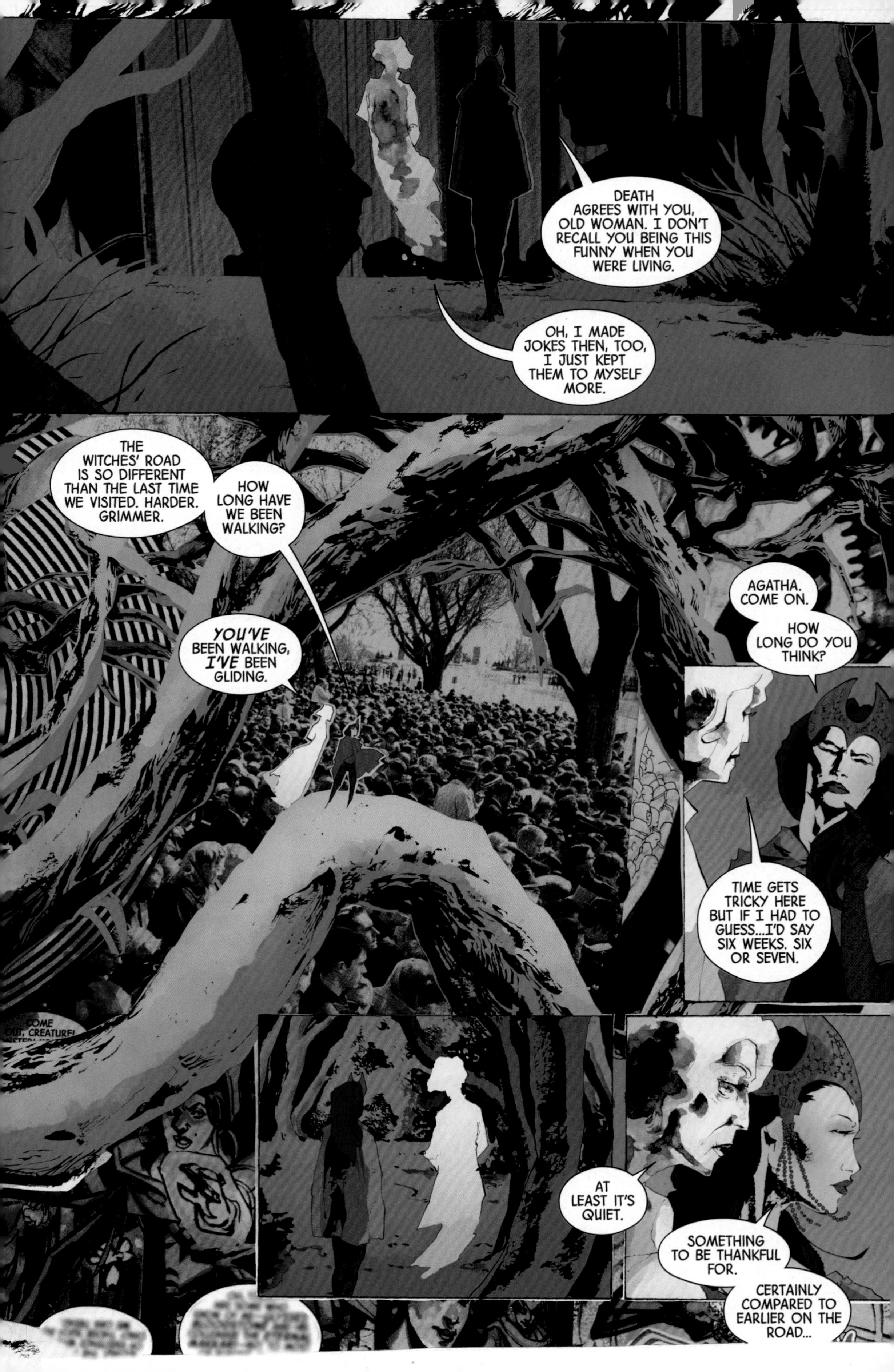
DEATH AGREES WITH YOU, OLD WOMAN. I DON'T RECALL YOU BEING THIS FUNNY WHEN YOU WERE LIVING.
OH, I MADE JOKES THEN, TOO, I JUST KEPT THEM TO MYSELF MORE.
THE WITCHES' ROAD IS SO DIFFERENT THAN THE LAST TIME WE VISITED. HARDER. GRIMMER.
HOW LONG HAVE WE BEEN WALKING?
YOU'VE BEEN WALKING, I'VE BEEN GLIDING.
AGATHA. COME ON.
HOW LONG DO YOU THINK?
TIME GETS TRICKY HERE BUT IF I HAD TO GUESS...I'D SAY SIX WEEKS. SIX OR SEVEN.
AT LEAST IT'S QUIET.
SOMETHING TO BE THANKFUL FOR.
CERTAINLY COMPARED TO EARLIER ON THE ROAD...

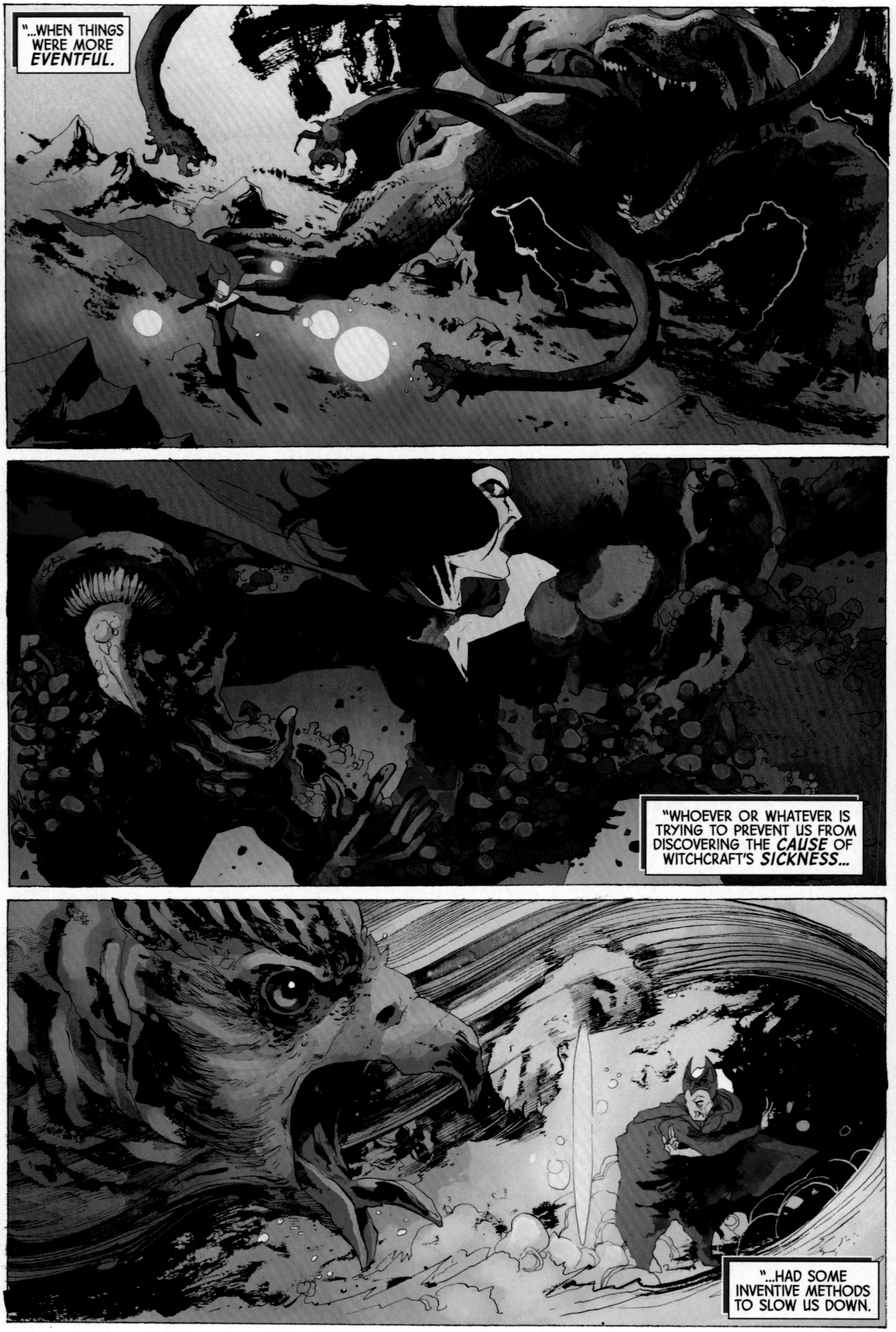
"...WHEN THINGS WERE MORE EVENTFUL.
"WHOEVER OR WHATEVER IS TRYING TO PREVENT US FROM DISCOVERING THE CAUSE OF WITCHCRAFT'S SICKNESS...
"...HAD SOME INVENTIVE METHODS TO SLOW US DOWN.

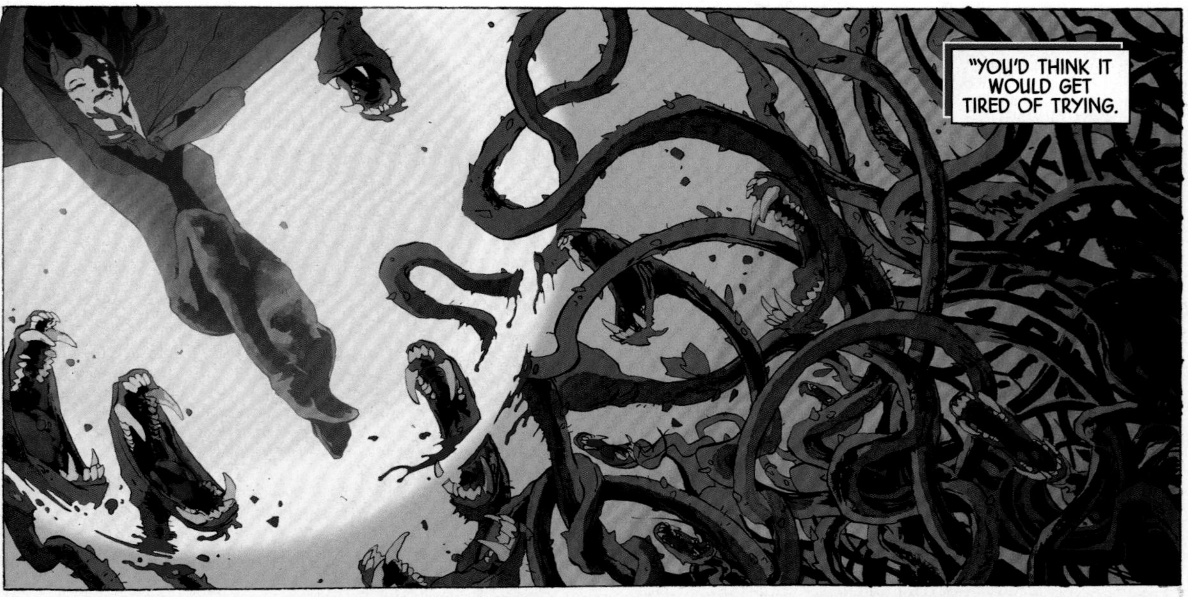
"YOU'D THINK IT WOULD GET TIRED OF TRYING.

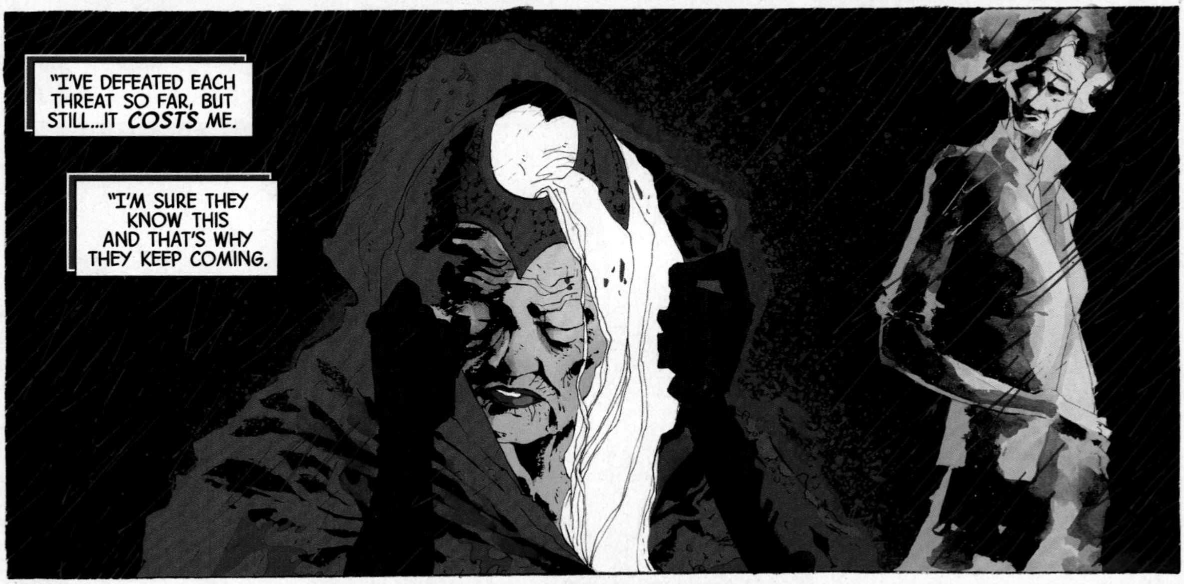
"I'VE DEFEATED EACH THREAT SO FAR, BUT STILL...IT *COSTS* ME.
"I'M SURE THEY KNOW THIS AND THAT'S WHY THEY KEEP COMING.

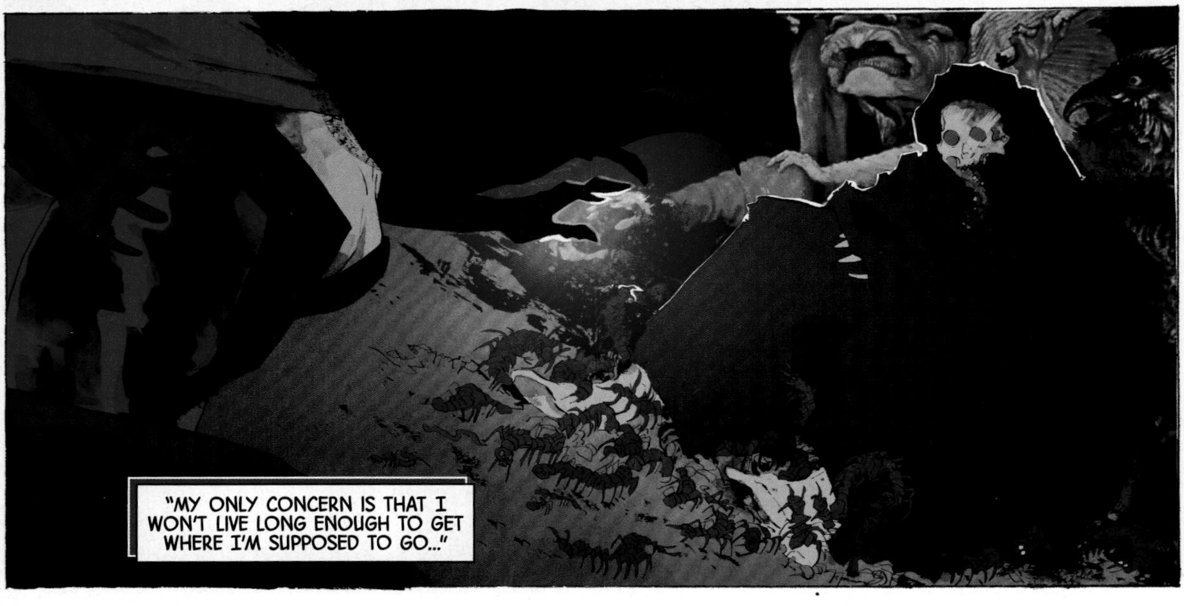
"MY ONLY CONCERN IS THAT I WON'T LIVE LONG ENOUGH TO GET WHERE I'M SUPPOSED TO GO..."

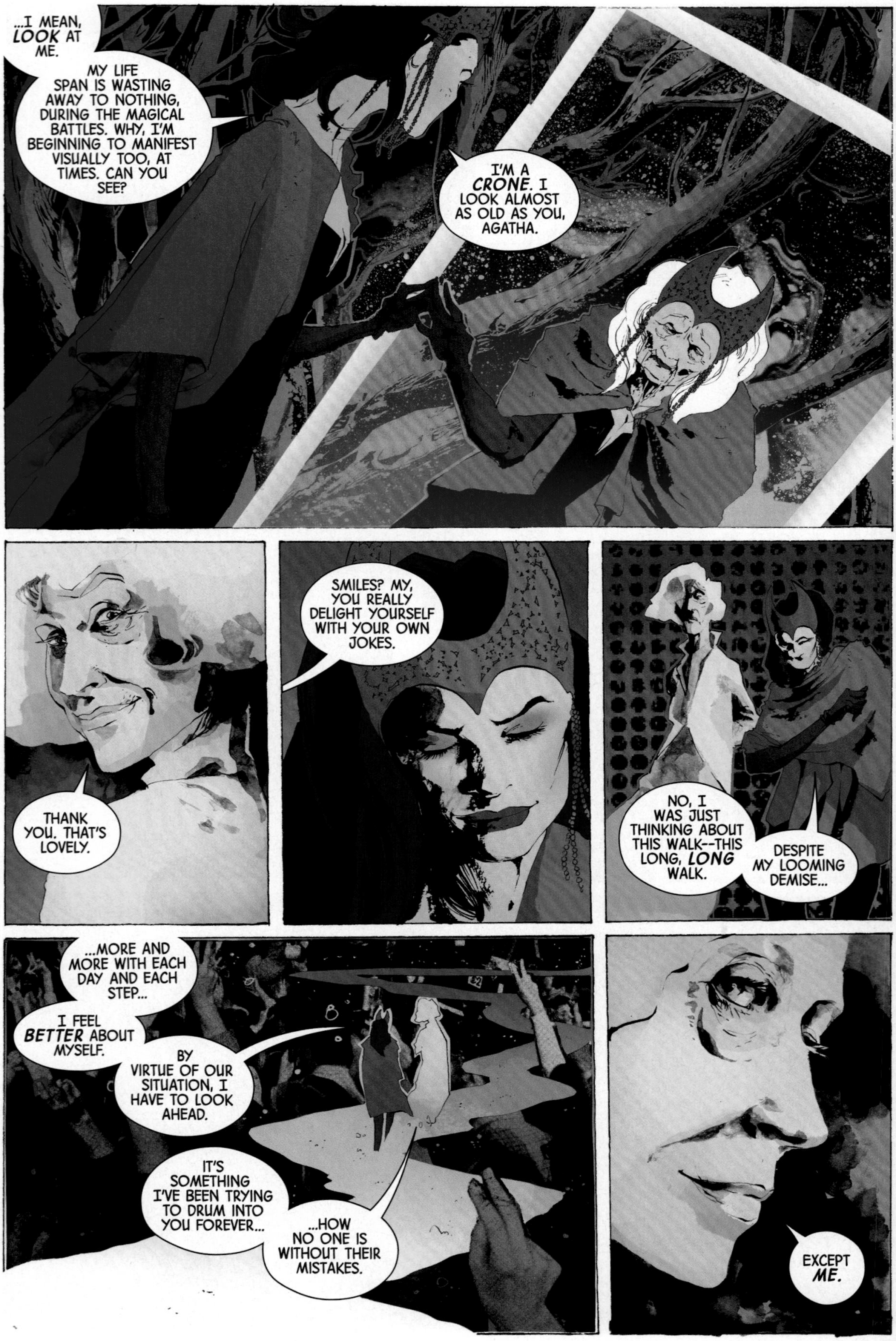
...I MEAN, LOOK AT ME.
MY LIFE SPAN IS WASTING AWAY TO NOTHING, DURING THE MAGICAL BATTLES. WHY, I'M BEGINNING TO MANIFEST VISUALLY TOO, AT TIMES. CAN YOU SEE?
I'M A CRONE. I LOOK ALMOST AS OLD AS YOU, AGATHA.
THANK YOU. THAT'S LOVELY.
SMILES? MY, YOU REALLY DELIGHT YOURSELF WITH YOUR OWN JOKES.
NO, I WAS JUST THINKING ABOUT THIS WALK--THIS LONG, LONG WALK.
DESPITE MY LOOMING DEMISE...
...MORE AND MORE WITH EACH DAY AND EACH STEP...
I FEEL BETTER ABOUT MYSELF.
BY VIRTUE OF OUR SITUATION, I HAVE TO LOOK AHEAD.
IT'S SOMETHING I'VE BEEN TRYING TO DRUM INTO YOU FOREVER...
...HOW NO ONE IS WITHOUT THEIR MISTAKES.
EXCEPT ME.

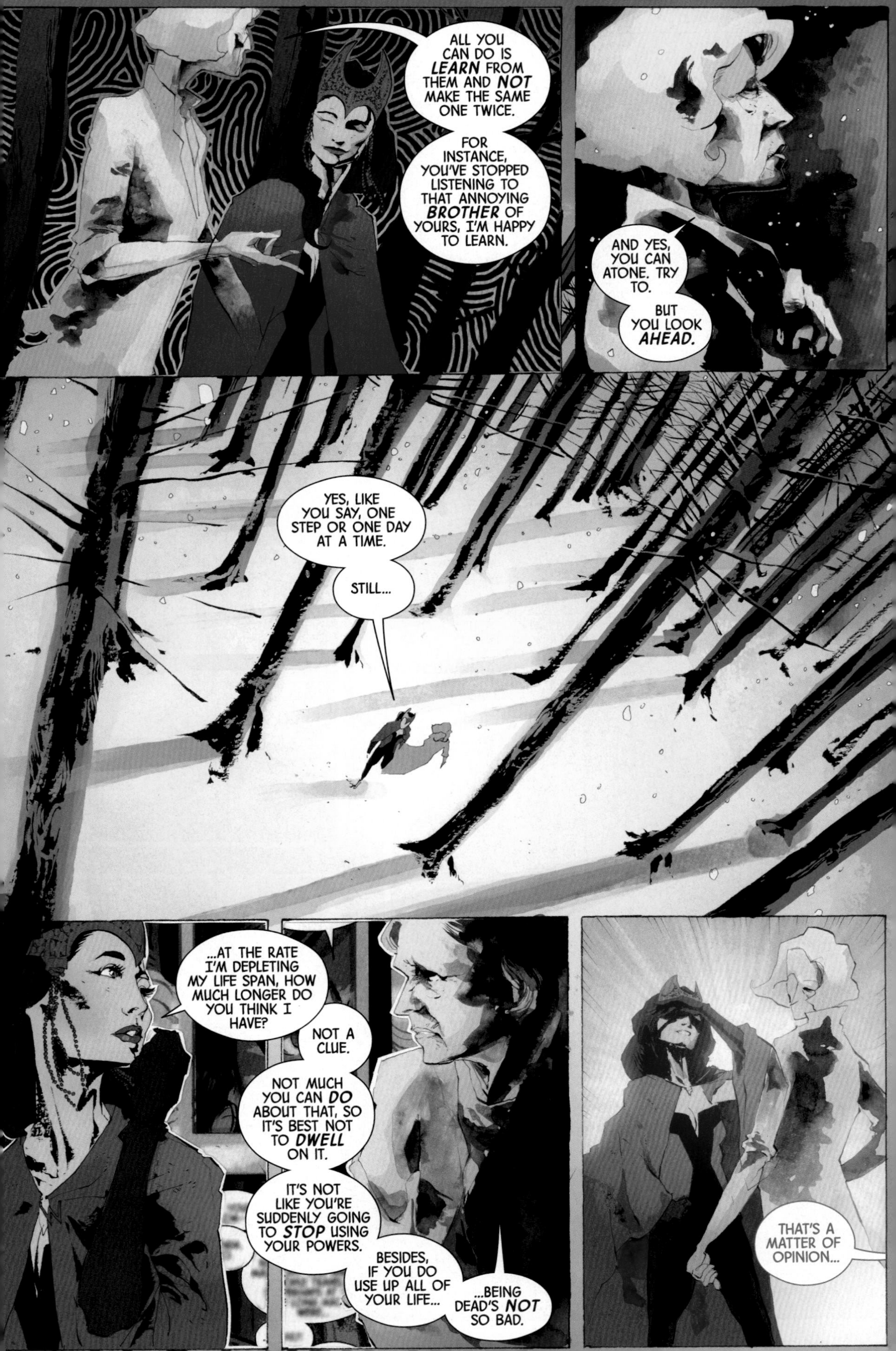
ALL YOU CAN DO IS LEARN FROM THEM AND NOT MAKE THE SAME ONE TWICE.
FOR INSTANCE, YOU'VE STOPPED LISTENING TO THAT ANNOYING BROTHER OF YOURS, I'M HAPPY TO LEARN.
AND YES, YOU CAN ATONE. TRY TO.
BUT YOU LOOK AHEAD.
YES, LIKE YOU SAY, ONE STEP OR ONE DAY AT A TIME.
STILL...
...AT THE RATE I'M DEPLETING MY LIFE SPAN, HOW MUCH LONGER DO YOU THINK I HAVE?
NOT A CLUE.
NOT MUCH YOU CAN DO ABOUT THAT, SO IT'S BEST NOT TO DWELL ON IT.
IT'S NOT LIKE YOU'RE SUDDENLY GOING TO STOP USING YOUR POWERS.
BESIDES, IF YOU DO USE UP ALL OF YOUR LIFE...
...BEING DEAD'S NOT SO BAD.
THAT'S A MATTER OF OPINION...

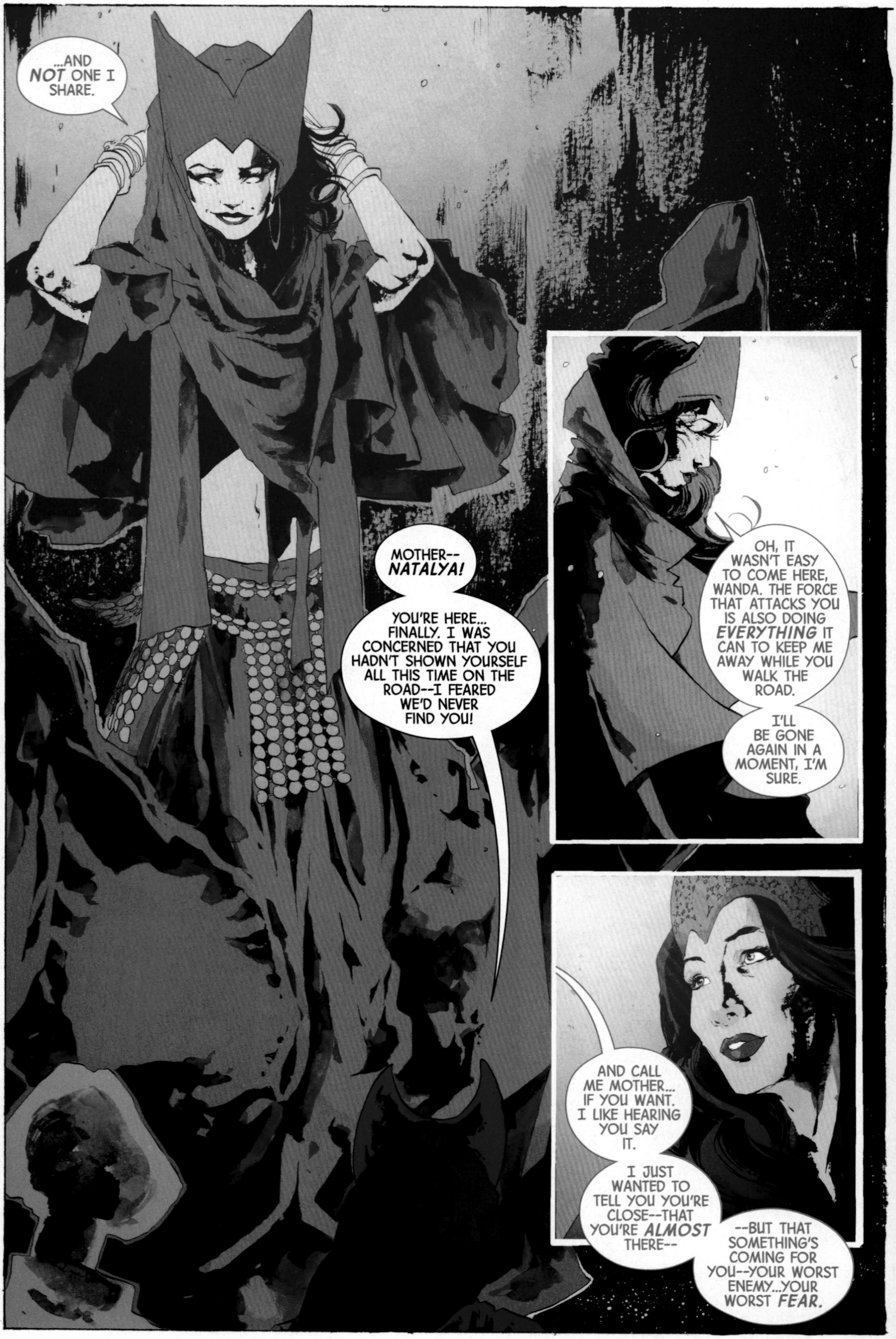

...AND NOT ONE I SHARE.
MOTHER-- NATALYA!
YOU'RE HERE... FINALLY. I WAS CONCERNED THAT YOU HADN'T SHOWN YOURSELF ALL THIS TIME ON THE ROAD--I FEARED WE'D NEVER FIND YOU!
OH, IT WASN'T EASY TO COME HERE, WANDA. THE FORCE THAT ATTACKS YOU IS ALSO DOING EVERYTHING IT CAN TO KEEP ME AWAY WHILE YOU WALK THE ROAD.
I'LL BE GONE AGAIN IN A MOMENT, I'M SURE.
AND CALL ME MOTHER... IF YOU WANT. I LIKE HEARING YOU SAY IT.
I JUST WANTED TO TELL YOU YOU'RE CLOSE--THAT YOU'RE ALMOST THERE--
--BUT THAT SOMETHING'S COMING FOR YOU--YOUR WORST ENEMY...YOUR WORST FEAR.

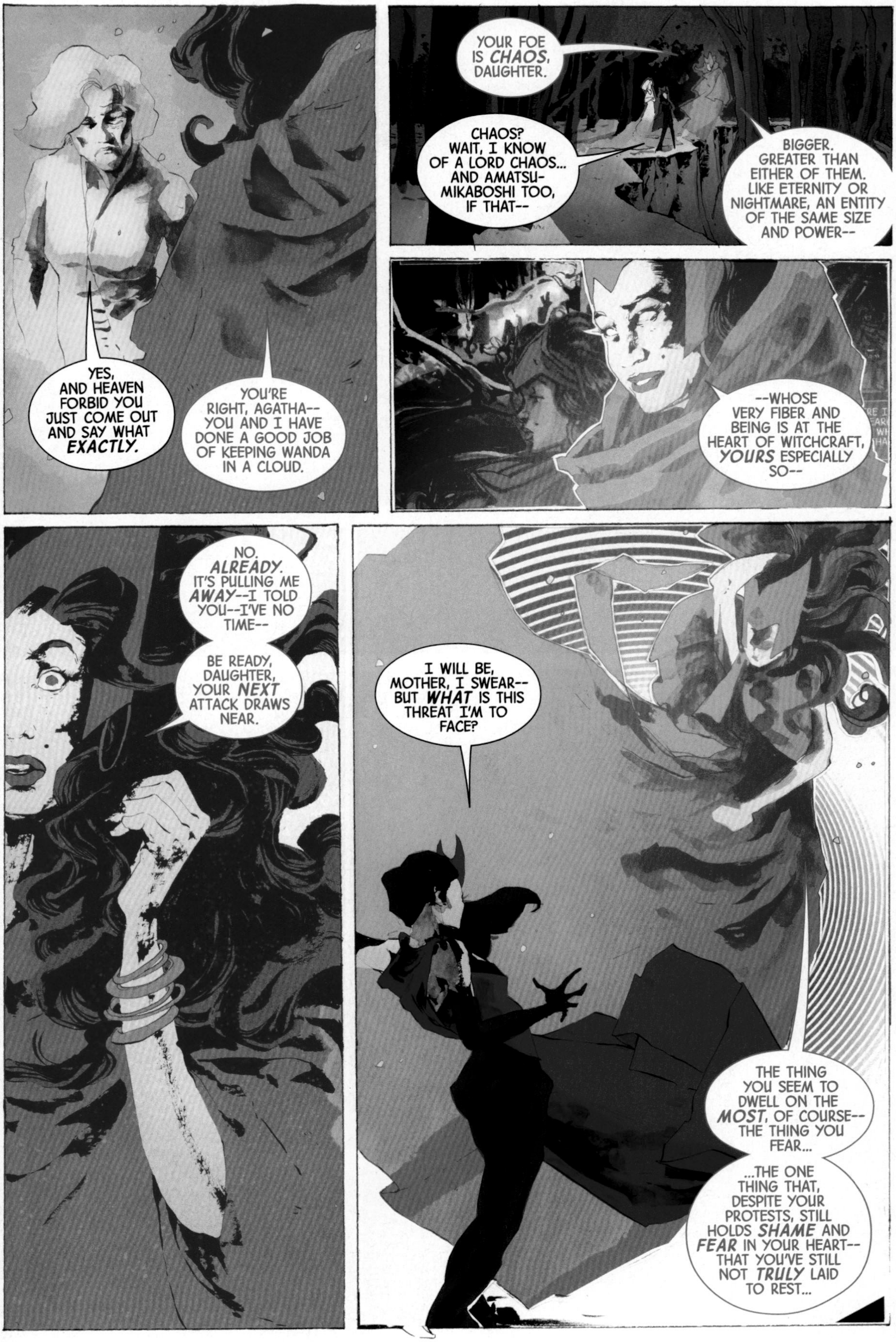
YES, AND HEAVEN FORBID YOU JUST COME OUT AND SAY WHAT EXACTLY.
YOU'RE RIGHT, AGATHA--YOU AND I HAVE DONE A GOOD JOB OF KEEPING WANDA IN A CLOUD.
YOUR FOE IS CHAOS, DAUGHTER.
CHAOS? WAIT, I KNOW OF A LORD CHAOS... AND AMATSU-MIKABOSHI TOO, IF THAT--
BIGGER. GREATER THAN EITHER OF THEM. LIKE ETERNITY OR NIGHTMARE, AN ENTITY OF THE SAME SIZE AND POWER--
--WHOSE VERY FIBER AND BEING IS AT THE HEART OF WITCHCRAFT, YOURS ESPECIALLY SO--
NO. ALREADY. IT'S PULLING ME AWAY--I TOLD YOU--I'VE NO TIME--
BE READY, DAUGHTER, YOUR NEXT ATTACK DRAWS NEAR.
I WILL BE, MOTHER, I SWEAR--BUT WHAT IS THIS THREAT I'M TO FACE?
THE THING YOU SEEM TO DWELL ON THE MOST, OF COURSE--THE THING YOU FEAR...
...THE ONE THING THAT, DESPITE YOUR PROTESTS, STILL HOLDS SHAME AND FEAR IN YOUR HEART--THAT YOU'VE STILL NOT TRULY LAID TO REST...

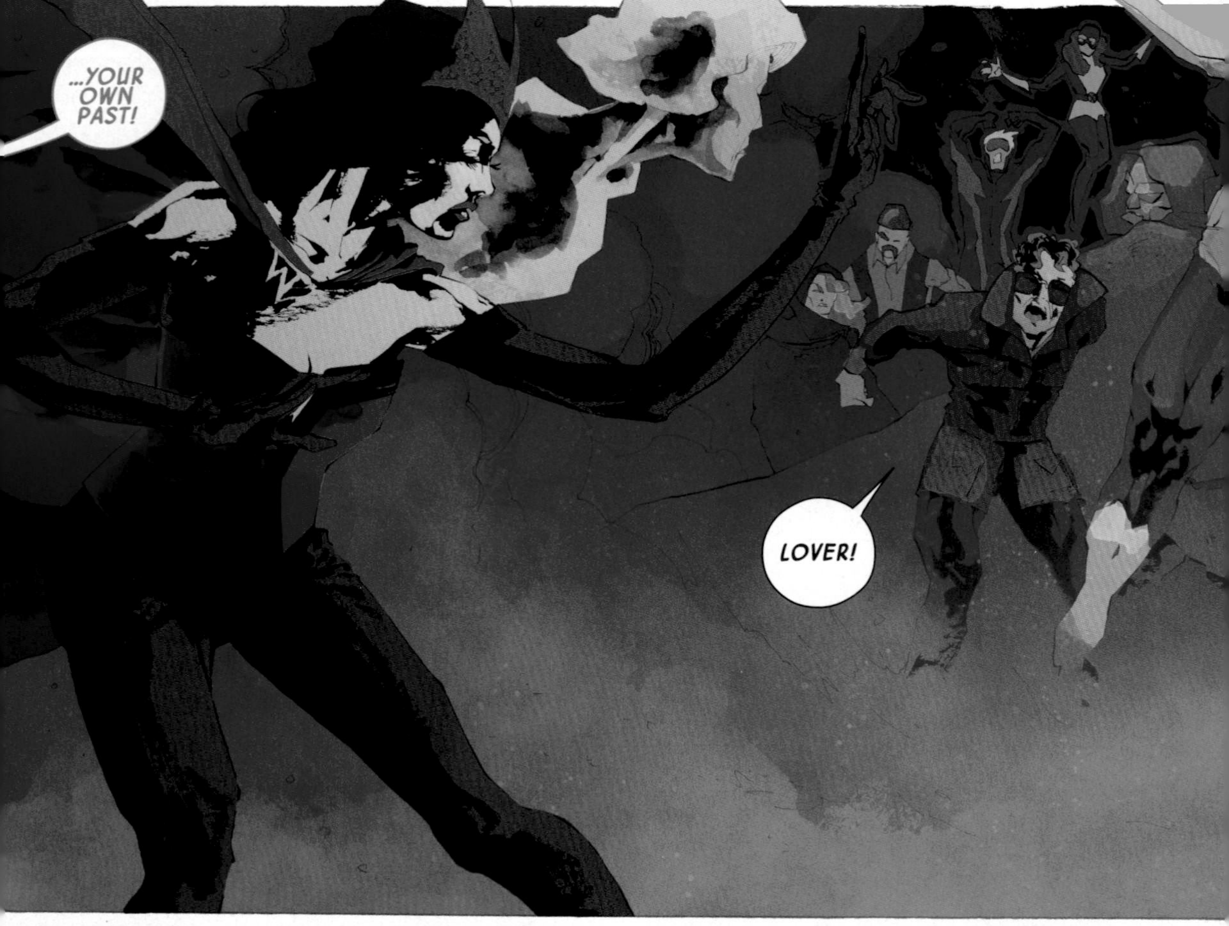
...YOUR OWN PAST!
LOVER!
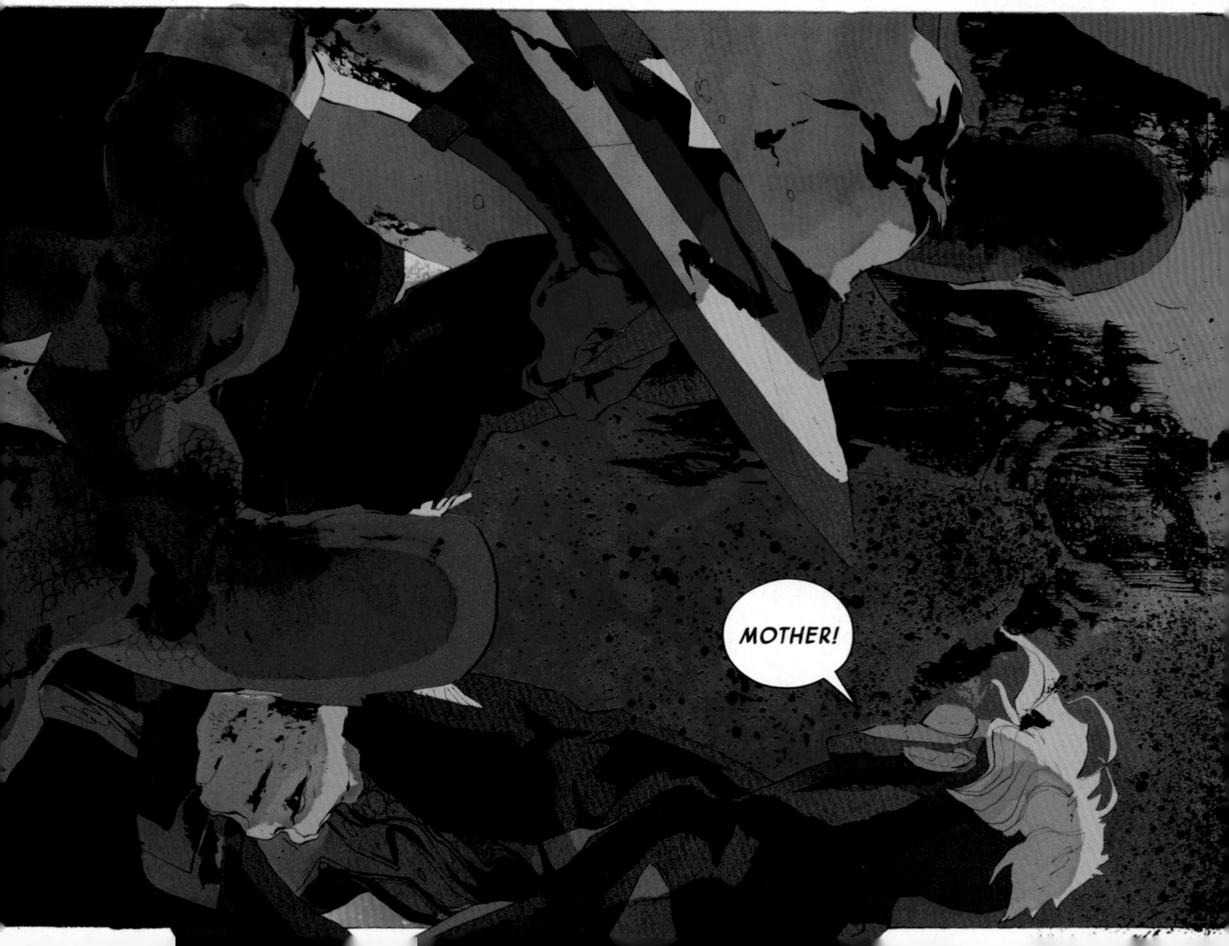
MOTHER!

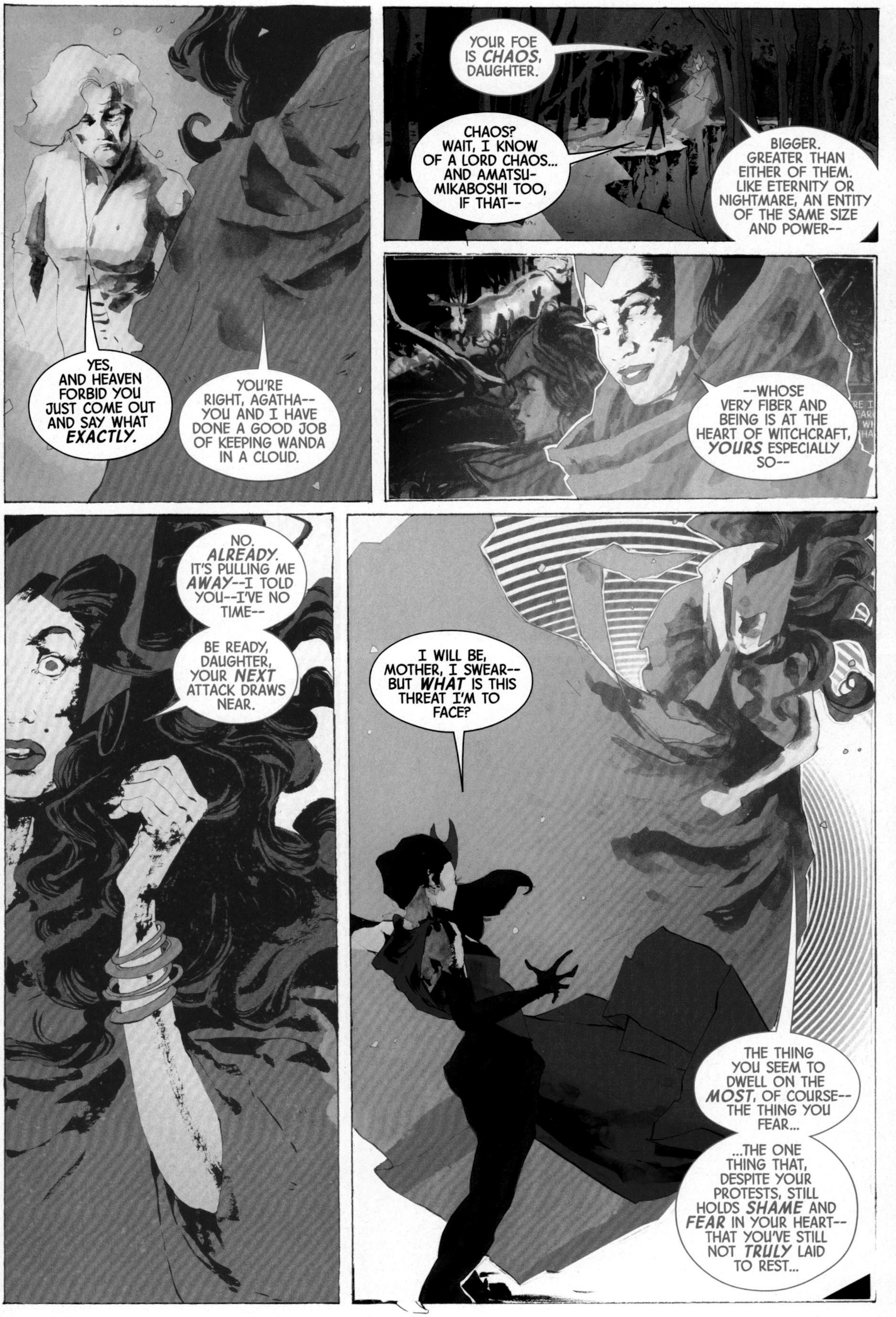
YES, AND HEAVEN FORBID YOU JUST COME OUT AND SAY WHAT EXACTLY.
YOU'RE RIGHT, AGATHA-- YOU AND I HAVE DONE A GOOD JOB OF KEEPING WANDA IN A CLOUD.
YOUR FOE IS CHAOS, DAUGHTER.
CHAOS? WAIT, I KNOW OF A LORD CHAOS... AND AMATSU-MIKABOSHI TOO, IF THAT--
BIGGER. GREATER THAN EITHER OF THEM. LIKE ETERNITY OR NIGHTMARE, AN ENTITY OF THE SAME SIZE AND POWER--
--WHOSE VERY FIBER AND BEING IS AT THE HEART OF WITCHCRAFT, YOURS ESPECIALLY SO--
NO. ALREADY. IT'S PULLING ME AWAY--I TOLD YOU--I'VE NO TIME--
BE READY, DAUGHTER, YOUR NEXT ATTACK DRAWS NEAR.
I WILL BE, MOTHER, I SWEAR-- BUT WHAT IS THIS THREAT I'M TO FACE?
THE THING YOU SEEM TO DWELL ON THE MOST, OF COURSE-- THE THING YOU FEAR...
...THE ONE THING THAT, DESPITE YOUR PROTESTS, STILL HOLDS SHAME AND FEAR IN YOUR HEART-- THAT YOU'VE STILL NOT TRULY LAID TO REST...

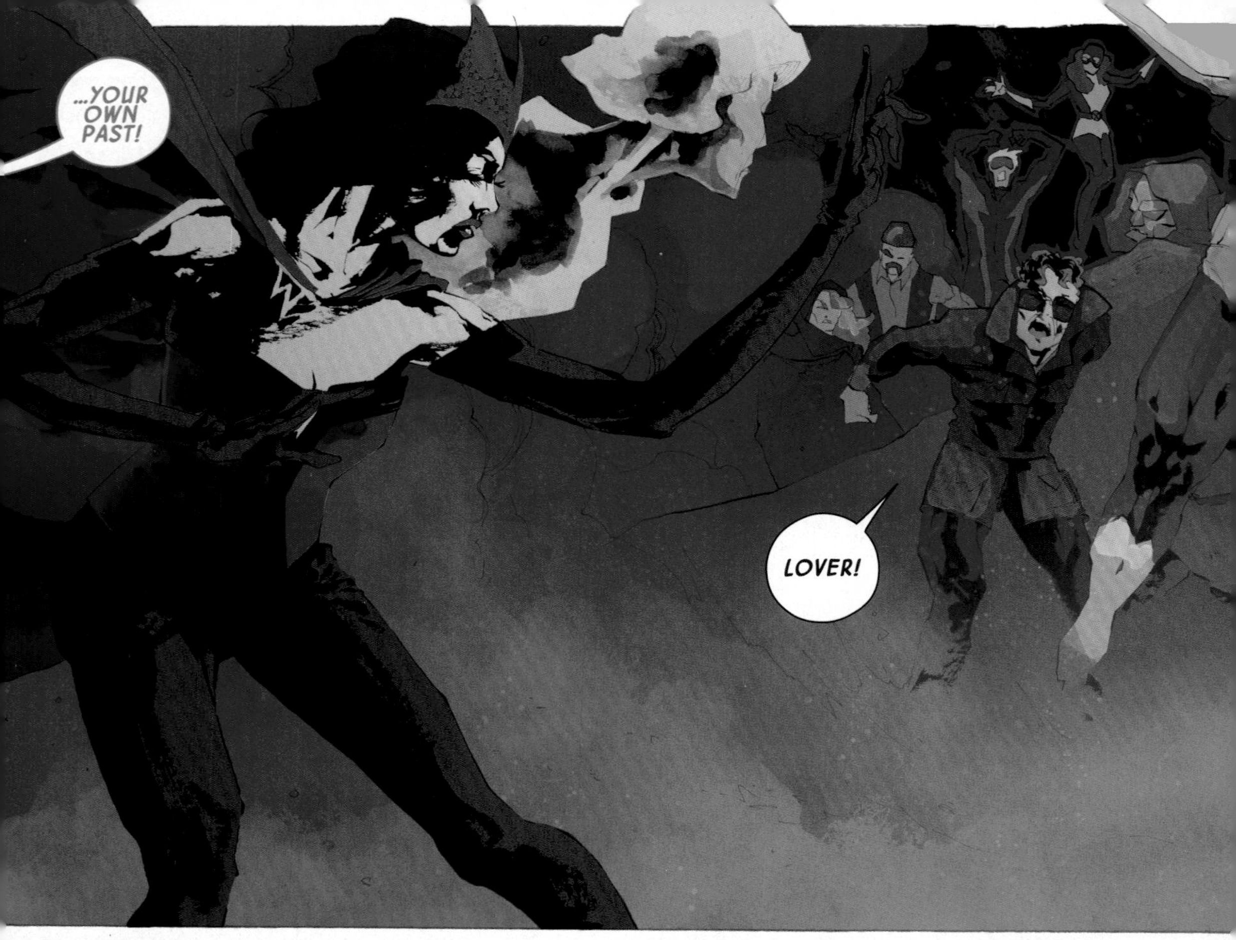
...YOUR OWN PAST!
LOVER!
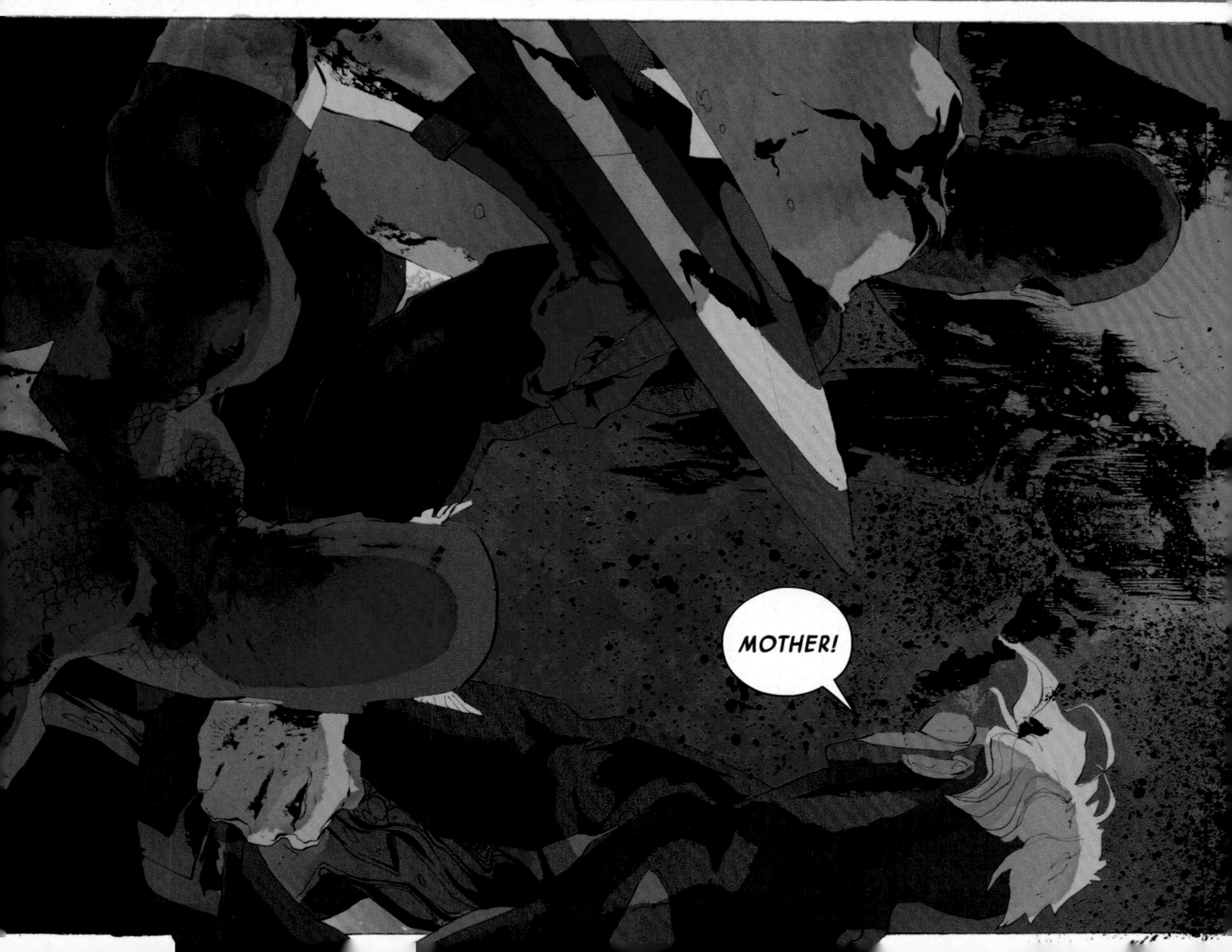
MOTHER!

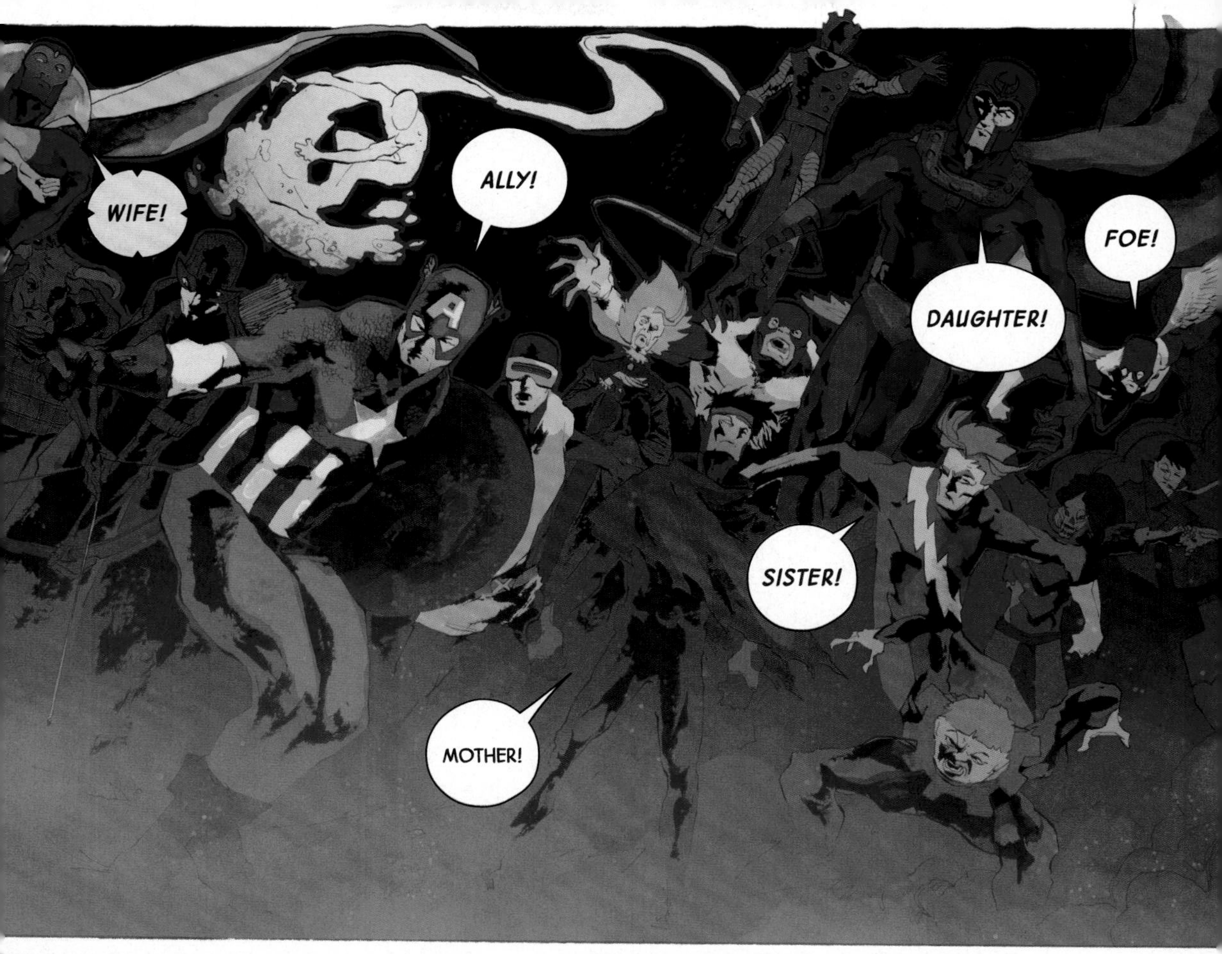
WIFE!
ALLY!
DAUGHTER!
FOE!
SISTER!
MOTHER!

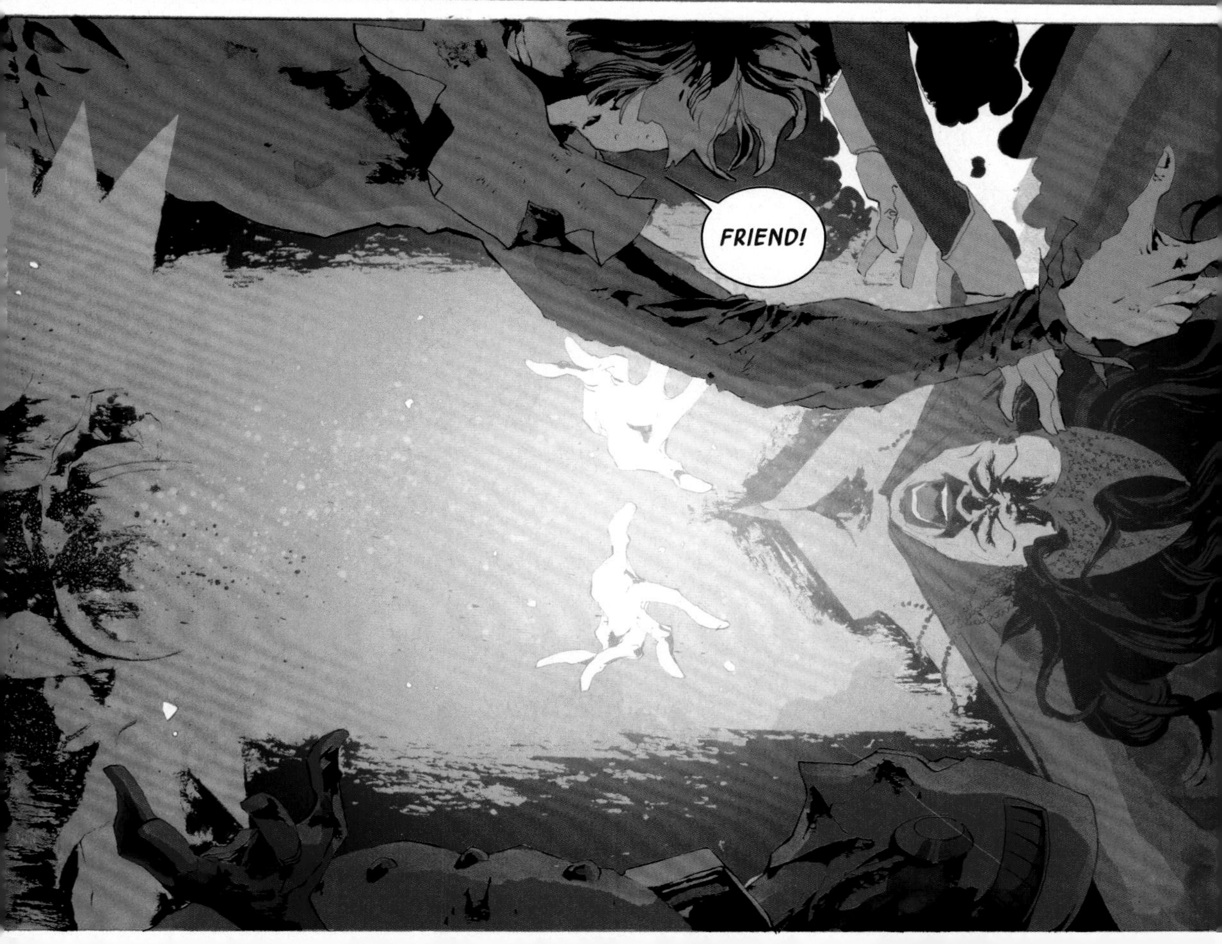
FRIEND!

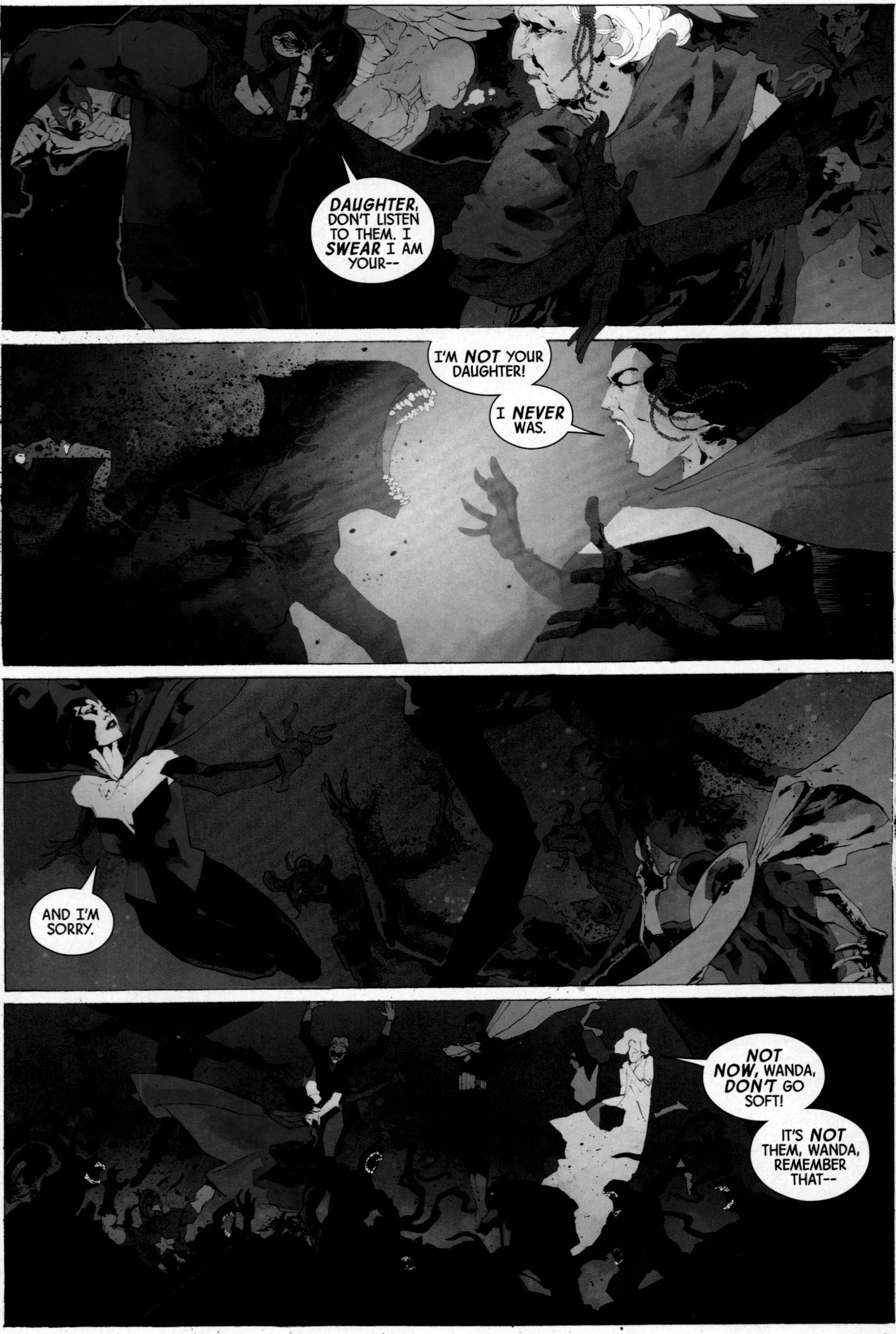
DAUGHTER, DON'T LISTEN TO THEM. I SWEAR I AM YOUR--
I'M NOT YOUR DAUGHTER!
I NEVER WAS.
AND I'M SORRY.
NOT NOW, WANDA, DON'T GO SOFT!
IT'S NOT THEM, WANDA, REMEMBER THAT--

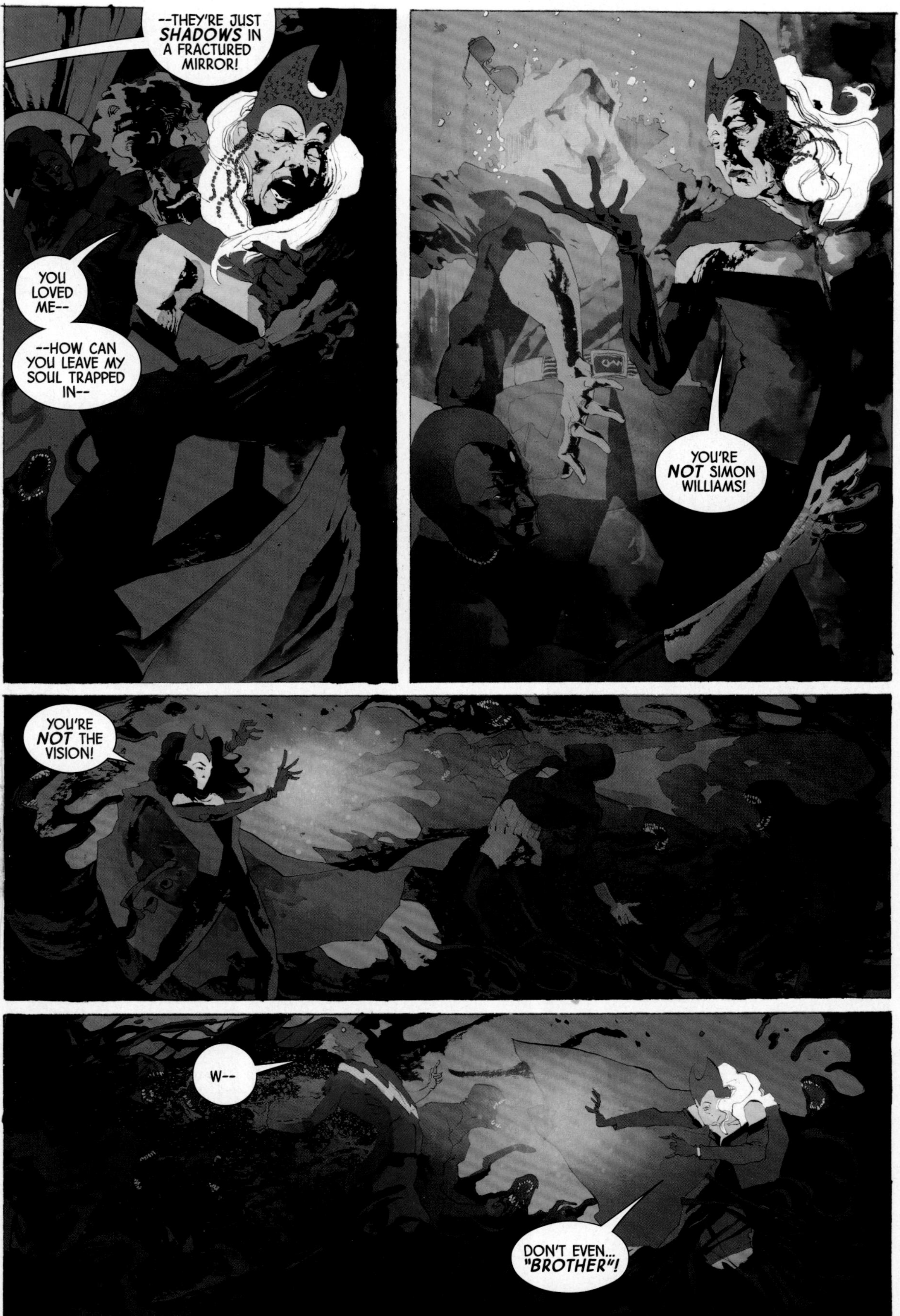
--THEY'RE JUST *SHADOWS* IN A FRACTURED MIRROR!
YOU LOVED ME--
--HOW CAN YOU LEAVE MY SOUL TRAPPED IN--
YOU'RE *NOT* SIMON WILLIAMS!
YOU'RE *NOT* THE VISION!
W--
DON'T EVEN... *"BROTHER"*!

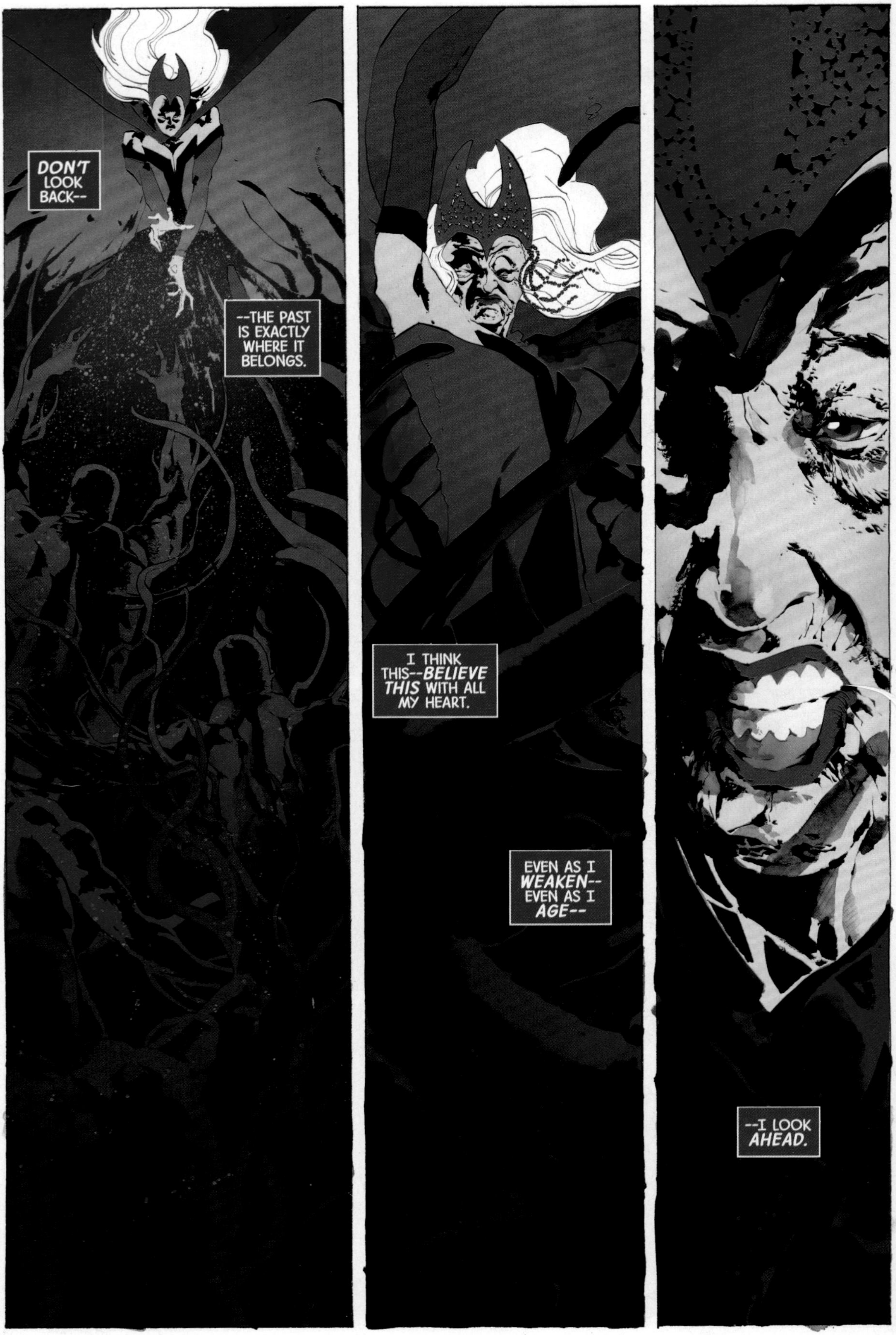
DON'T LOOK BACK--
--THE PAST IS EXACTLY WHERE IT BELONGS.
I THINK THIS--BELIEVE THIS WITH ALL MY HEART.
EVEN AS I WEAKEN-- EVEN AS I AGE--
--I LOOK AHEAD.

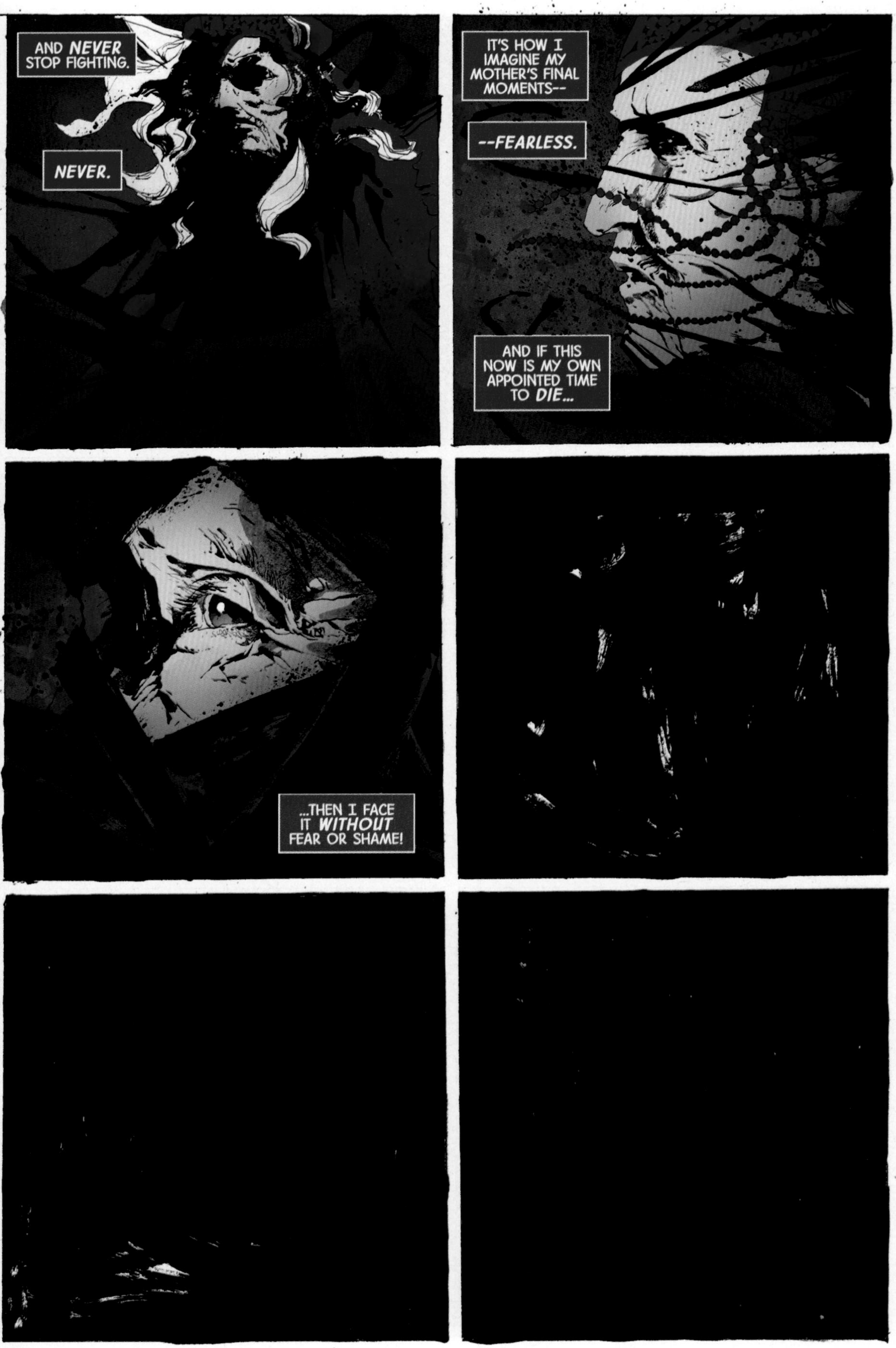
AND NEVER STOP FIGHTING.
NEVER.
IT'S HOW I IMAGINE MY MOTHER'S FINAL MOMENTS--
--FEARLESS.
AND IF THIS NOW IS MY OWN APPOINTED TIME TO DIE...
...THEN I FACE IT WITHOUT FEAR OR SHAME!

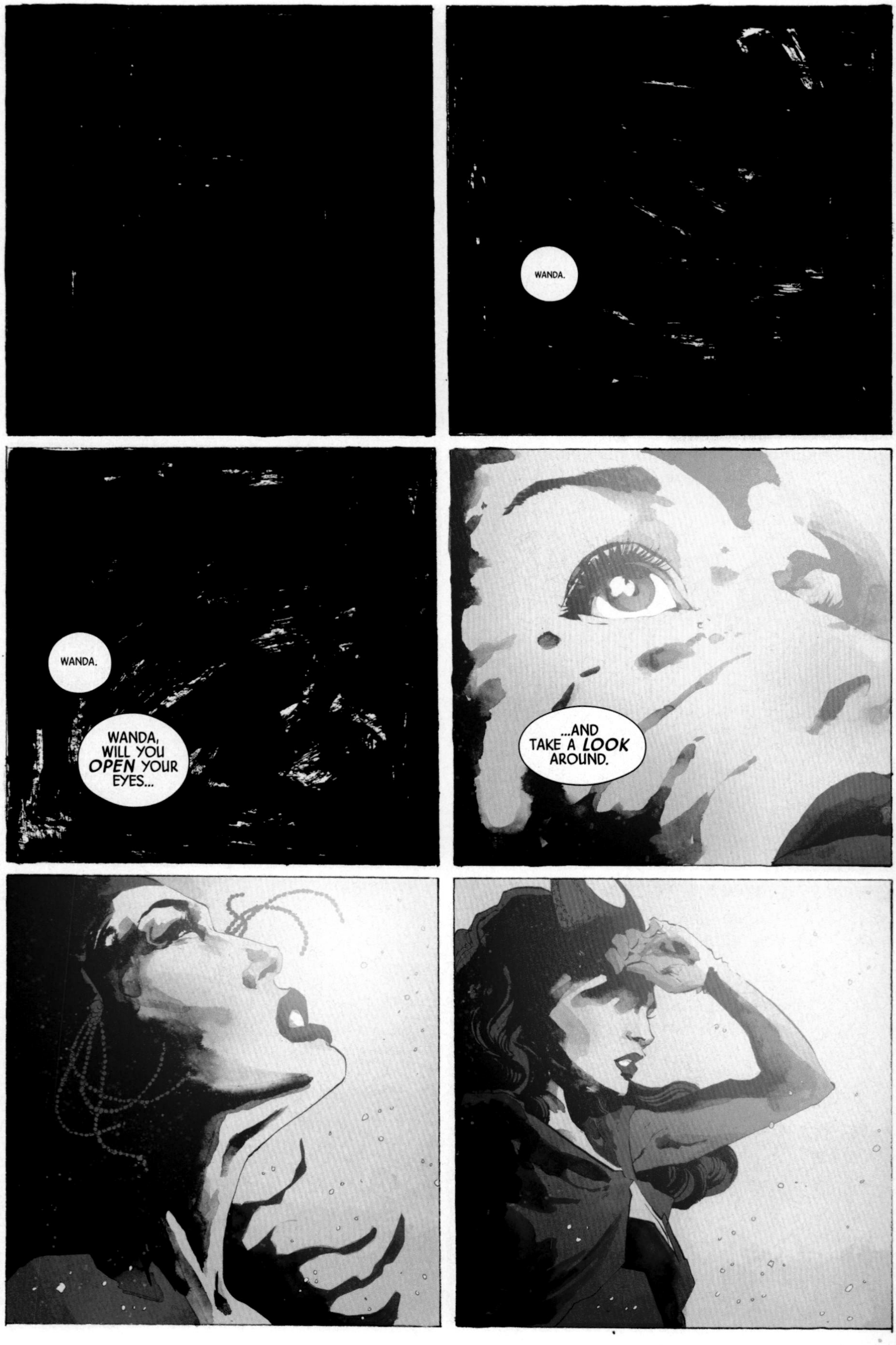
WANDA.
WANDA.
WANDA, WILL YOU OPEN YOUR EYES...
...AND TAKE A LOOK AROUND.

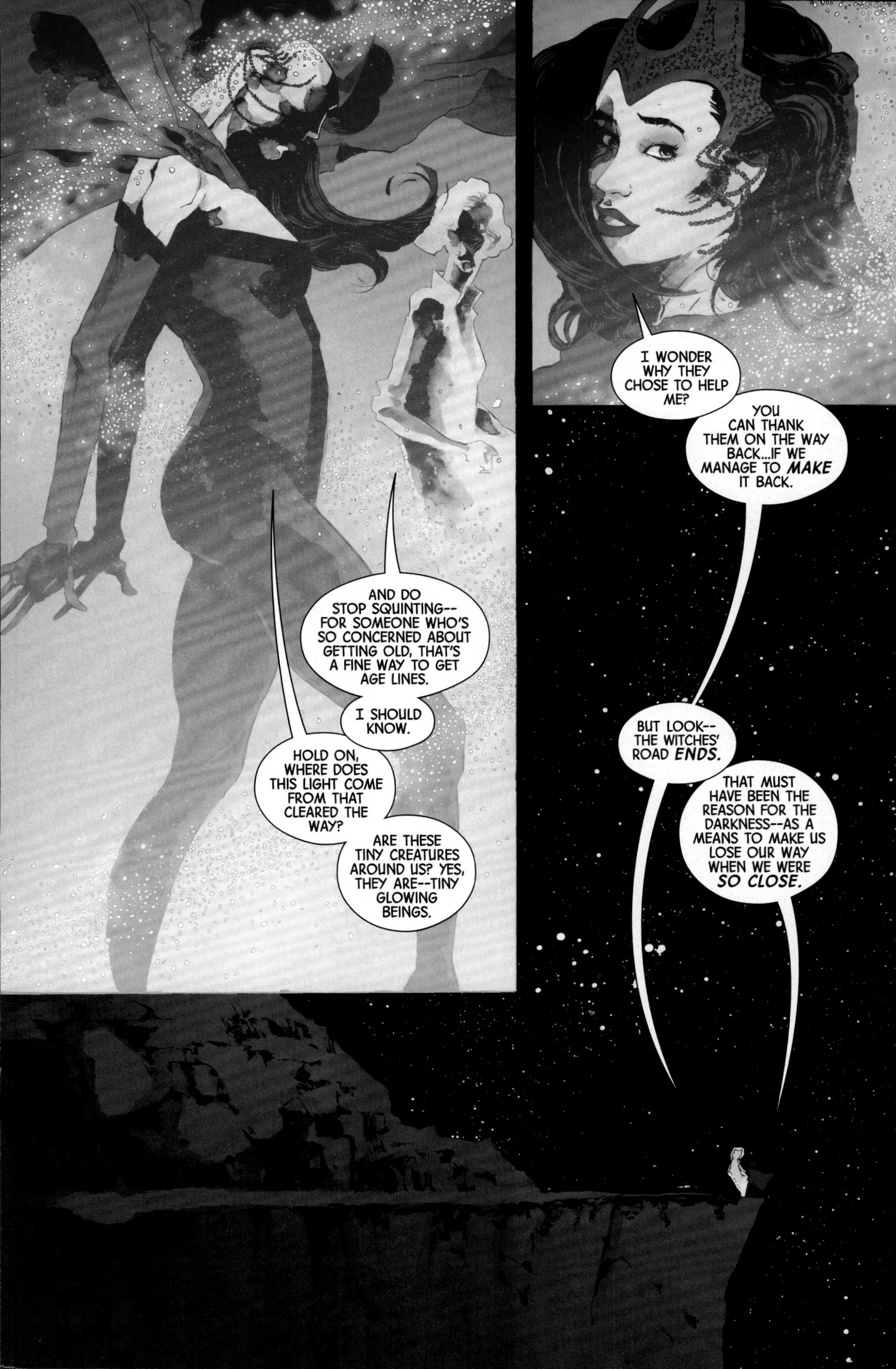
I WONDER WHY THEY CHOSE TO HELP ME?
YOU CAN THANK THEM ON THE WAY BACK...IF WE MANAGE TO *MAKE* IT BACK.
AND DO STOP SQUINTING--FOR SOMEONE WHO'S SO CONCERNED ABOUT GETTING OLD, THAT'S A FINE WAY TO GET AGE LINES.
I SHOULD KNOW.
HOLD ON, WHERE DOES THIS LIGHT COME FROM THAT CLEARED THE WAY?
ARE THESE TINY CREATURES AROUND US? YES, THEY ARE--TINY GLOWING BEINGS.
BUT LOOK--THE WITCHES' ROAD *ENDS.*
THAT MUST HAVE BEEN THE REASON FOR THE DARKNESS--AS A MEANS TO MAKE US LOSE OUR WAY WHEN WE WERE *SO CLOSE.*

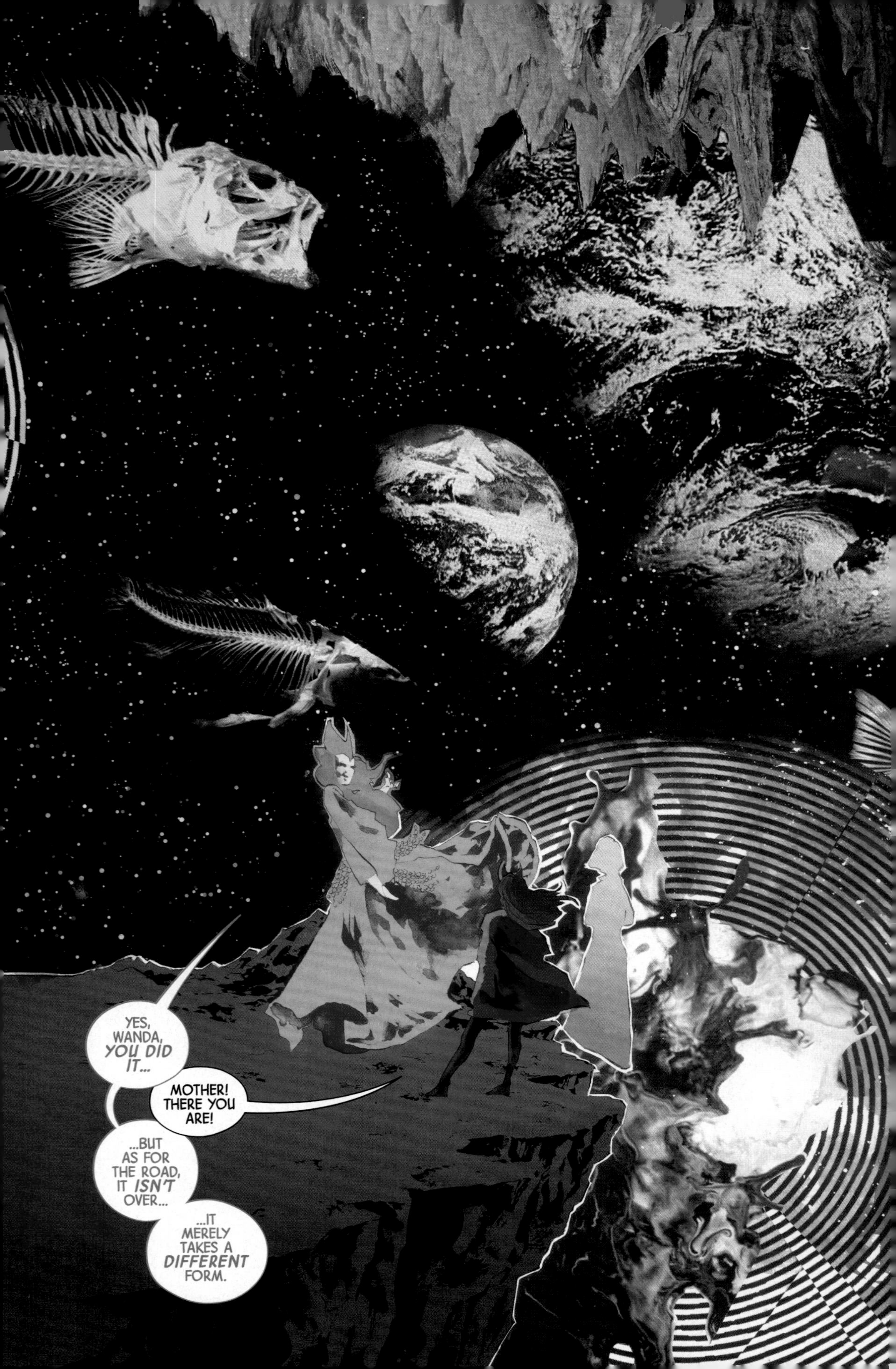
YES, WANDA, YOU DID IT...
MOTHER! THERE YOU ARE!
...BUT AS FOR THE ROAD, IT ISN'T OVER...
...IT MERELY TAKES A DIFFERENT FORM.

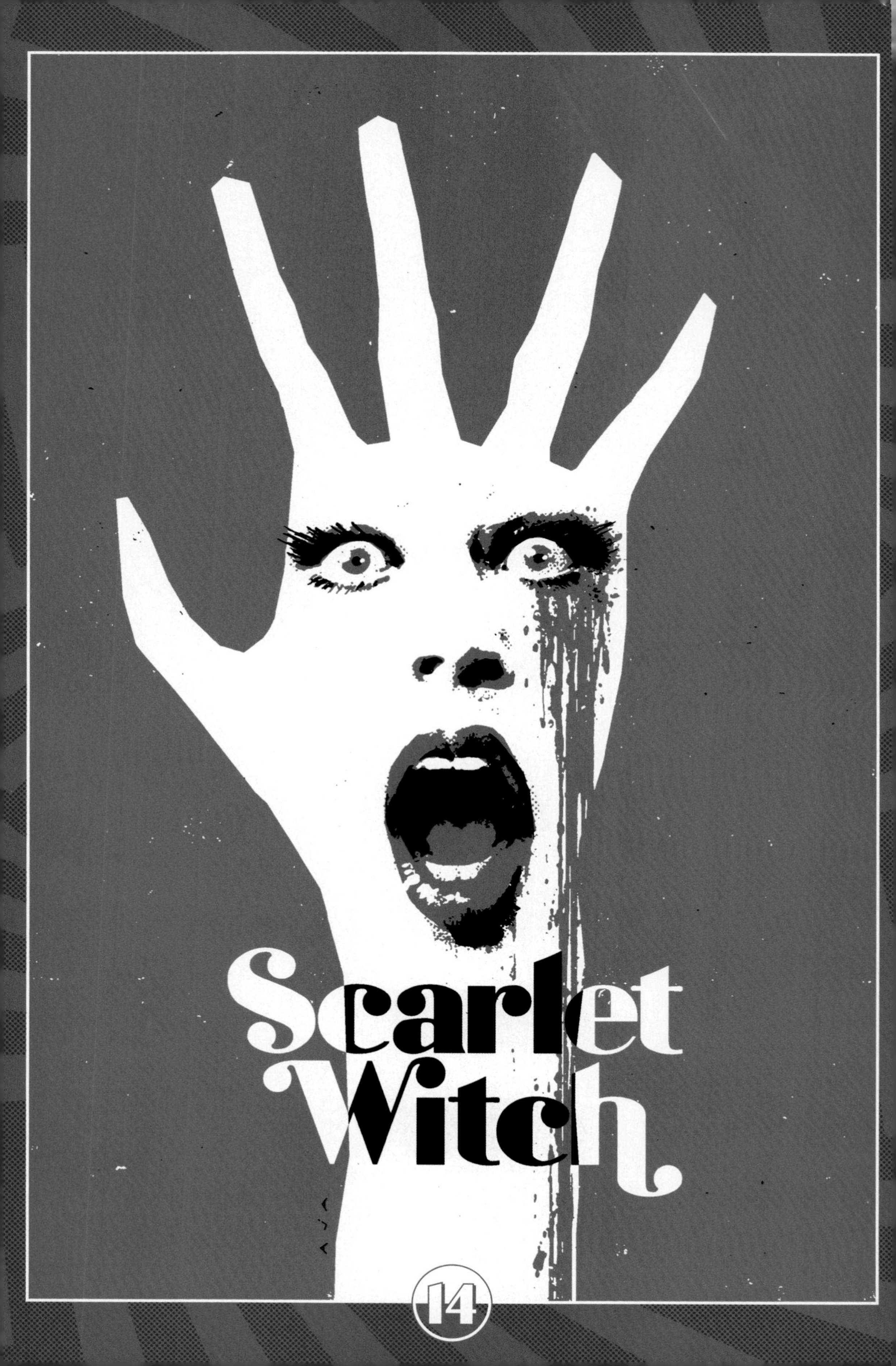

Scarlet Witch
14

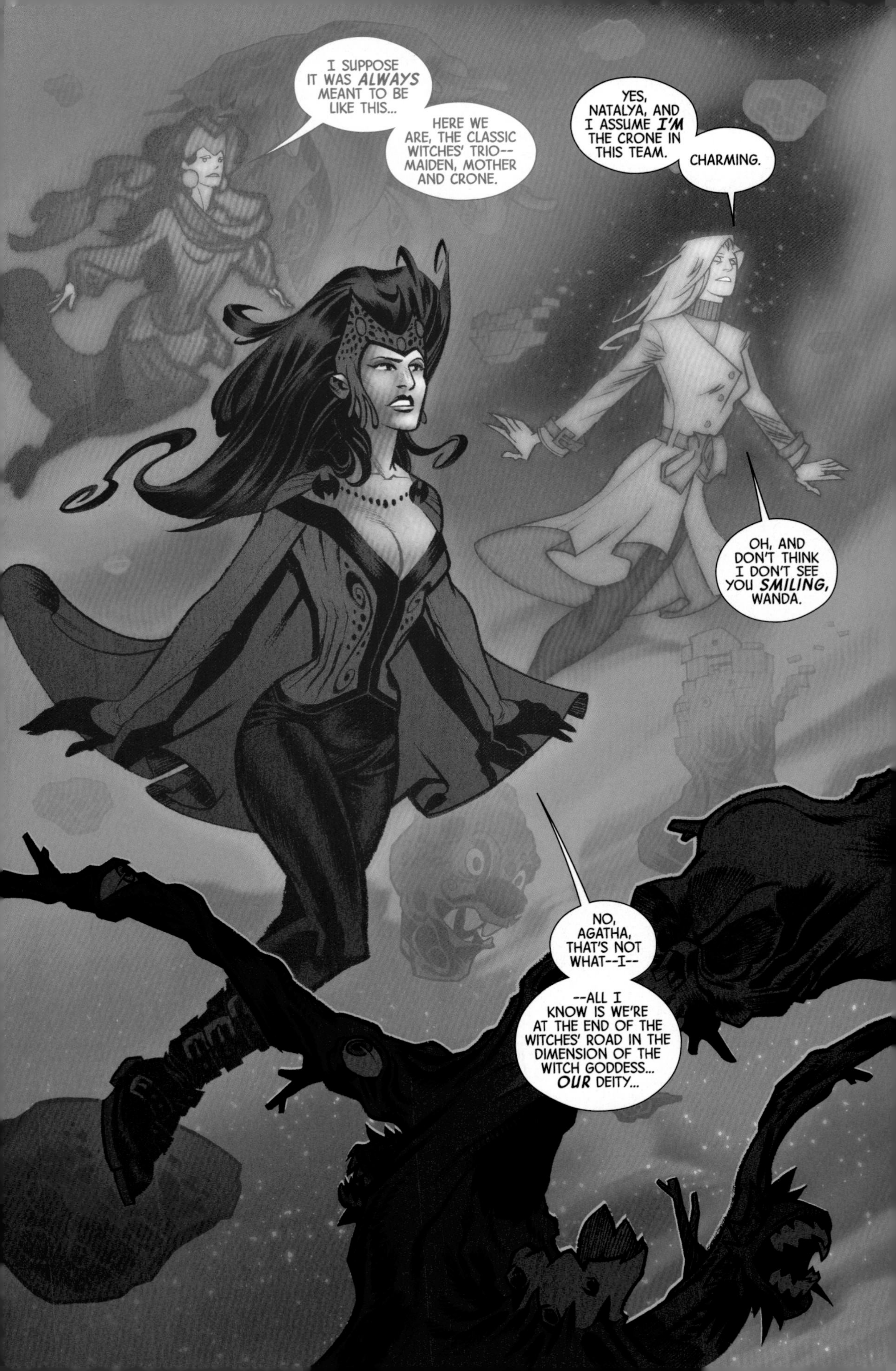

I SUPPOSE IT WAS ALWAYS MEANT TO BE LIKE THIS...
HERE WE ARE, THE CLASSIC WITCHES' TRIO-- MAIDEN, MOTHER AND CRONE.
YES, NATALYA, AND I ASSUME I'M THE CRONE IN THIS TEAM.
CHARMING.
OH, AND DON'T THINK I DON'T SEE YOU SMILING, WANDA.
NO, AGATHA, THAT'S NOT WHAT--I--
--ALL I KNOW IS WE'RE AT THE END OF THE WITCHES' ROAD IN THE DIMENSION OF THE WITCH GODDESS... OUR DEITY...

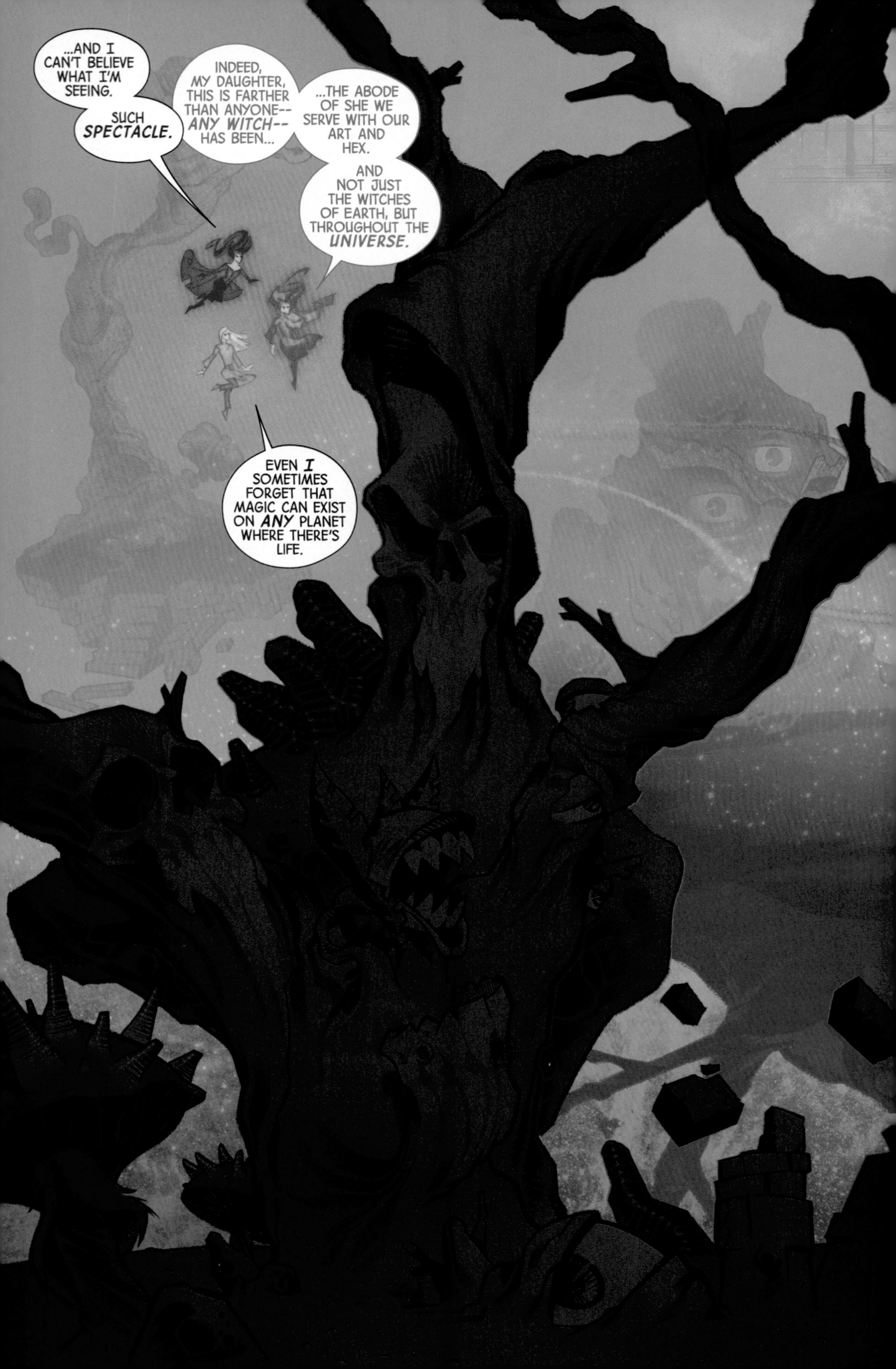
...AND I CAN'T BELIEVE WHAT I'M SEEING.
SUCH *SPECTACLE.*
INDEED, MY DAUGHTER, THIS IS FARTHER THAN ANYONE-- *ANY WITCH--* HAS BEEN...
...THE ABODE OF SHE WE SERVE WITH OUR ART AND HEX.
AND NOT JUST THE WITCHES OF EARTH, BUT THROUGHOUT THE *UNIVERSE.*
EVEN *I* SOMETIMES FORGET THAT MAGIC CAN EXIST ON *ANY* PLANET WHERE THERE'S LIFE.

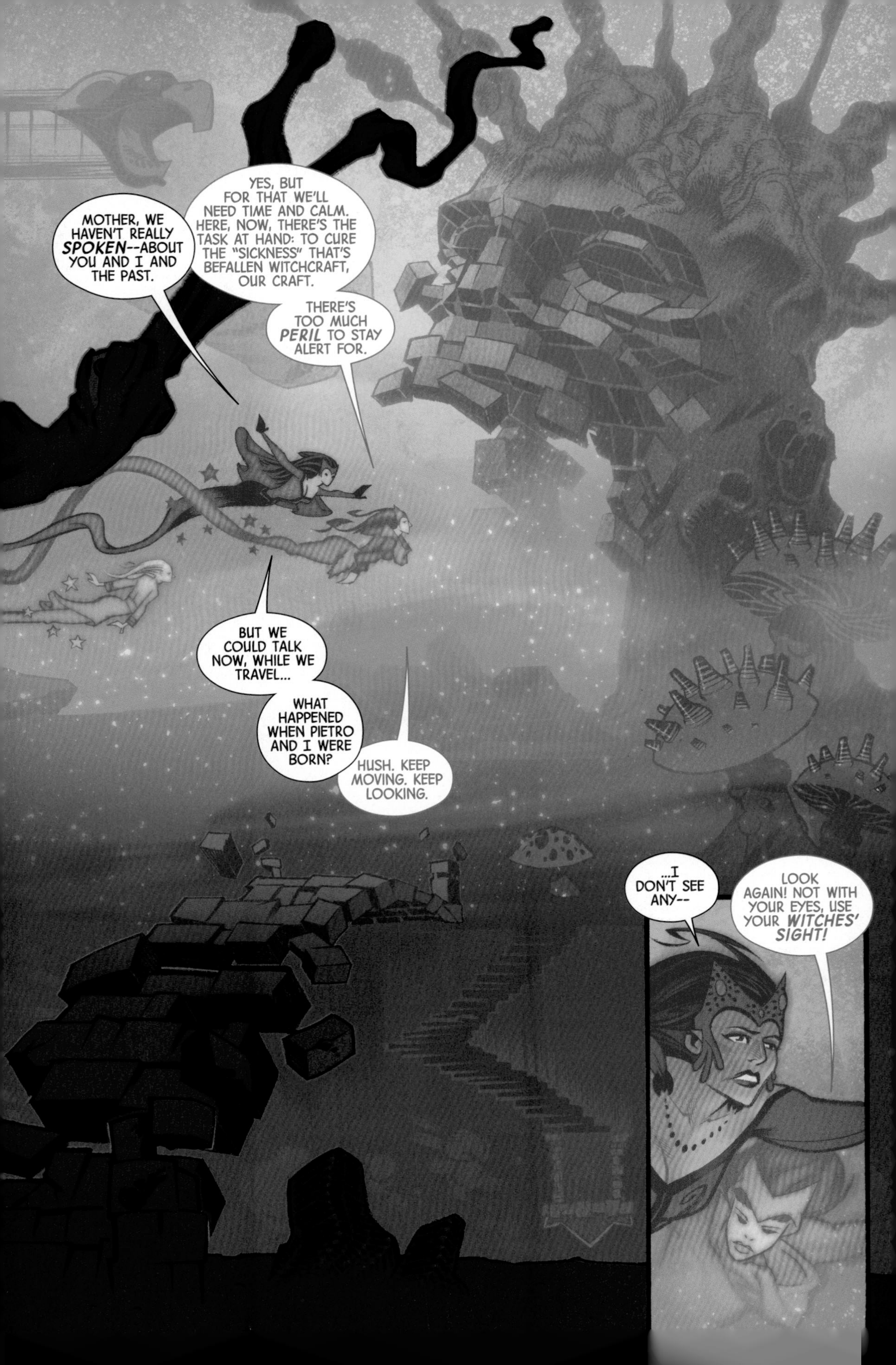
MOTHER, WE HAVEN'T REALLY SPOKEN--ABOUT YOU AND I AND THE PAST.
YES, BUT FOR THAT WE'LL NEED TIME AND CALM. HERE, NOW, THERE'S THE TASK AT HAND: TO CURE THE "SICKNESS" THAT'S BEFALLEN WITCHCRAFT, OUR CRAFT.
THERE'S TOO MUCH PERIL TO STAY ALERT FOR.
BUT WE COULD TALK NOW, WHILE WE TRAVEL...
WHAT HAPPENED WHEN PIETRO AND I WERE BORN?
HUSH. KEEP MOVING. KEEP LOOKING.
...I DON'T SEE ANY--
LOOK AGAIN! NOT WITH YOUR EYES, USE YOUR WITCHES' SIGHT!

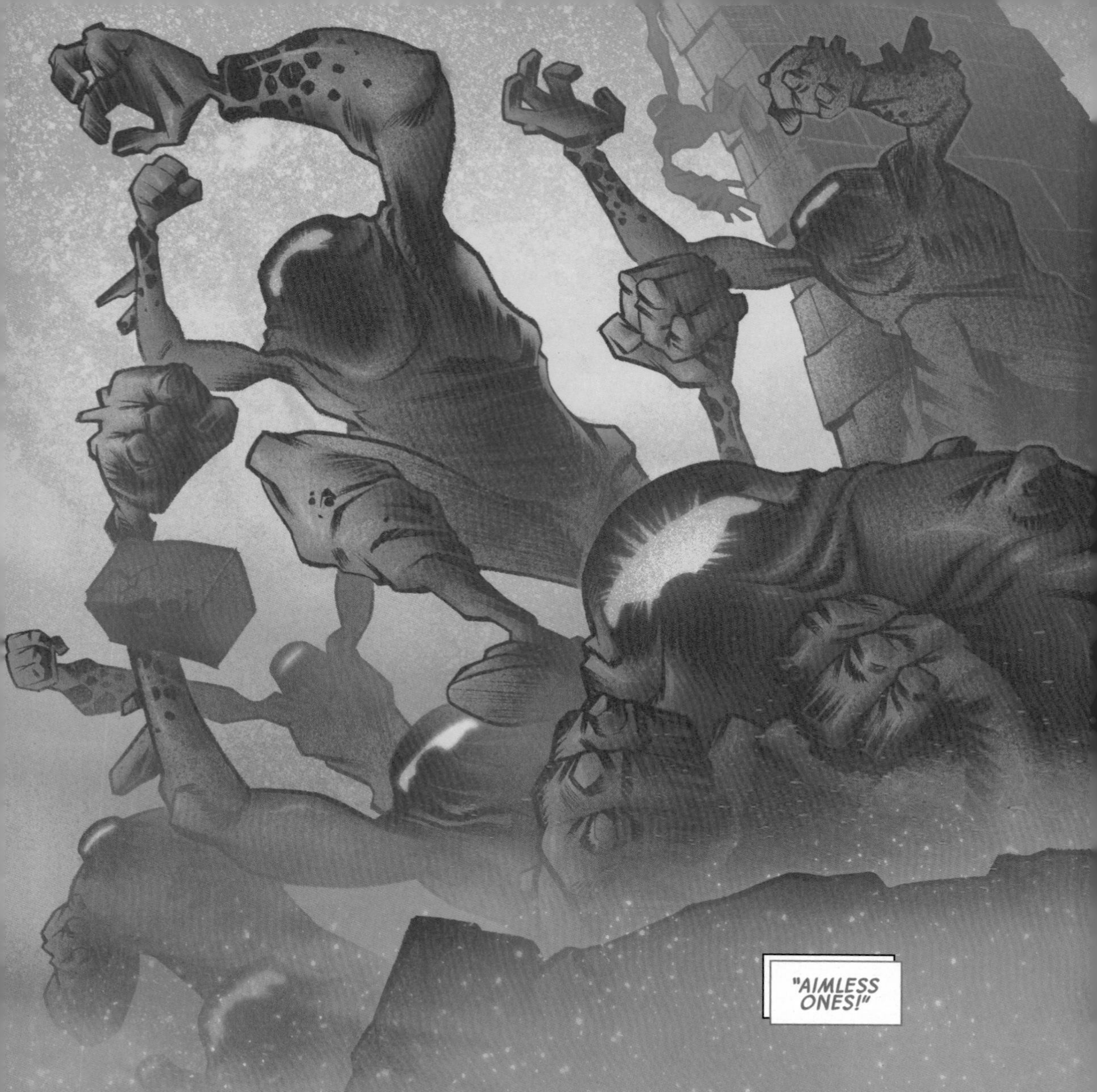
"AIMLESS ONES!"

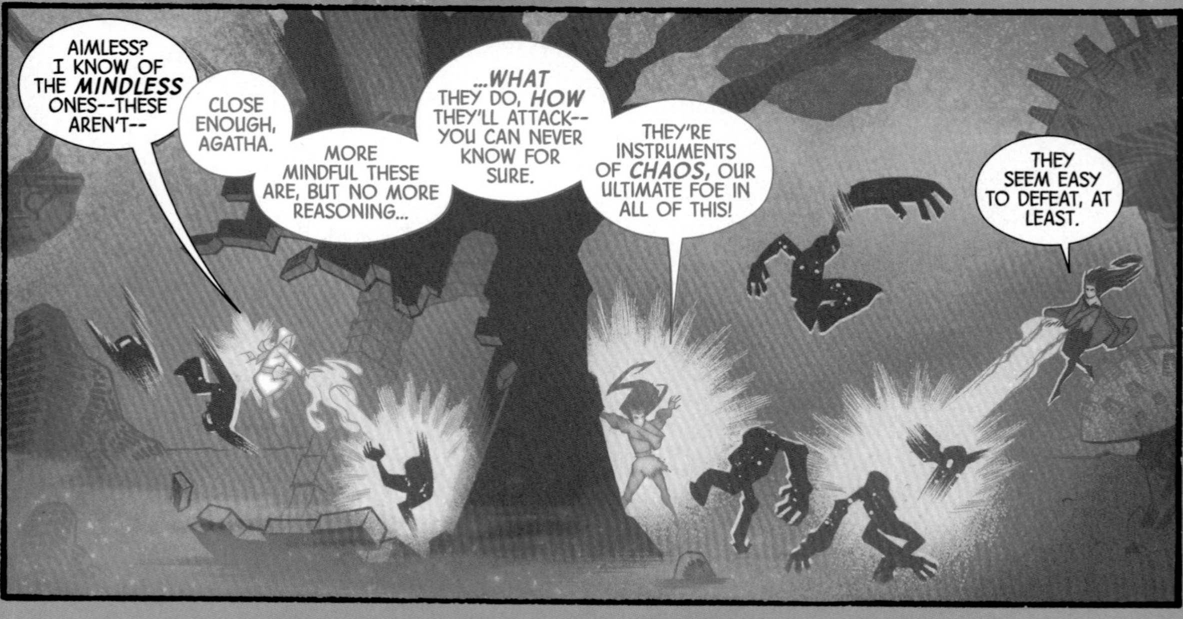
AIMLESS? I KNOW OF THE MINDLESS ONES--THESE AREN'T--
CLOSE ENOUGH, AGATHA.
MORE MINDFUL THESE ARE, BUT NO MORE REASONING...
...WHAT THEY DO, HOW THEY'LL ATTACK-- YOU CAN NEVER KNOW FOR SURE.
THEY'RE INSTRUMENTS OF CHAOS, OUR ULTIMATE FOE IN ALL OF THIS!
THEY SEEM EASY TO DEFEAT, AT LEAST.

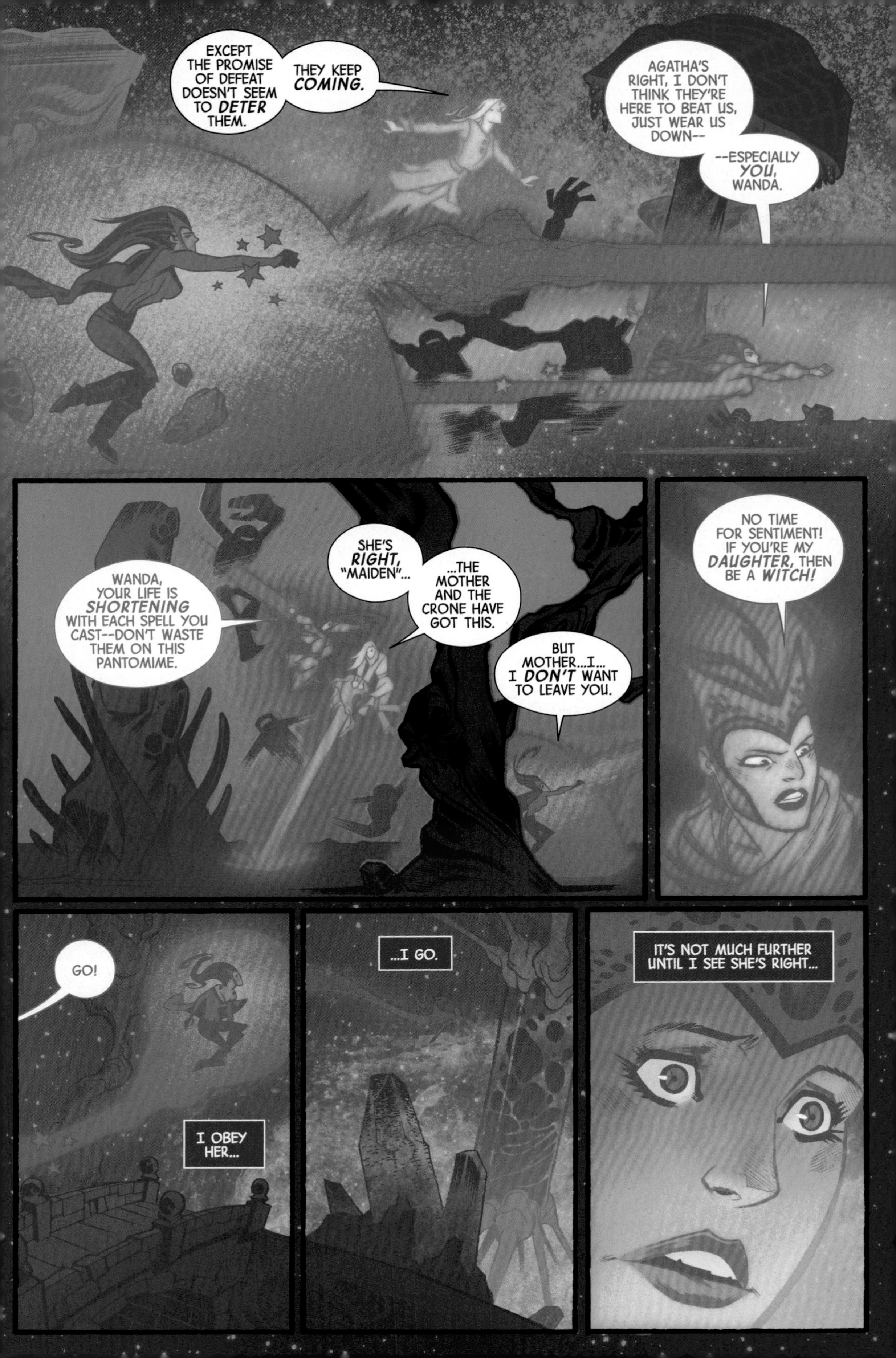
EXCEPT THE PROMISE OF DEFEAT DOESN'T SEEM TO DETER THEM.
THEY KEEP COMING.
AGATHA'S RIGHT, I DON'T THINK THEY'RE HERE TO BEAT US, JUST WEAR US DOWN--
--ESPECIALLY YOU, WANDA.
WANDA, YOUR LIFE IS SHORTENING WITH EACH SPELL YOU CAST--DON'T WASTE THEM ON THIS PANTOMIME.
SHE'S RIGHT, "MAIDEN"...
...THE MOTHER AND THE CRONE HAVE GOT THIS.
BUT MOTHER...I... I DON'T WANT TO LEAVE YOU.
NO TIME FOR SENTIMENT! IF YOU'RE MY DAUGHTER, THEN BE A WITCH!
GO!
I OBEY HER...
...I GO.
IT'S NOT MUCH FURTHER UNTIL I SEE SHE'S RIGHT...

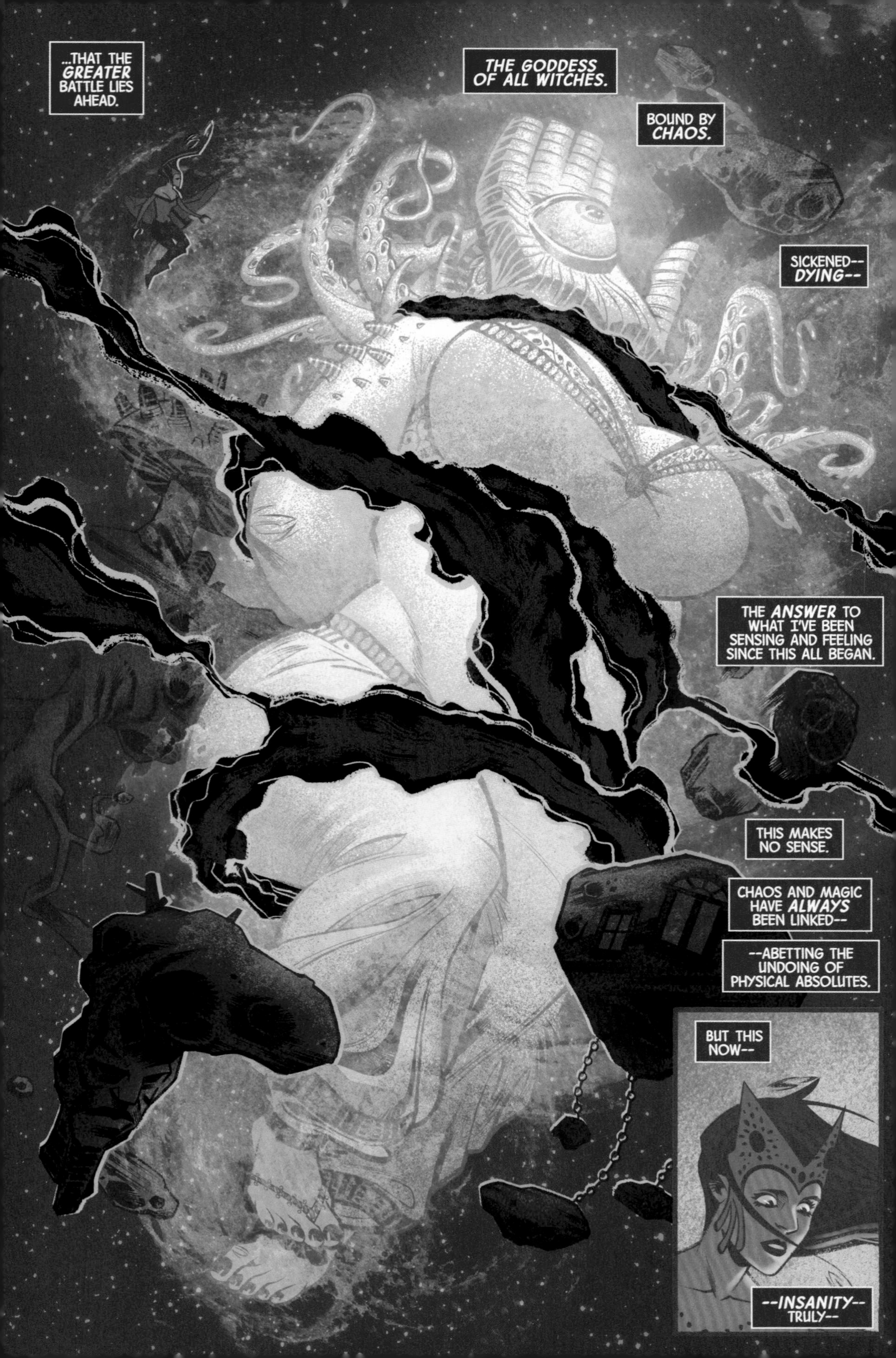

...THAT THE GREATER BATTLE LIES AHEAD.
THE GODDESS OF ALL WITCHES.
BOUND BY CHAOS.
SICKENED-- DYING--
THE ANSWER TO WHAT I'VE BEEN SENSING AND FEELING SINCE THIS ALL BEGAN.
THIS MAKES NO SENSE.
CHAOS AND MAGIC HAVE ALWAYS BEEN LINKED--
--ABETTING THE UNDOING OF PHYSICAL ABSOLUTES.
BUT THIS NOW--
--INSANITY-- TRULY--

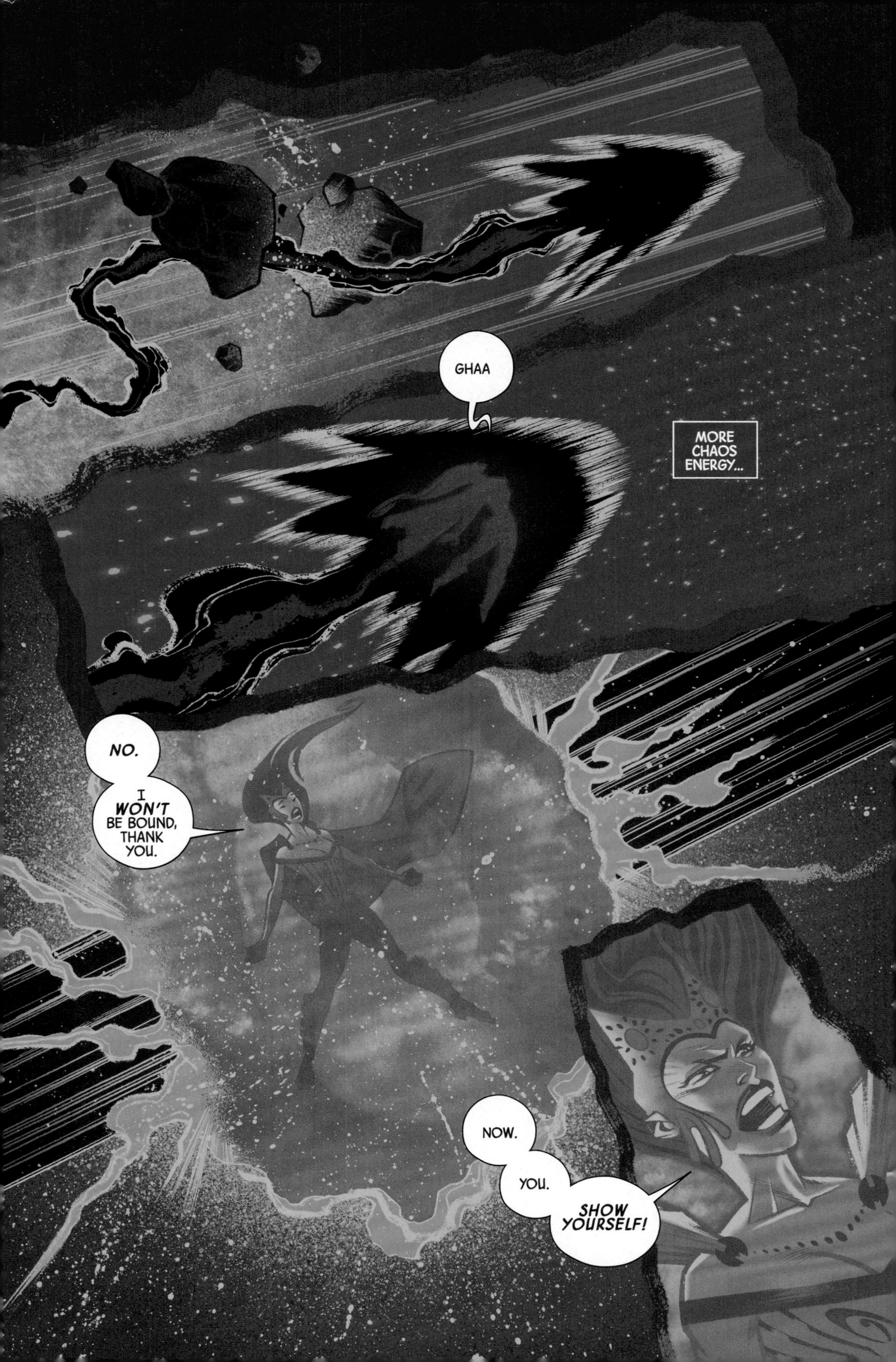
GHAA
MORE CHAOS ENERGY...
NO.
I WON'T BE BOUND, THANK YOU.
NOW.
YOU.
SHOW YOURSELF!

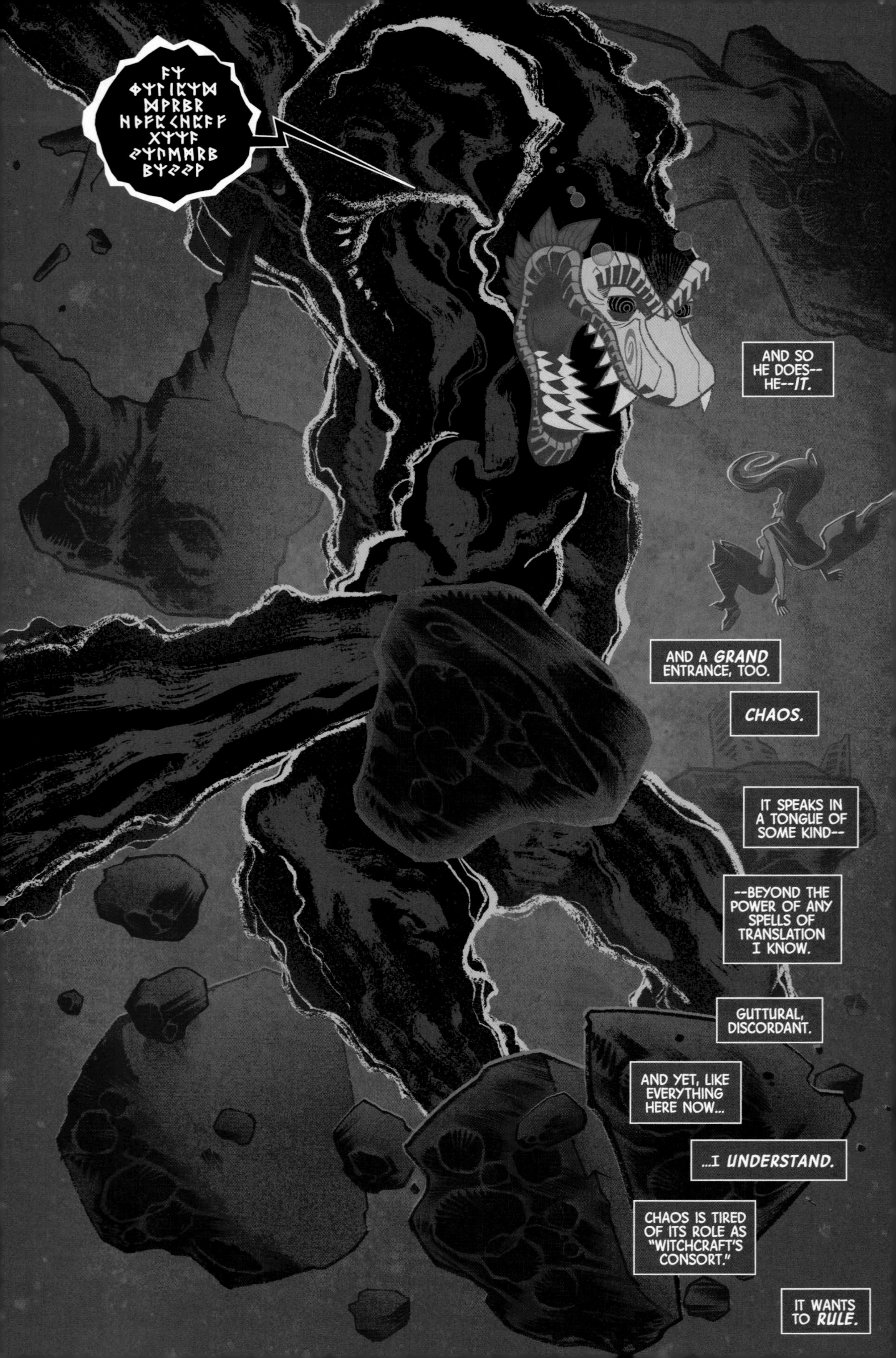
AND SO HE DOES-- HE--IT.
AND A GRAND ENTRANCE, TOO.
CHAOS.
IT SPEAKS IN A TONGUE OF SOME KIND--
--BEYOND THE POWER OF ANY SPELLS OF TRANSLATION I KNOW.
GUTTURAL, DISCORDANT.
AND YET, LIKE EVERYTHING HERE NOW...
...I UNDERSTAND.
CHAOS IS TIRED OF ITS ROLE AS "WITCHCRAFT'S CONSORT."
IT WANTS TO RULE.

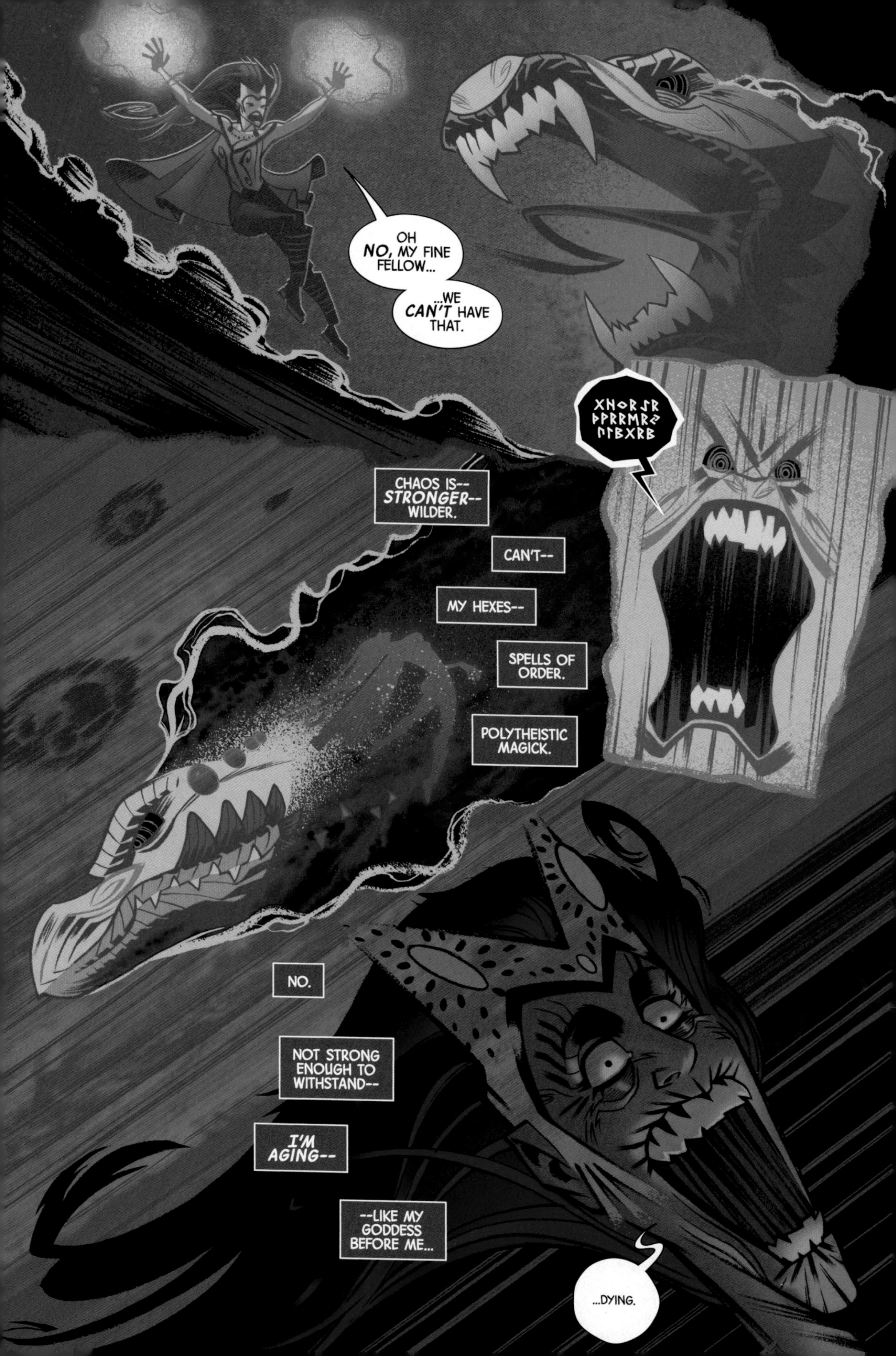

OH NO, MY FINE FELLOW...
...WE CAN'T HAVE THAT.
CHAOS IS-- STRONGER-- WILDER.
CAN'T--
MY HEXES--
SPELLS OF ORDER.
POLYTHEISTIC MAGICK.
NO.
NOT STRONG ENOUGH TO WITHSTAND--
I'M AGING--
--LIKE MY GODDESS BEFORE ME...
...DYING.

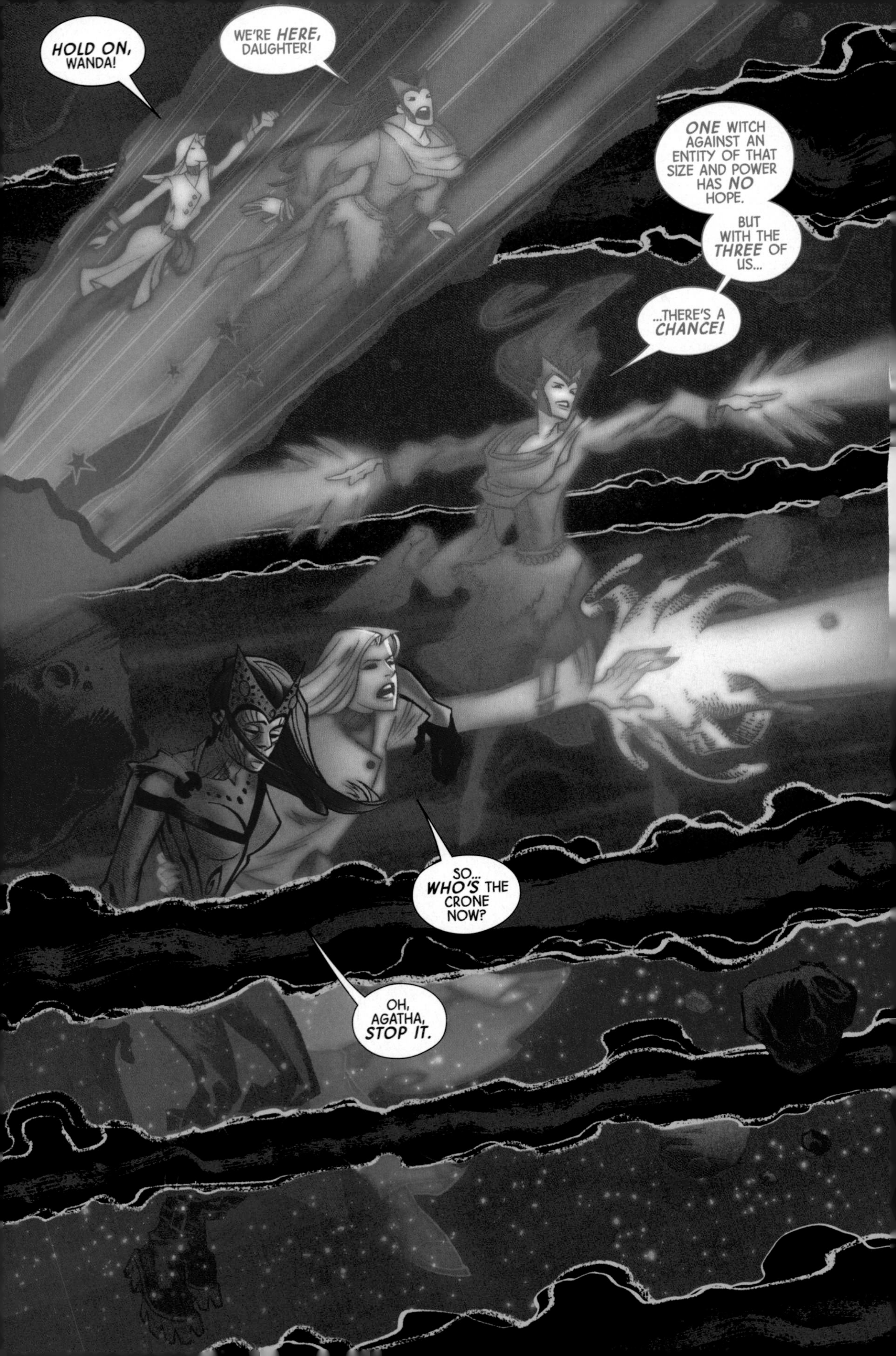
HOLD ON, WANDA!
WE'RE HERE, DAUGHTER!
ONE WITCH AGAINST AN ENTITY OF THAT SIZE AND POWER HAS NO HOPE.
BUT WITH THE THREE OF US...
...THERE'S A CHANCE!
SO... WHO'S THE CRONE NOW?
OH, AGATHA, STOP IT.

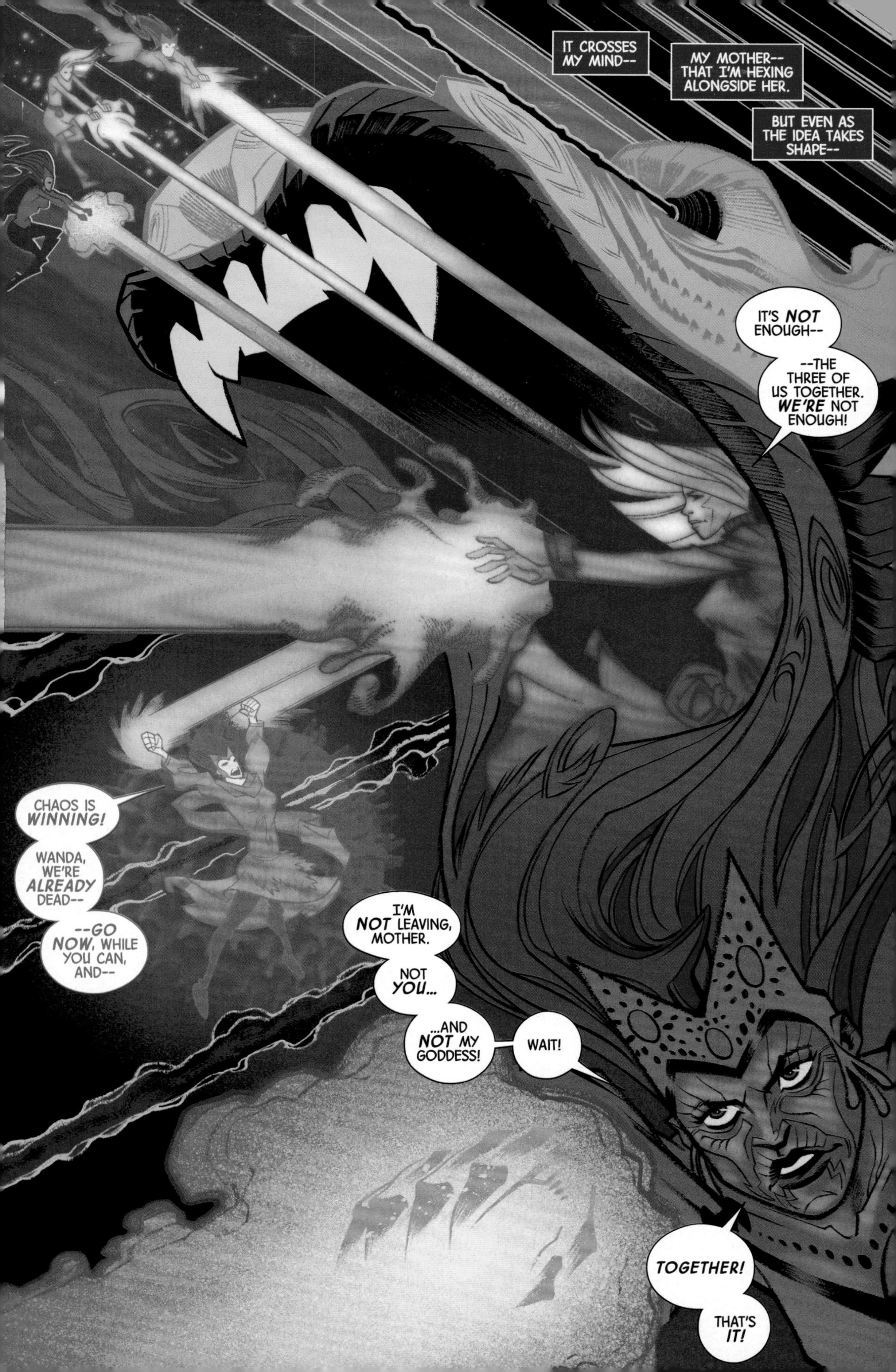

IT CROSSES MY MIND--
MY MOTHER-- THAT I'M HEXING ALONGSIDE HER.
BUT EVEN AS THE IDEA TAKES SHAPE--
IT'S NOT ENOUGH--
--THE THREE OF US TOGETHER. WE'RE NOT ENOUGH!
CHAOS IS WINNING!
WANDA, WE'RE ALREADY DEAD--
--GO NOW, WHILE YOU CAN, AND--
I'M NOT LEAVING, MOTHER.
NOT YOU...
...AND NOT MY GODDESS!
WAIT!
TOGETHER!
THAT'S IT!

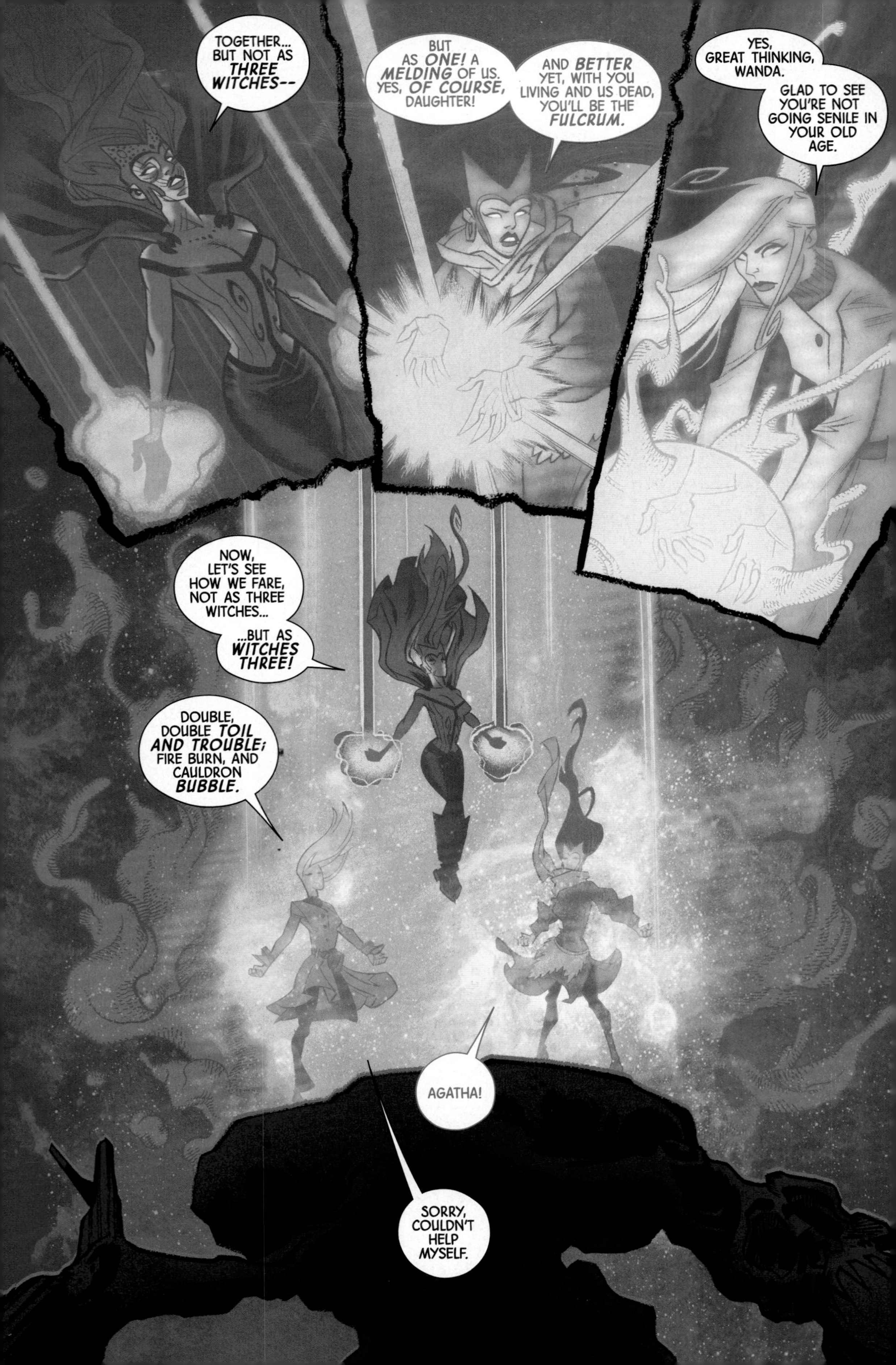
TOGETHER... BUT NOT AS THREE WITCHES--
BUT AS ONE! A MELDING OF US. YES, OF COURSE, DAUGHTER!
AND BETTER YET, WITH YOU LIVING AND US DEAD, YOU'LL BE THE FULCRUM.
YES, GREAT THINKING, WANDA.
GLAD TO SEE YOU'RE NOT GOING SENILE IN YOUR OLD AGE.
NOW, LET'S SEE HOW WE FARE, NOT AS THREE WITCHES...
...BUT AS WITCHES THREE!
DOUBLE, DOUBLE TOIL AND TROUBLE; FIRE BURN, AND CAULDRON BUBBLE.
AGATHA!
SORRY, COULDN'T HELP MYSELF.

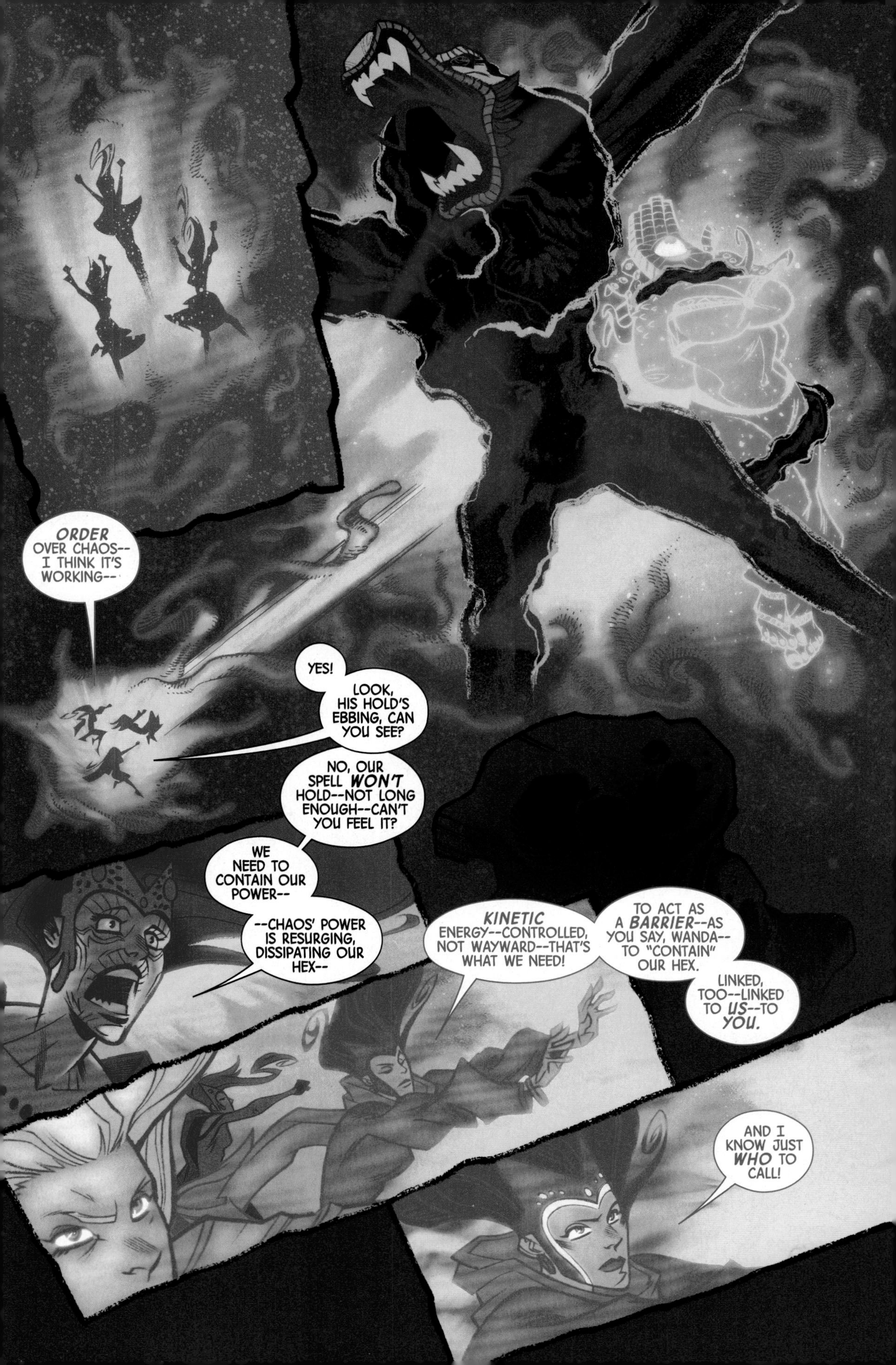
ORDER OVER CHAOS-- I THINK IT'S WORKING--
YES!
LOOK, HIS HOLD'S EBBING, CAN YOU SEE?
NO, OUR SPELL WON'T HOLD--NOT LONG ENOUGH--CAN'T YOU FEEL IT?
WE NEED TO CONTAIN OUR POWER--
--CHAOS' POWER IS RESURGING, DISSIPATING OUR HEX--
KINETIC ENERGY--CONTROLLED, NOT WAYWARD--THAT'S WHAT WE NEED!
TO ACT AS A BARRIER--AS YOU SAY, WANDA-- TO "CONTAIN" OUR HEX.
LINKED, TOO--LINKED TO US--TO YOU.
AND I KNOW JUST WHO TO CALL!

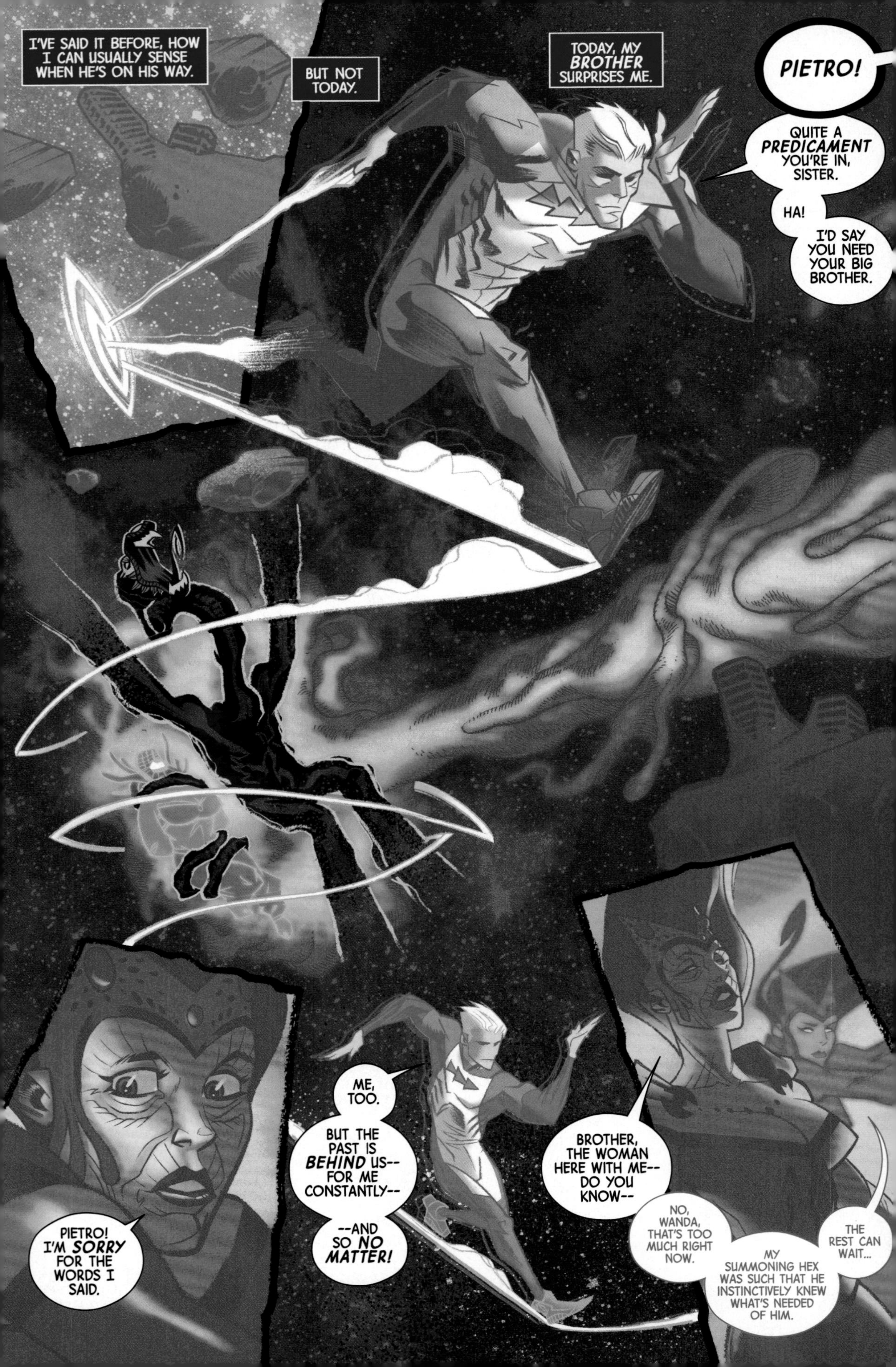

I'VE SAID IT BEFORE, HOW I CAN USUALLY SENSE WHEN HE'S ON HIS WAY.
BUT NOT TODAY.
TODAY, MY BROTHER SURPRISES ME.
PIETRO!
QUITE A PREDICAMENT YOU'RE IN, SISTER.
HA!
I'D SAY YOU NEED YOUR BIG BROTHER.
PIETRO! I'M SORRY FOR THE WORDS I SAID.
ME, TOO.
BUT THE PAST IS BEHIND US-- FOR ME CONSTANTLY--
--AND SO NO MATTER!
BROTHER, THE WOMAN HERE WITH ME-- DO YOU KNOW--
NO, WANDA, THAT'S TOO MUCH RIGHT NOW.
THE REST CAN WAIT...
MY SUMMONING HEX WAS SUCH THAT HE INSTINCTIVELY KNEW WHAT'S NEEDED OF HIM.

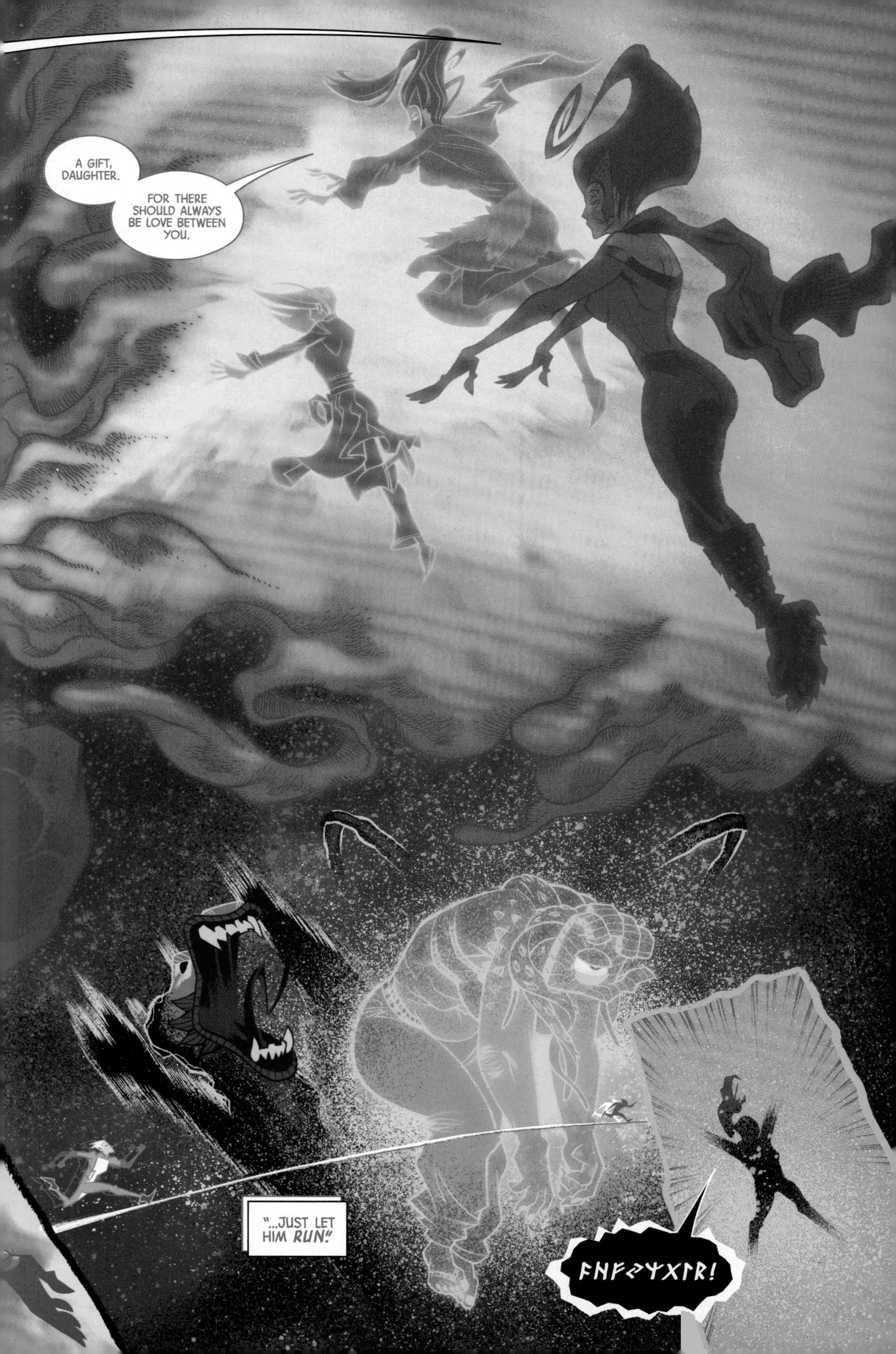
A GIFT, DAUGHTER.
FOR THERE SHOULD ALWAYS BE LOVE BETWEEN YOU.
"...JUST LET HIM RUN!"

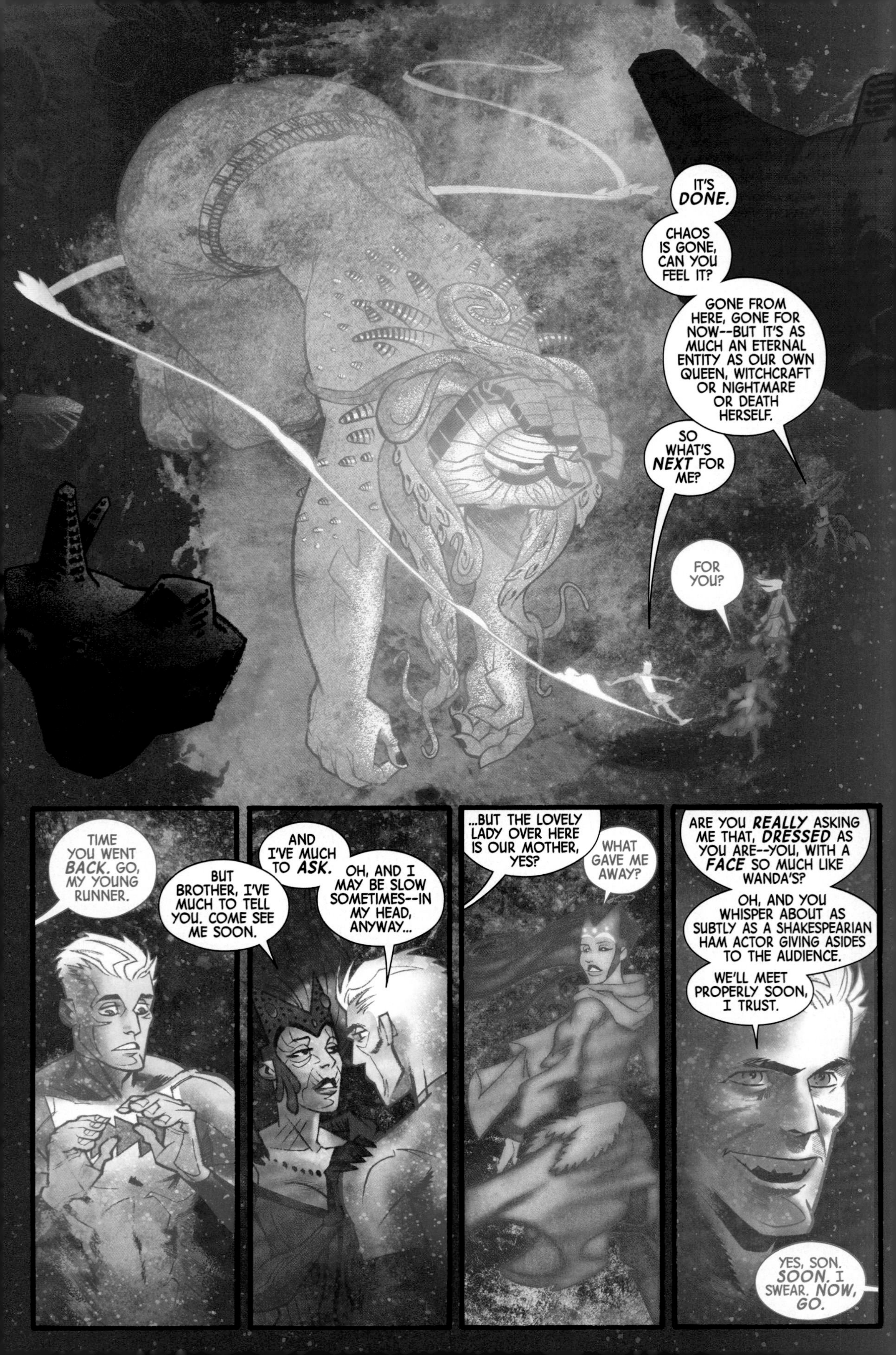
IT'S DONE.
CHAOS IS GONE, CAN YOU FEEL IT?
GONE FROM HERE, GONE FOR NOW--BUT IT'S AS MUCH AN ETERNAL ENTITY AS OUR OWN QUEEN, WITCHCRAFT OR NIGHTMARE OR DEATH HERSELF.
SO WHAT'S NEXT FOR ME?
FOR YOU?
TIME YOU WENT BACK. GO, MY YOUNG RUNNER.
BUT BROTHER, I'VE MUCH TO TELL YOU. COME SEE ME SOON.
AND I'VE MUCH TO ASK.
OH, AND I MAY BE SLOW SOMETIMES--IN MY HEAD, ANYWAY...
...BUT THE LOVELY LADY OVER HERE IS OUR MOTHER, YES?
WHAT GAVE ME AWAY?
ARE YOU REALLY ASKING ME THAT, DRESSED AS YOU ARE--YOU, WITH A FACE SO MUCH LIKE WANDA'S?
OH, AND YOU WHISPER ABOUT AS SUBTLY AS A SHAKESPEARIAN HAM ACTOR GIVING ASIDES TO THE AUDIENCE.
WE'LL MEET PROPERLY SOON, I TRUST.
YES, SON. SOON. I SWEAR. NOW, GO.

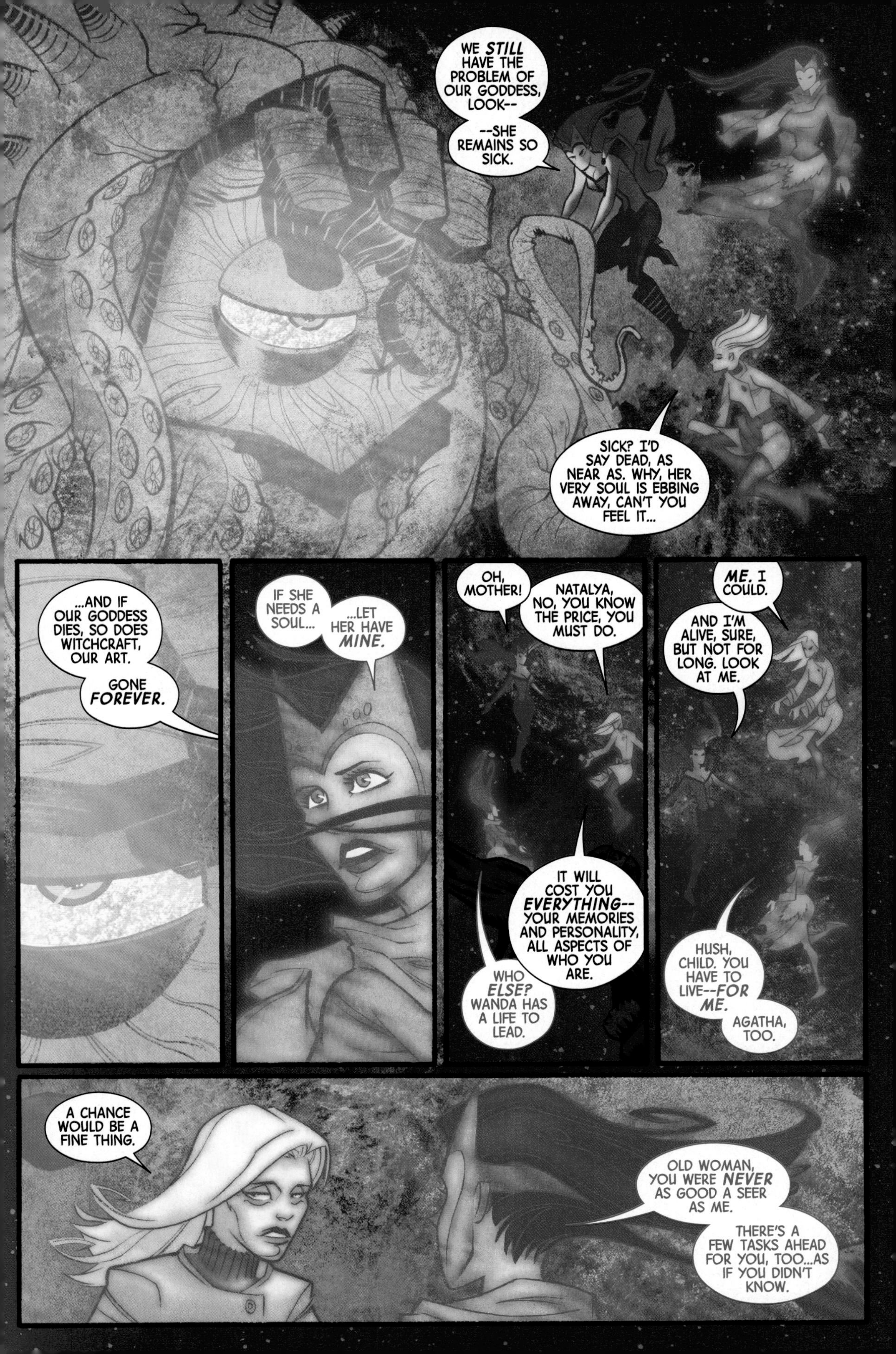
WE STILL HAVE THE PROBLEM OF OUR GODDESS, LOOK--
--SHE REMAINS SO SICK.
SICK? I'D SAY DEAD, AS NEAR AS. WHY, HER VERY SOUL IS EBBING AWAY, CAN'T YOU FEEL IT...
...AND IF OUR GODDESS DIES, SO DOES WITCHCRAFT, OUR ART.
GONE FOREVER.
IF SHE NEEDS A SOUL...
...LET HER HAVE MINE.
OH, MOTHER!
NATALYA, NO, YOU KNOW THE PRICE, YOU MUST DO.
IT WILL COST YOU EVERYTHING--YOUR MEMORIES AND PERSONALITY, ALL ASPECTS OF WHO YOU ARE.
WHO ELSE? WANDA HAS A LIFE TO LEAD.
ME. I COULD.
AND I'M ALIVE, SURE, BUT NOT FOR LONG. LOOK AT ME.
HUSH, CHILD. YOU HAVE TO LIVE--FOR ME.
AGATHA, TOO.
A CHANCE WOULD BE A FINE THING.
OLD WOMAN, YOU WERE NEVER AS GOOD A SEER AS ME.
THERE'S A FEW TASKS AHEAD FOR YOU, TOO...AS IF YOU DIDN'T KNOW.

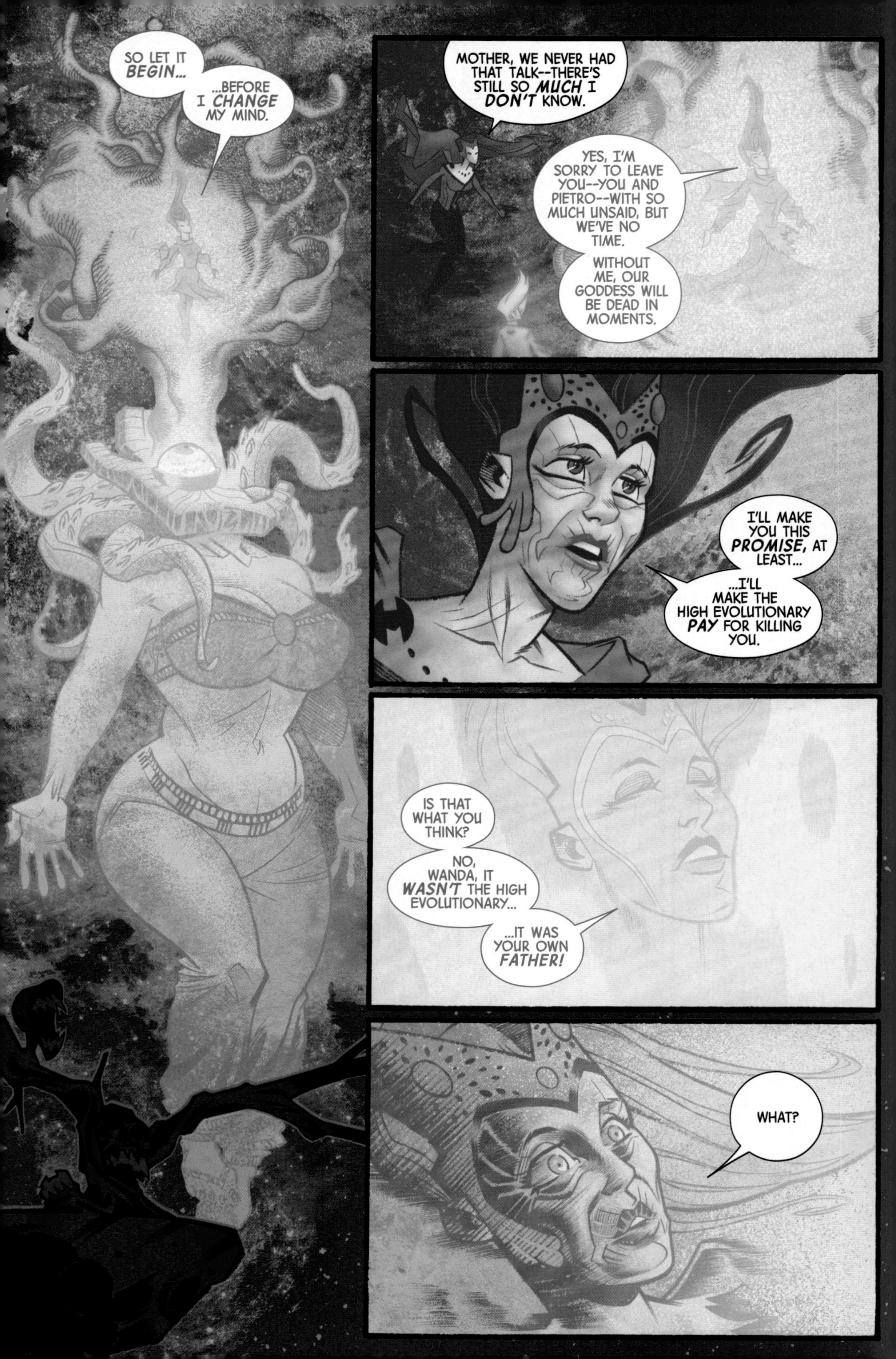
SO LET IT BEGIN...
...BEFORE I CHANGE MY MIND.
MOTHER, WE NEVER HAD THAT TALK--THERE'S STILL SO MUCH I DON'T KNOW.
YES, I'M SORRY TO LEAVE YOU--YOU AND PIETRO--WITH SO MUCH UNSAID, BUT WE'VE NO TIME.
WITHOUT ME, OUR GODDESS WILL BE DEAD IN MOMENTS.
I'LL MAKE YOU THIS PROMISE, AT LEAST...
...I'LL MAKE THE HIGH EVOLUTIONARY PAY FOR KILLING YOU.
IS THAT WHAT YOU THINK?
NO, WANDA, IT WASN'T THE HIGH EVOLUTIONARY...
...IT WAS YOUR OWN FATHER!
WHAT?

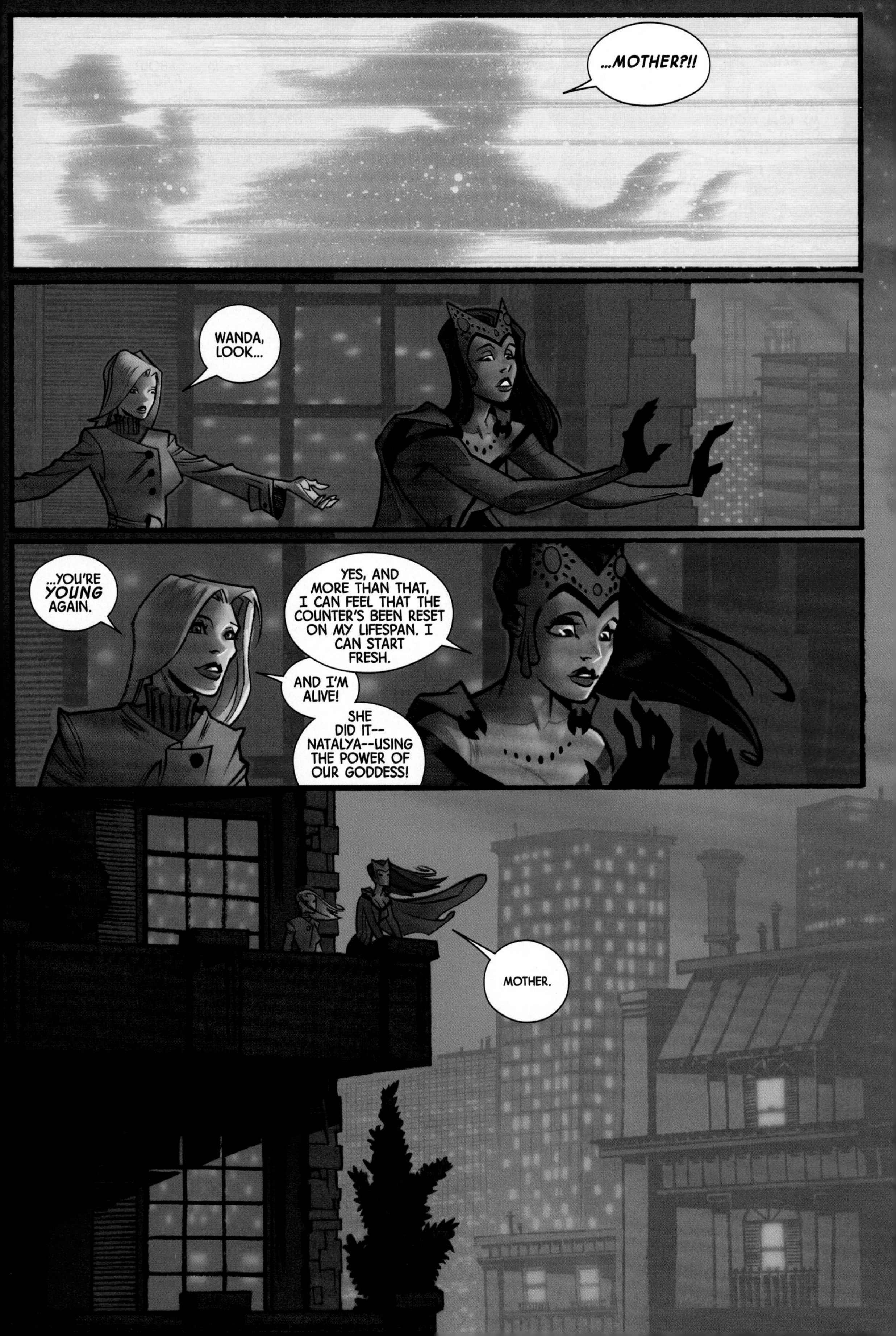
...MOTHER?!!
WANDA, LOOK...
...YOU'RE *YOUNG* AGAIN.
YES, AND MORE THAN THAT, I CAN FEEL THAT THE COUNTER'S BEEN RESET ON MY LIFESPAN. I CAN START FRESH.
AND I'M ALIVE!
SHE DID IT-- NATALYA--USING THE POWER OF OUR GODDESS!
MOTHER.

Scarlet Witch

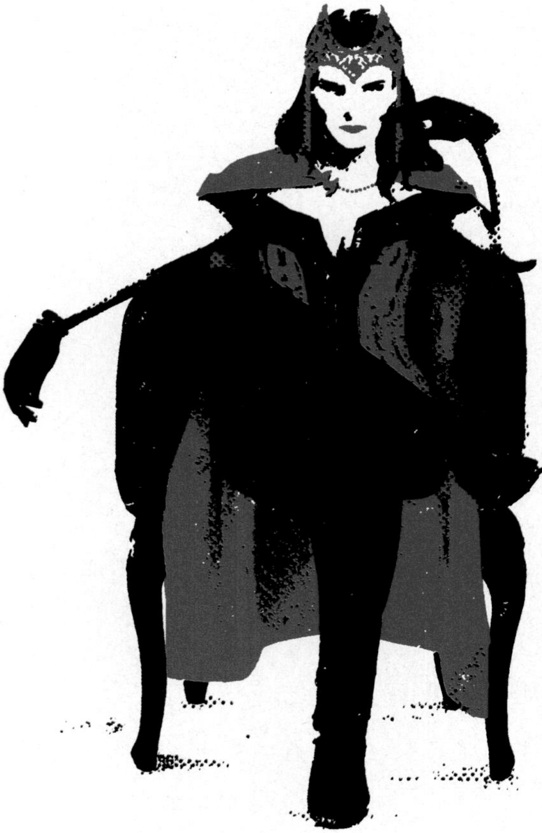

15

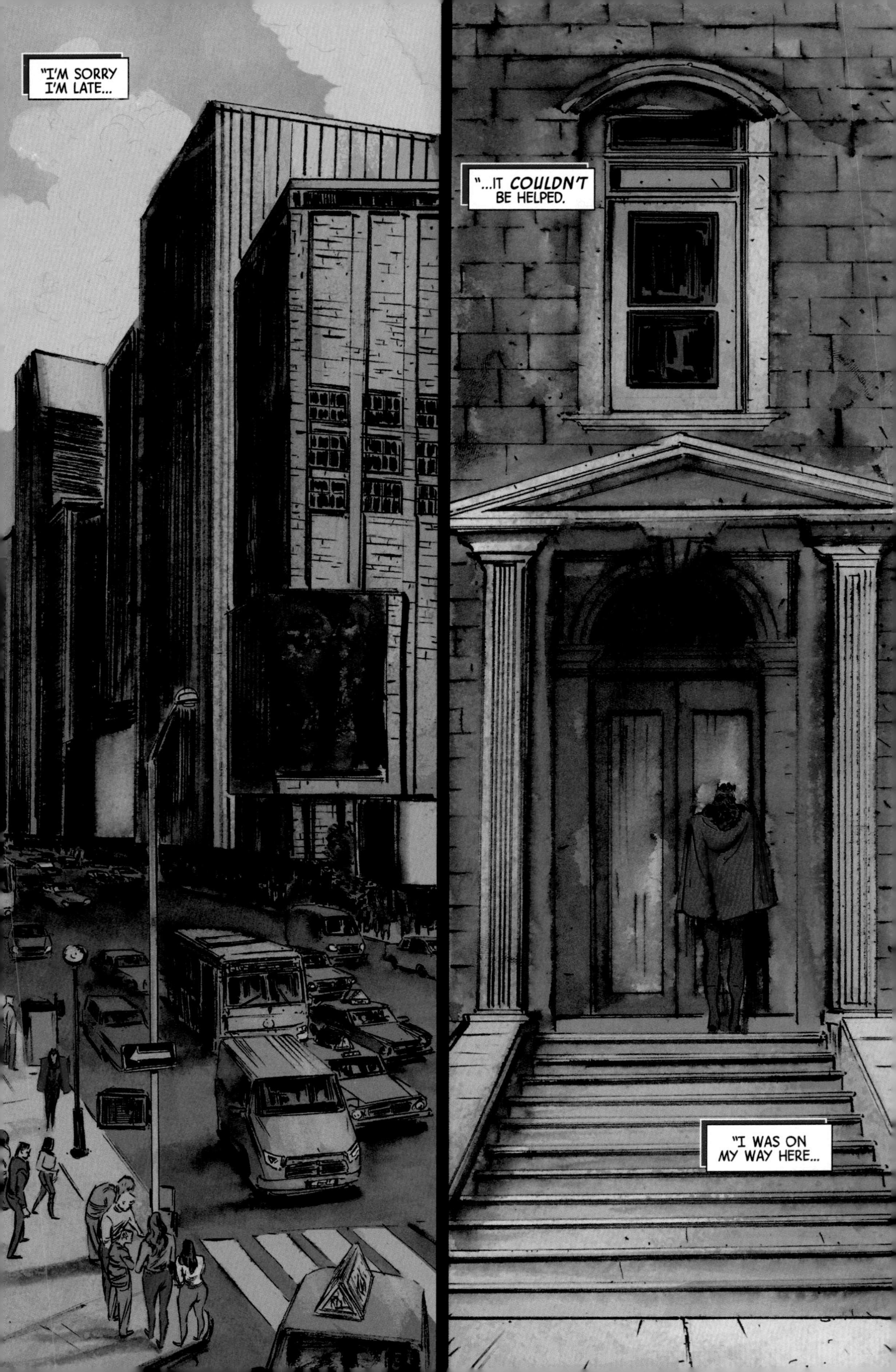
"I'M SORRY I'M LATE...
"...IT *COULDN'T* BE HELPED.
"I WAS ON MY WAY HERE...

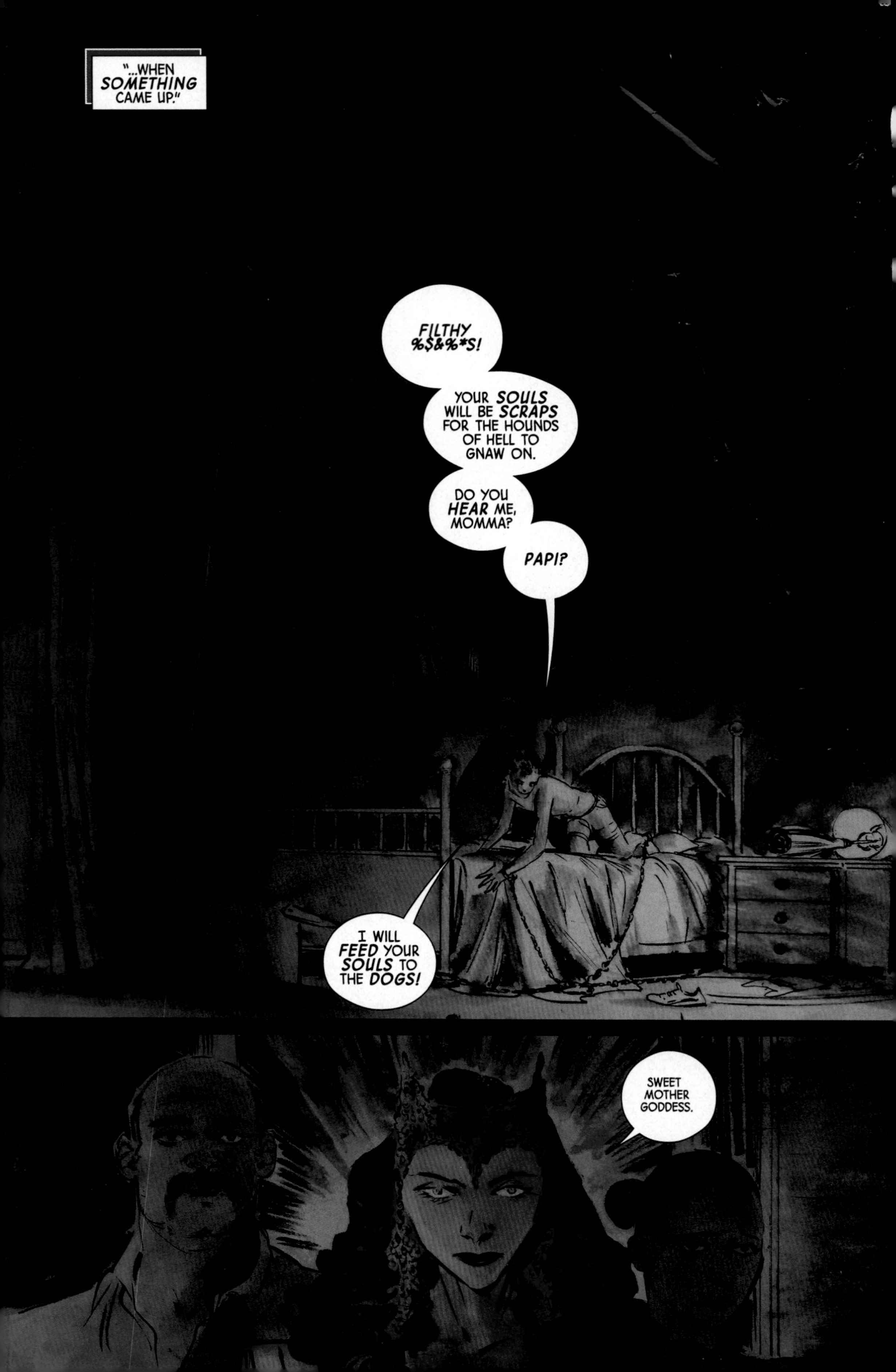
"...WHEN SOMETHING CAME UP."
FILTHY %$&%*S!
YOUR SOULS WILL BE SCRAPS FOR THE HOUNDS OF HELL TO GNAW ON.
DO YOU HEAR ME, MOMMA?
PAPI?
I WILL FEED YOUR SOULS TO THE DOGS!
SWEET MOTHER GODDESS.

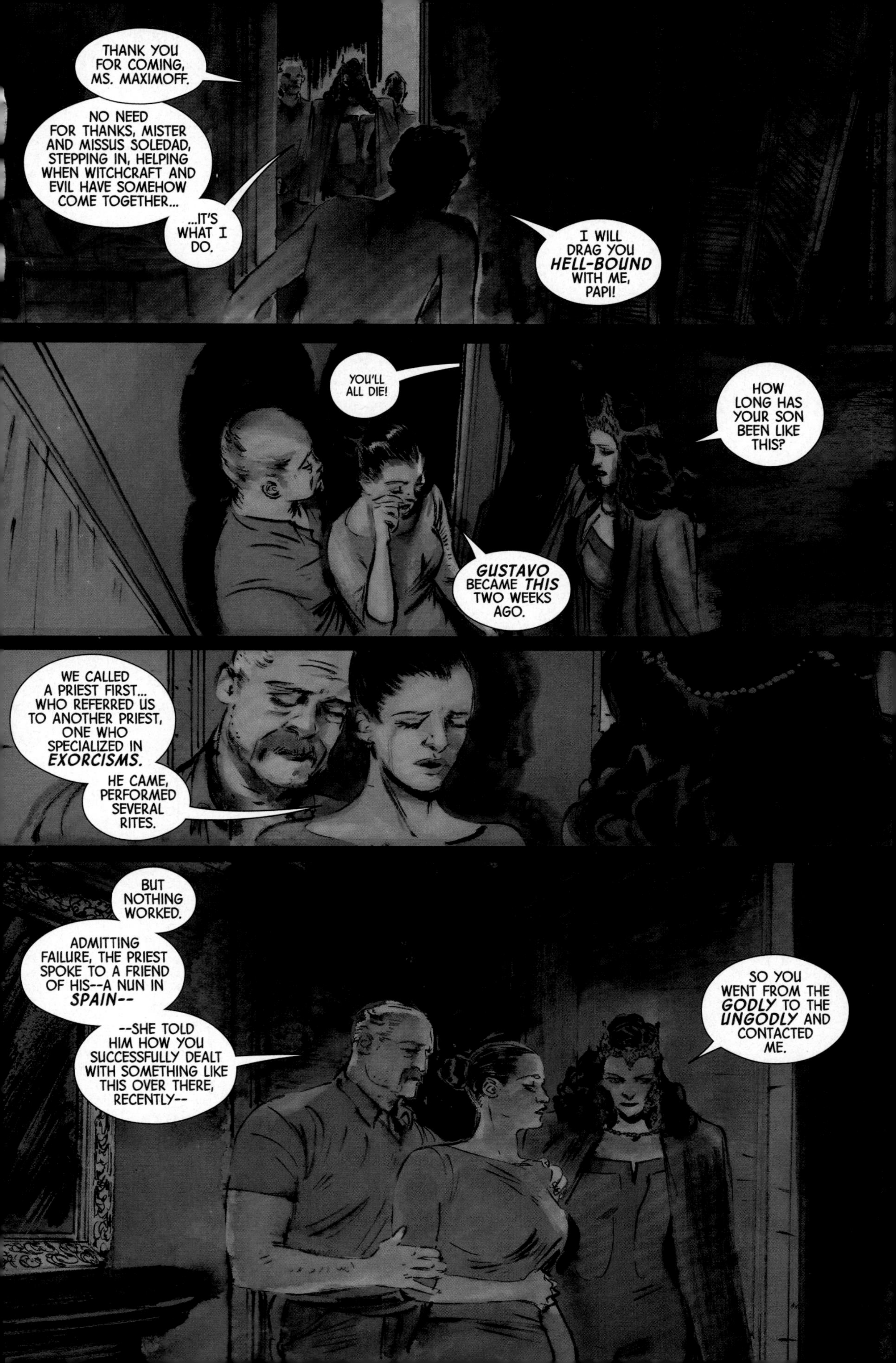

THANK YOU FOR COMING, MS. MAXIMOFF.
NO NEED FOR THANKS, MISTER AND MISSUS SOLEDAD, STEPPING IN, HELPING WHEN WITCHCRAFT AND EVIL HAVE SOMEHOW COME TOGETHER...
...IT'S WHAT I DO.
I WILL DRAG YOU ***HELL-BOUND*** WITH ME, PAPI!
YOU'LL ALL DIE!
HOW LONG HAS YOUR SON BEEN LIKE THIS?
GUSTAVO BECAME ***THIS*** TWO WEEKS AGO.
WE CALLED A PRIEST FIRST... WHO REFERRED US TO ANOTHER PRIEST, ONE WHO SPECIALIZED IN ***EXORCISMS.***
HE CAME, PERFORMED SEVERAL RITES.
BUT NOTHING WORKED.
ADMITTING FAILURE, THE PRIEST SPOKE TO A FRIEND OF HIS--A NUN IN ***SPAIN--***
--SHE TOLD HIM HOW YOU SUCCESSFULLY DEALT WITH SOMETHING LIKE THIS OVER THERE, RECENTLY--
SO YOU WENT FROM THE ***GODLY*** TO THE ***UNGODLY*** AND CONTACTED ME.

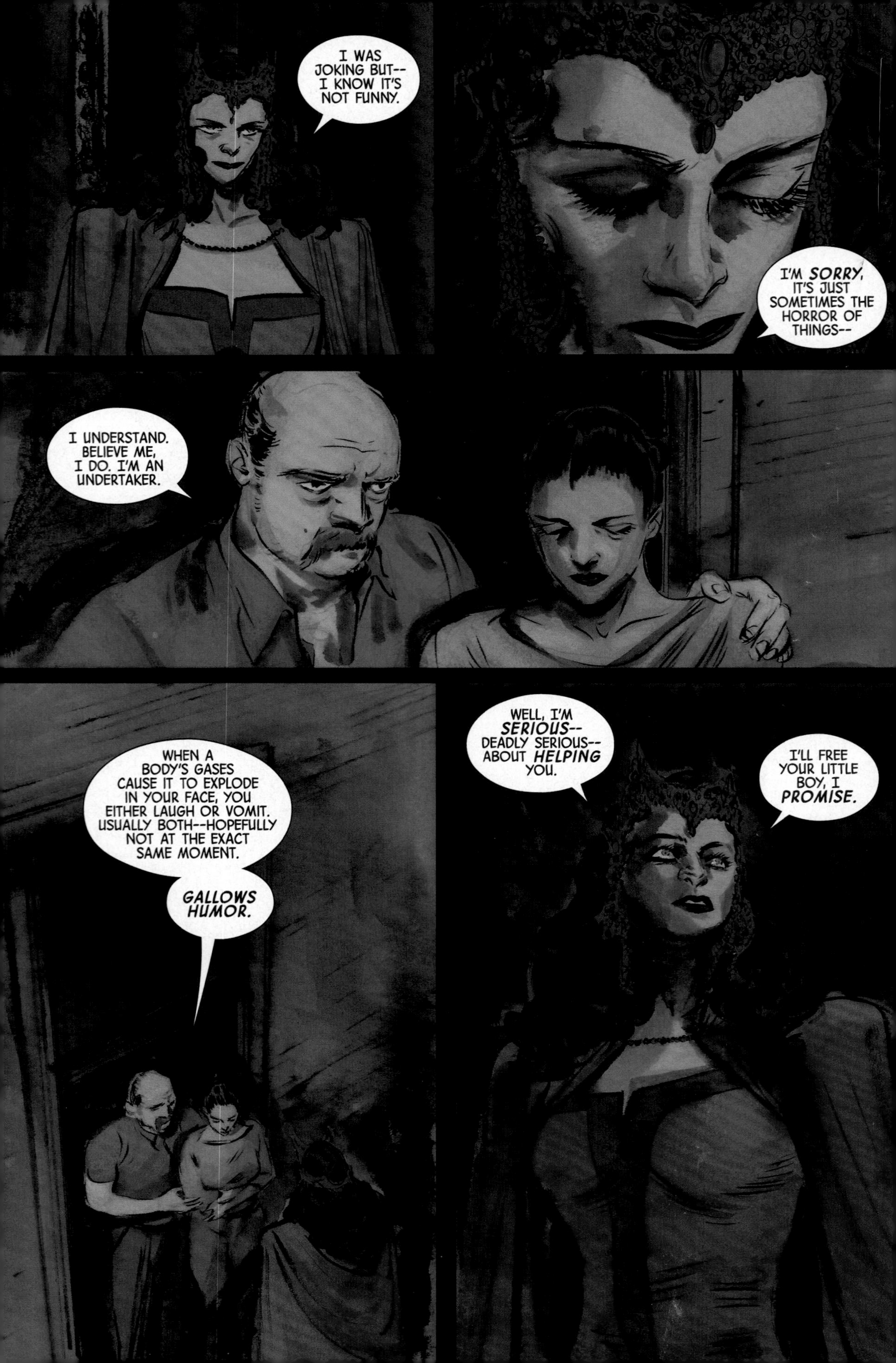
I WAS JOKING BUT-- I KNOW IT'S NOT FUNNY.
I'M *SORRY*, IT'S JUST SOMETIMES THE HORROR OF THINGS--
I UNDERSTAND. BELIEVE ME, I DO. I'M AN UNDERTAKER.
WHEN A BODY'S GASES CAUSE IT TO EXPLODE IN YOUR FACE, YOU EITHER LAUGH OR VOMIT. USUALLY BOTH--HOPEFULLY NOT AT THE EXACT SAME MOMENT.
GALLOWS HUMOR.
WELL, I'M *SERIOUS*-- DEADLY SERIOUS-- ABOUT *HELPING* YOU.
I'LL FREE YOUR LITTLE BOY, I *PROMISE.*

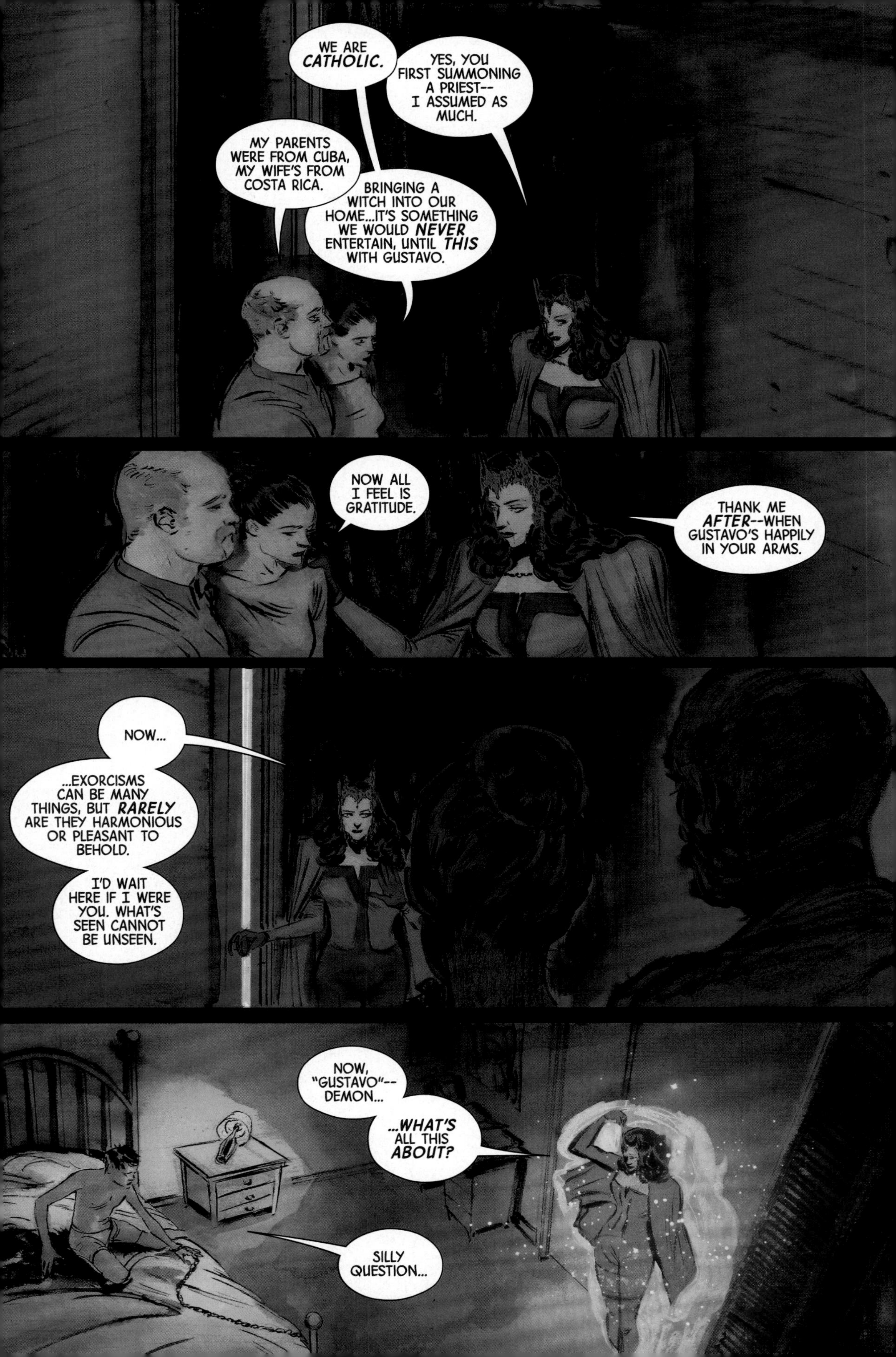
WE ARE CATHOLIC.
YES, YOU FIRST SUMMONING A PRIEST-- I ASSUMED AS MUCH.
MY PARENTS WERE FROM CUBA, MY WIFE'S FROM COSTA RICA.
BRINGING A WITCH INTO OUR HOME...IT'S SOMETHING WE WOULD NEVER ENTERTAIN, UNTIL THIS WITH GUSTAVO.
NOW ALL I FEEL IS GRATITUDE.
THANK ME AFTER--WHEN GUSTAVO'S HAPPILY IN YOUR ARMS.
NOW...
...EXORCISMS CAN BE MANY THINGS, BUT RARELY ARE THEY HARMONIOUS OR PLEASANT TO BEHOLD.
I'D WAIT HERE IF I WERE YOU. WHAT'S SEEN CANNOT BE UNSEEN.
NOW, "GUSTAVO"-- DEMON...
...WHAT'S ALL THIS ABOUT?
SILLY QUESTION...

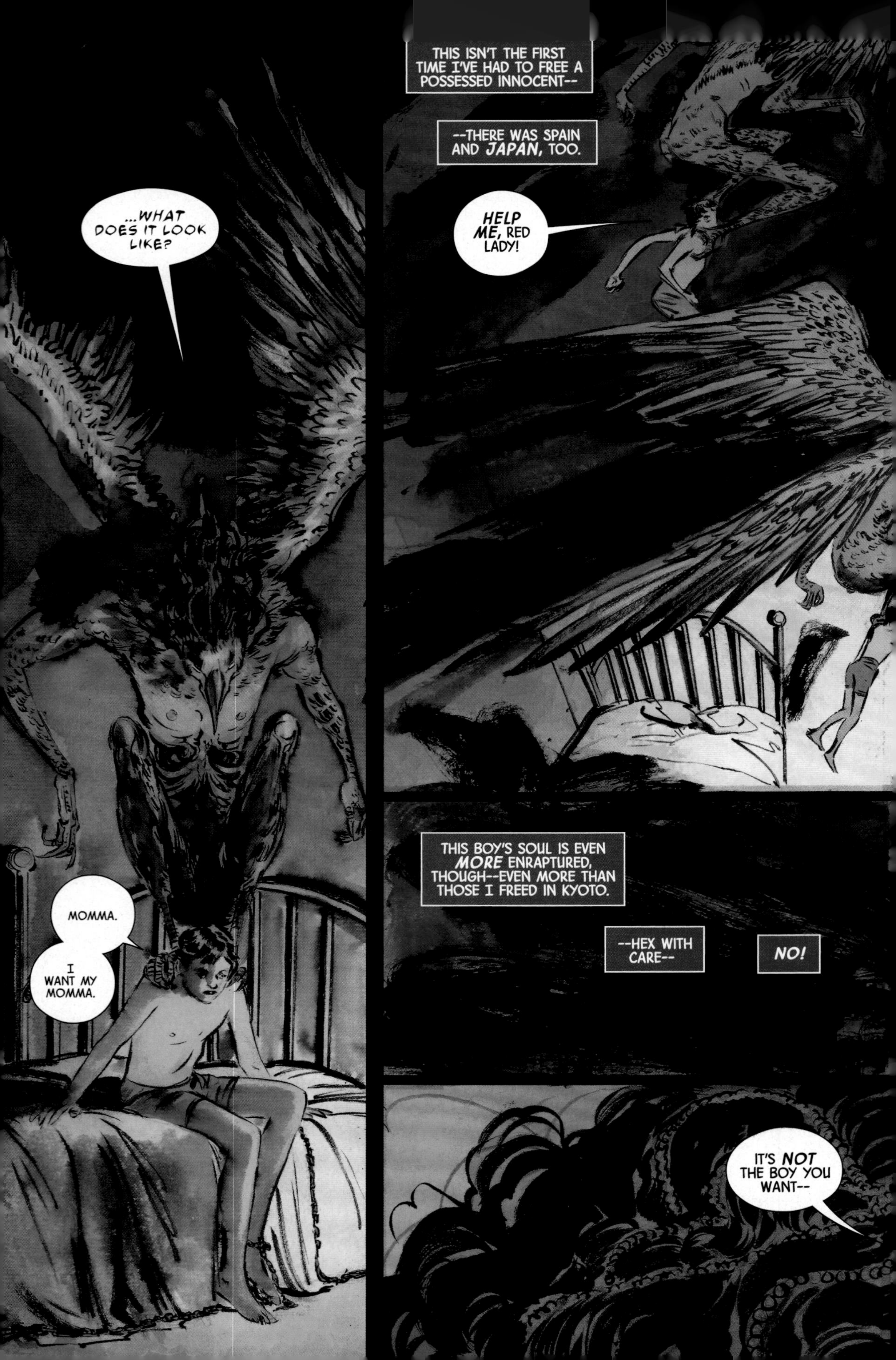
...WHAT DOES IT LOOK LIKE?
MOMMA.
I WANT MY MOMMA.
THIS ISN'T THE FIRST TIME I'VE HAD TO FREE A POSSESSED INNOCENT--
--THERE WAS SPAIN AND JAPAN, TOO.
HELP ME, RED LADY!
THIS BOY'S SOUL IS EVEN MORE ENRAPTURED, THOUGH--EVEN MORE THAN THOSE I FREED IN KYOTO.
--HEX WITH CARE--
NO!
IT'S NOT THE BOY YOU WANT--

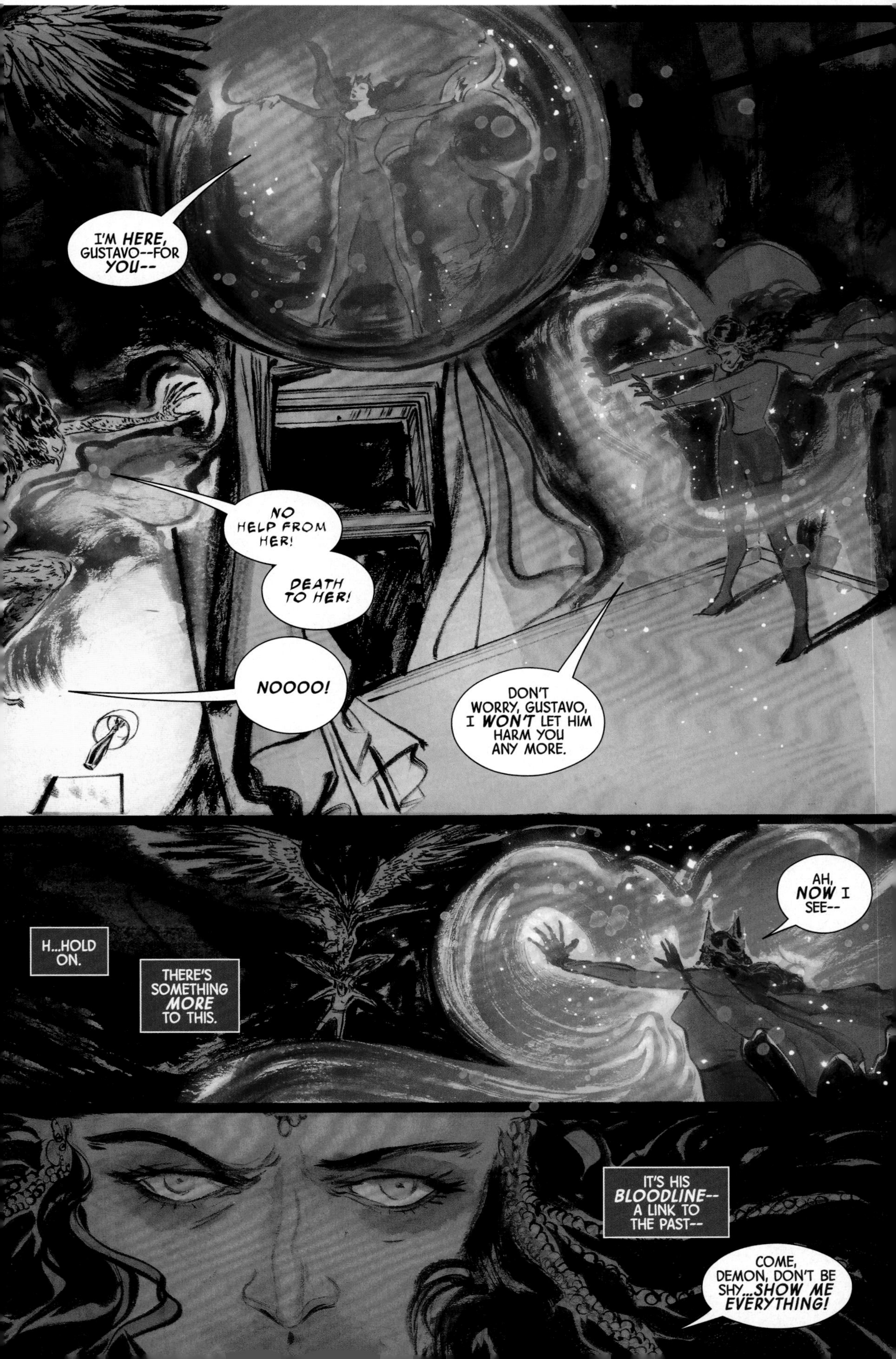

I'M *HERE*, GUSTAVO--FOR *YOU*--
NO HELP FROM HER!
DEATH TO HER!
NOOOO!
DON'T WORRY, GUSTAVO, I *WON'T* LET HIM HARM YOU ANY MORE.
H...HOLD ON.
THERE'S SOMETHING *MORE* TO THIS.
AH, *NOW* I SEE--
IT'S HIS *BLOODLINE*-- A LINK TO THE PAST--
COME, DEMON, DON'T BE SHY...*SHOW ME EVERYTHING!*

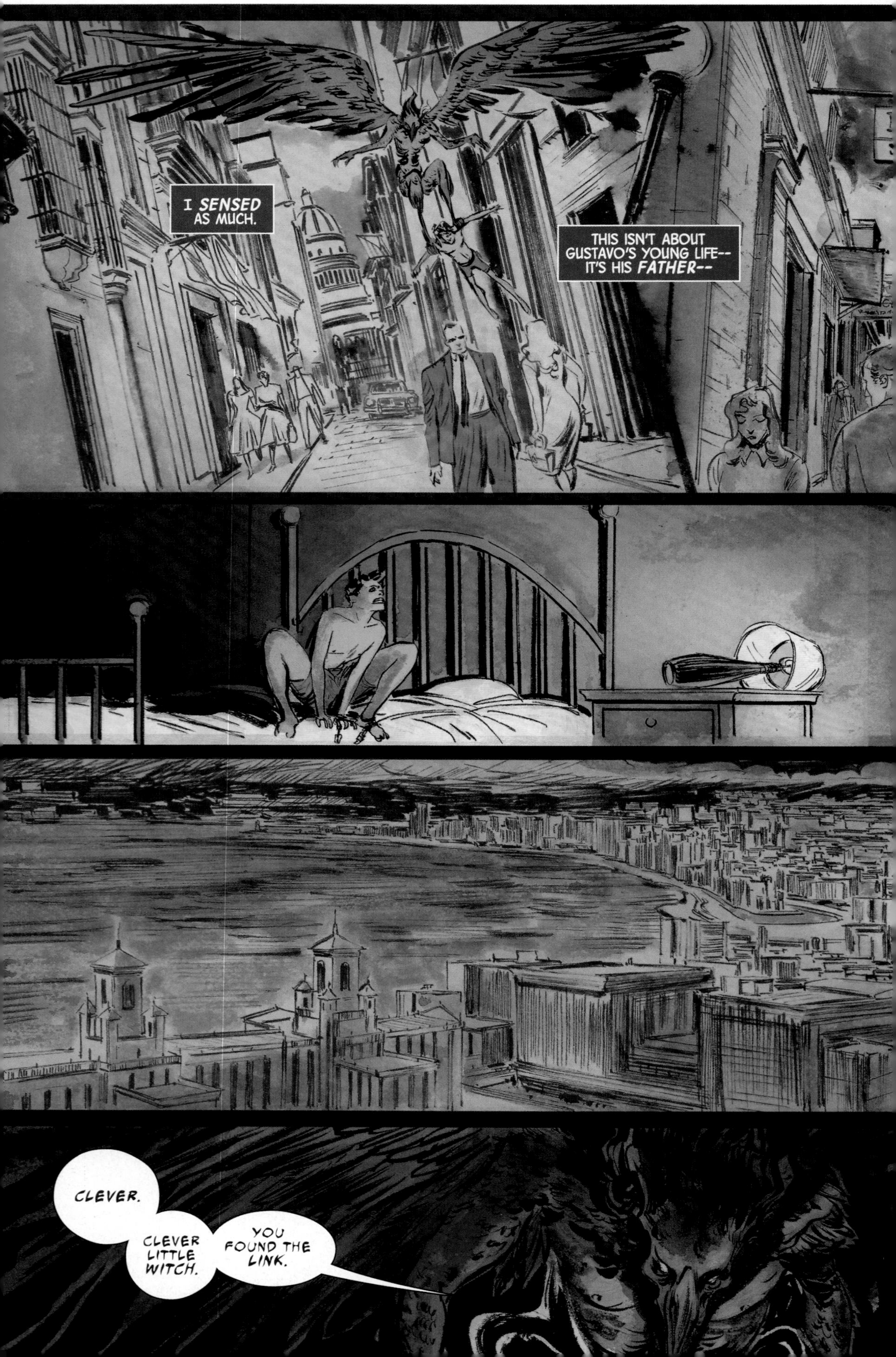
I SENSED AS MUCH.
THIS ISN'T ABOUT GUSTAVO'S YOUNG LIFE-- IT'S HIS FATHER--
CLEVER.
CLEVER LITTLE WITCH.
YOU FOUND THE LINK.

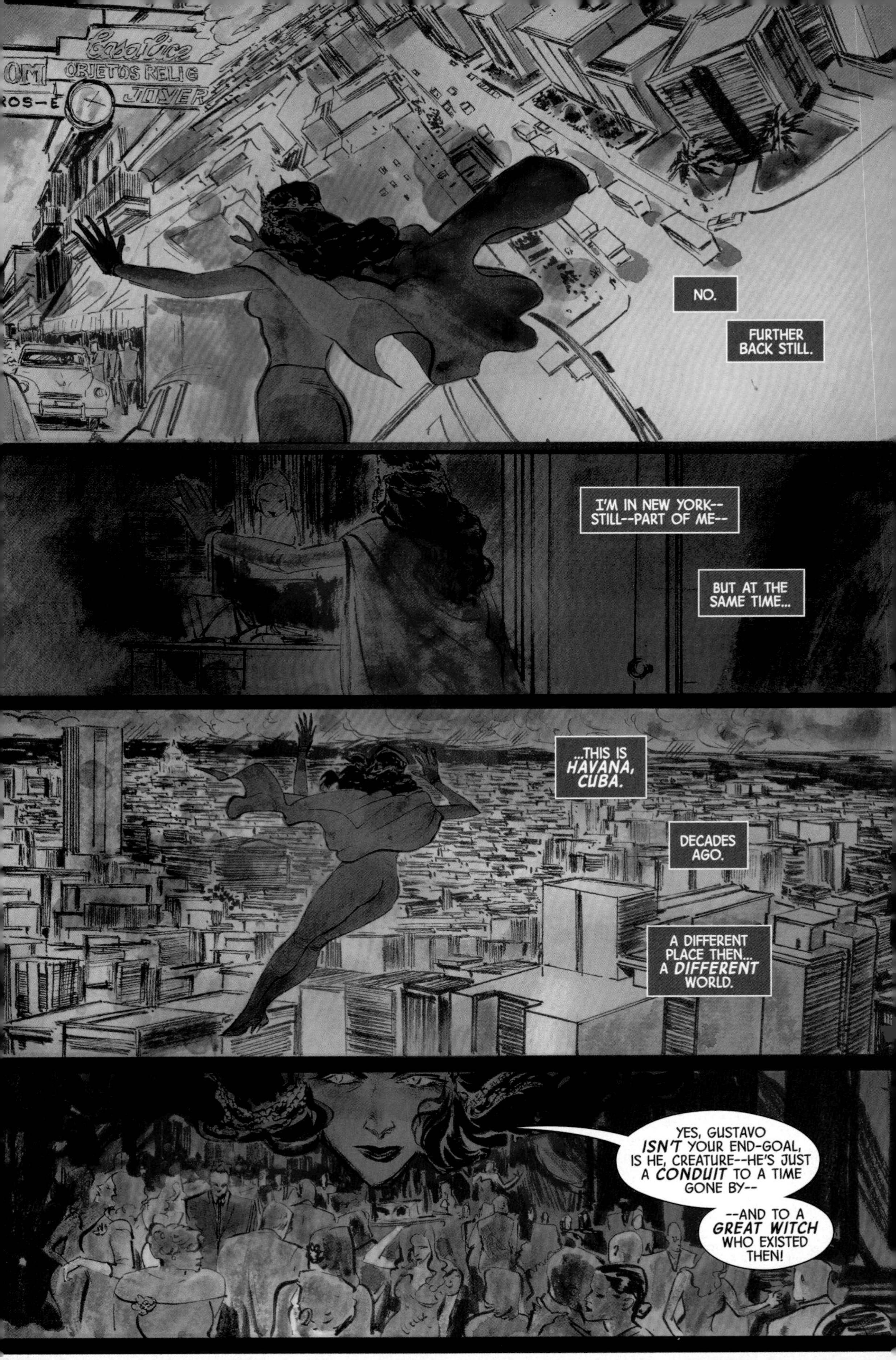
Casa Pice
OBJETOS RELIG
JOYER
NO.
FURTHER BACK STILL.
I'M IN NEW YORK--STILL--PART OF ME--
BUT AT THE SAME TIME...
...THIS IS HAVANA, CUBA.
DECADES AGO.
A DIFFERENT PLACE THEN... A DIFFERENT WORLD.
YES, GUSTAVO ISN'T YOUR END-GOAL, IS HE, CREATURE--HE'S JUST A CONDUIT TO A TIME GONE BY--
--AND TO A GREAT WITCH WHO EXISTED THEN!

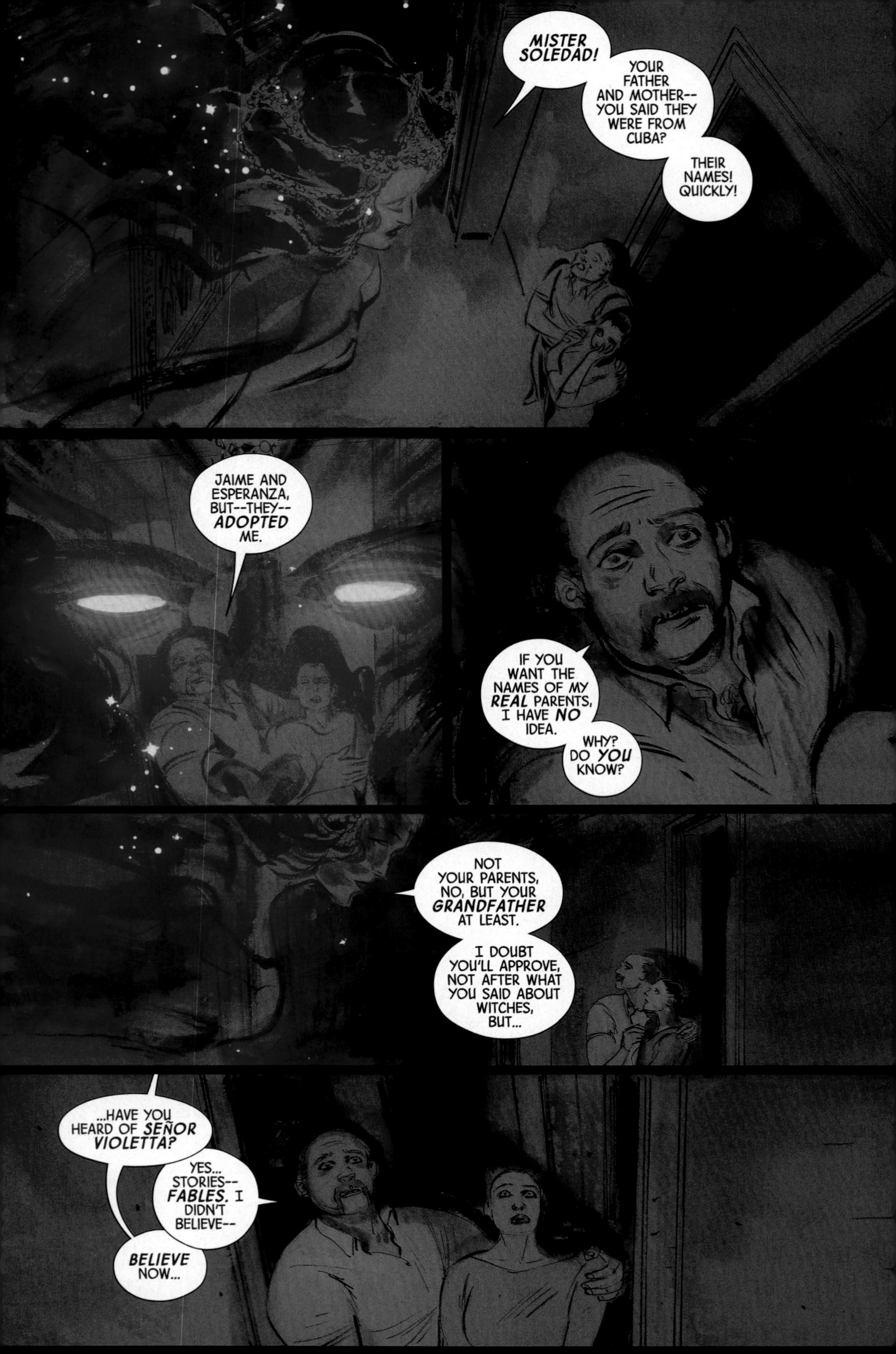
MISTER SOLEDAD!
YOUR FATHER AND MOTHER--YOU SAID THEY WERE FROM CUBA?
THEIR NAMES! QUICKLY!
JAIME AND ESPERANZA, BUT--THEY--ADOPTED ME.
IF YOU WANT THE NAMES OF MY REAL PARENTS, I HAVE NO IDEA.
WHY? DO YOU KNOW?
NOT YOUR PARENTS, NO, BUT YOUR GRANDFATHER AT LEAST.
I DOUBT YOU'LL APPROVE, NOT AFTER WHAT YOU SAID ABOUT WITCHES, BUT...
...HAVE YOU HEARD OF SEÑOR VIOLETTA?
YES... STORIES--FABLES. I DIDN'T BELIEVE--
BELIEVE NOW...

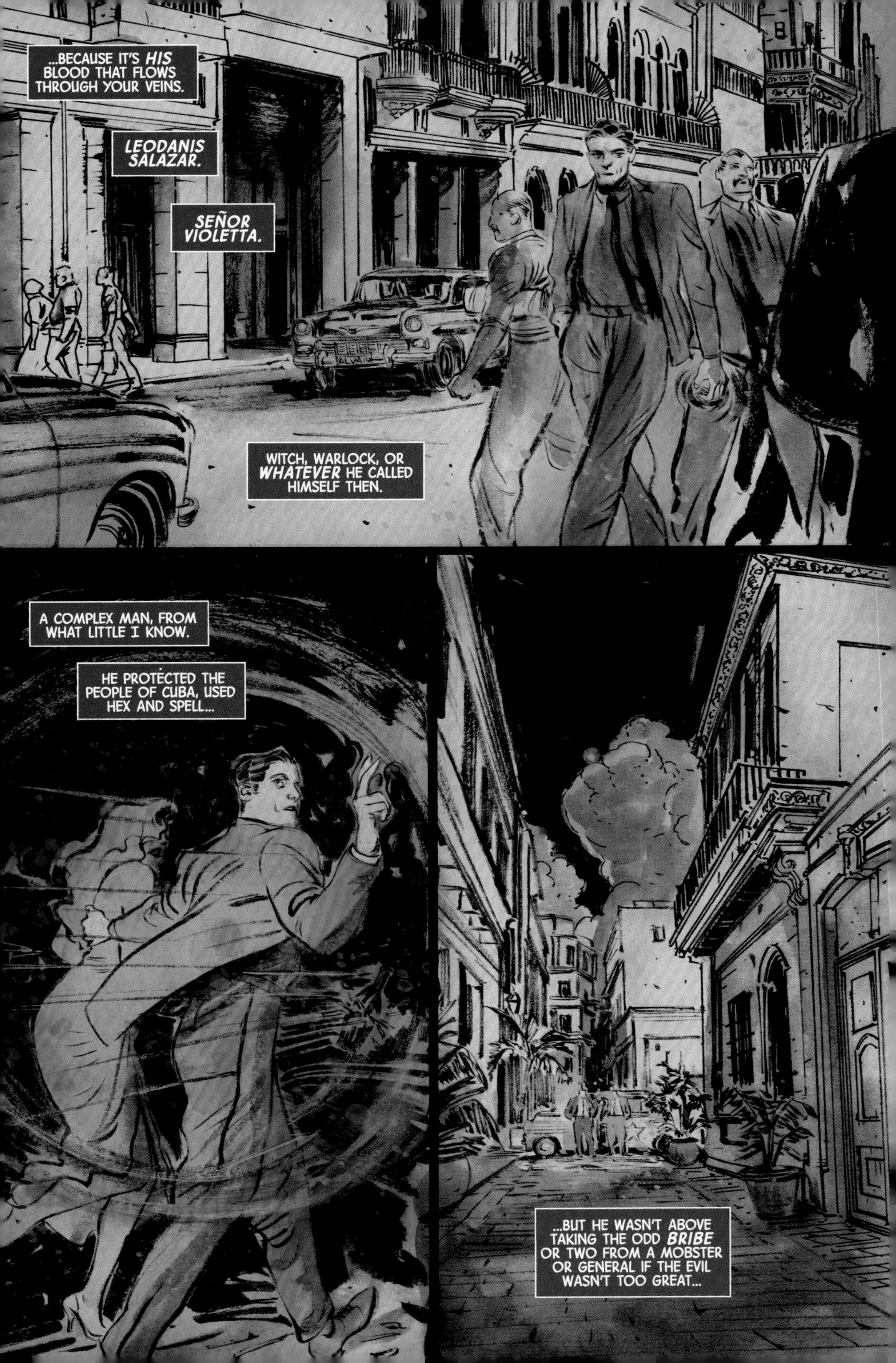
...BECAUSE IT'S HIS BLOOD THAT FLOWS THROUGH YOUR VEINS.
LEODANIS SALAZAR.
SEÑOR VIOLETTA.
WITCH, WARLOCK, OR WHATEVER HE CALLED HIMSELF THEN.
A COMPLEX MAN, FROM WHAT LITTLE I KNOW.
HE PROTECTED THE PEOPLE OF CUBA, USED HEX AND SPELL...
...BUT HE WASN'T ABOVE TAKING THE ODD BRIBE OR TWO FROM A MOBSTER OR GENERAL IF THE EVIL WASN'T TOO GREAT...

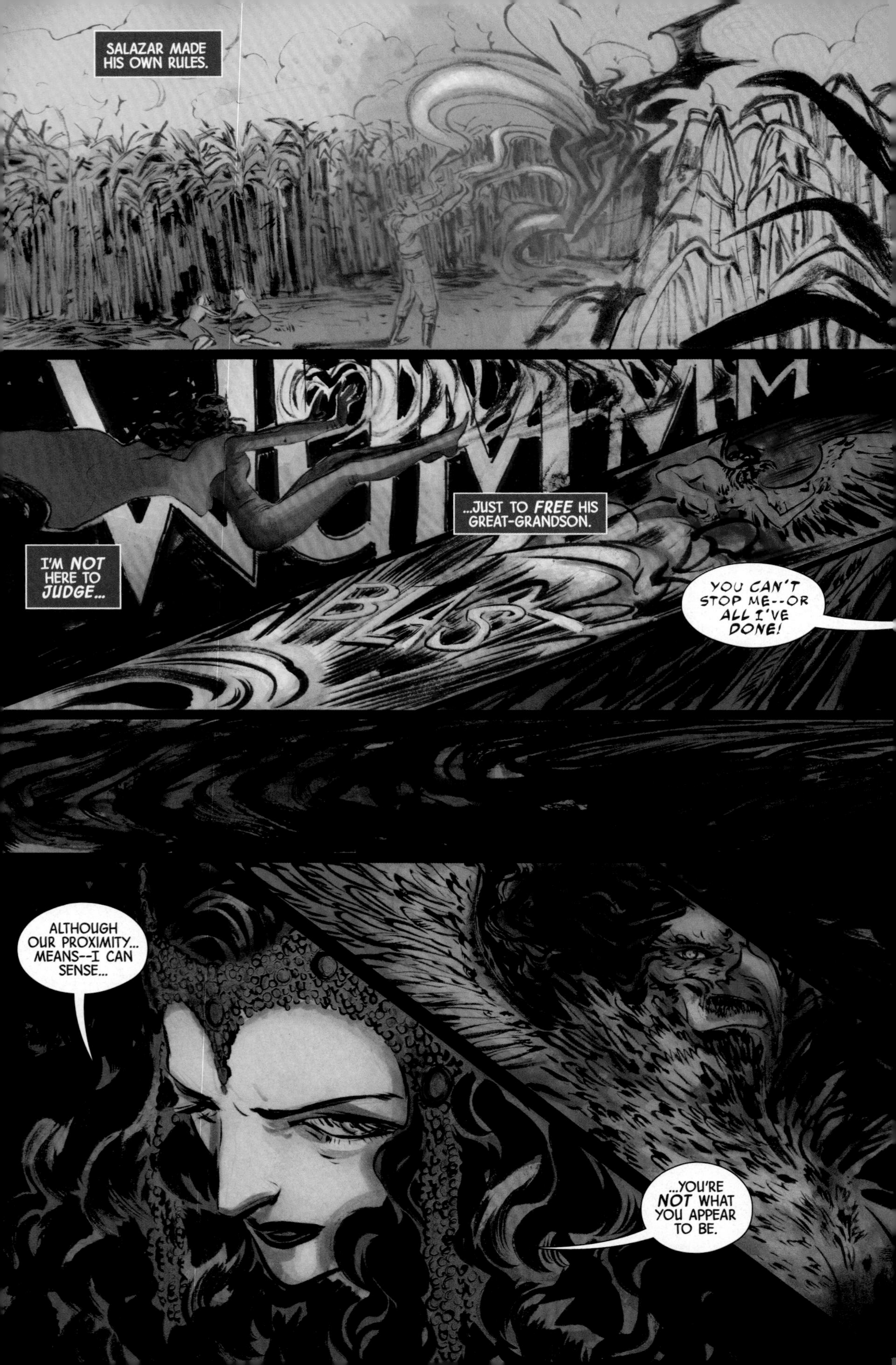
SALAZAR MADE HIS OWN RULES.
VRRRMMMM
I'M NOT HERE TO JUDGE...
...JUST TO FREE HIS GREAT-GRANDSON.
BLAST
YOU CAN'T STOP ME--OR ALL I'VE DONE!
ALTHOUGH OUR PROXIMITY... MEANS--I CAN SENSE...
...YOU'RE NOT WHAT YOU APPEAR TO BE.

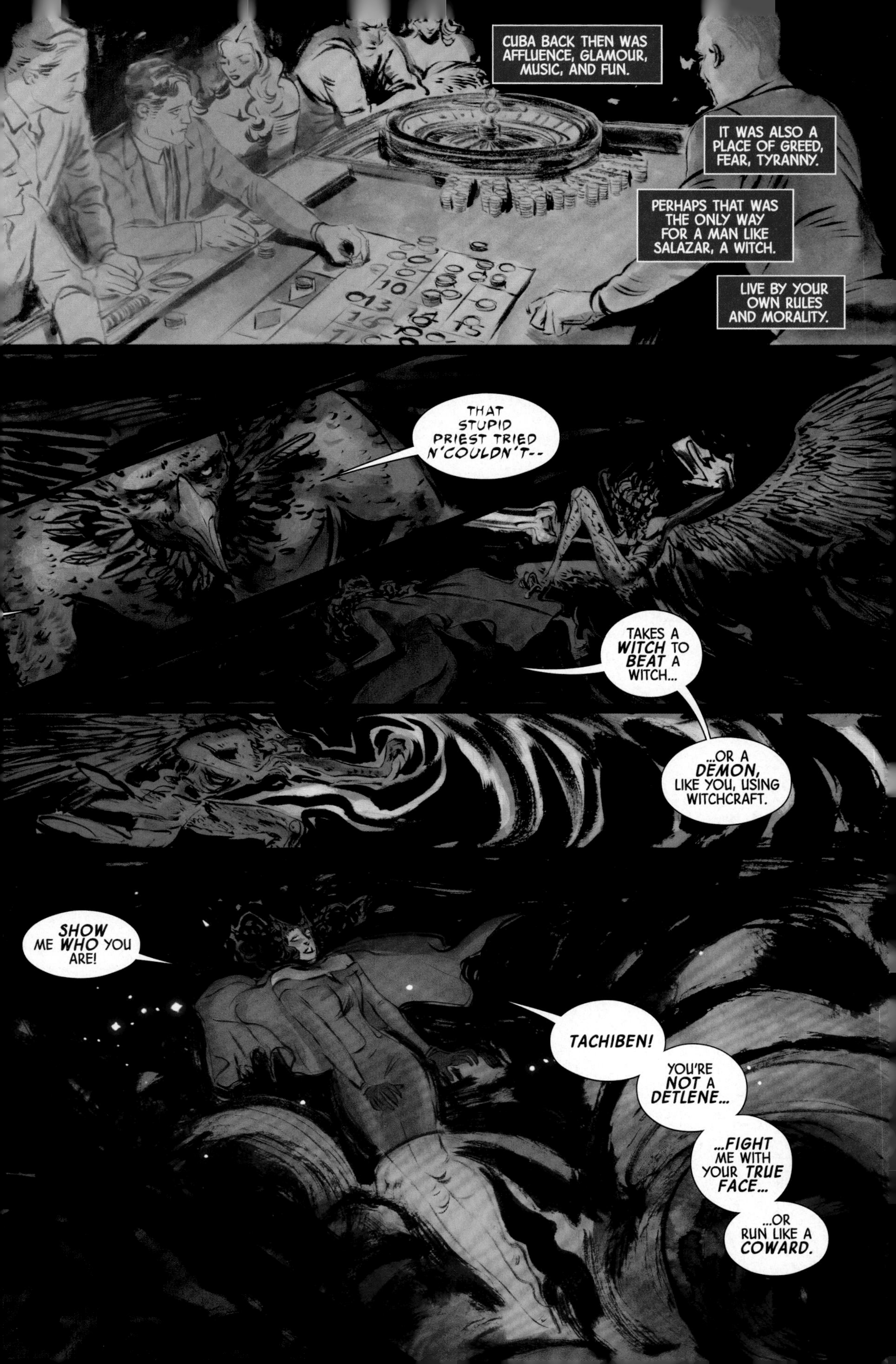
CUBA BACK THEN WAS AFFLUENCE, GLAMOUR, MUSIC, AND FUN.
IT WAS ALSO A PLACE OF GREED, FEAR, TYRANNY.
PERHAPS THAT WAS THE ONLY WAY FOR A MAN LIKE SALAZAR, A WITCH.
LIVE BY YOUR OWN RULES AND MORALITY.
THAT STUPID PRIEST TRIED N'COULDN'T--
TAKES A WITCH TO BEAT A WITCH...
...OR A DEMON, LIKE YOU, USING WITCHCRAFT.
SHOW ME WHO YOU ARE!
TACHIBEN!
YOU'RE NOT A DETLENE...
...FIGHT ME WITH YOUR TRUE FACE...
...OR RUN LIKE A COWARD.

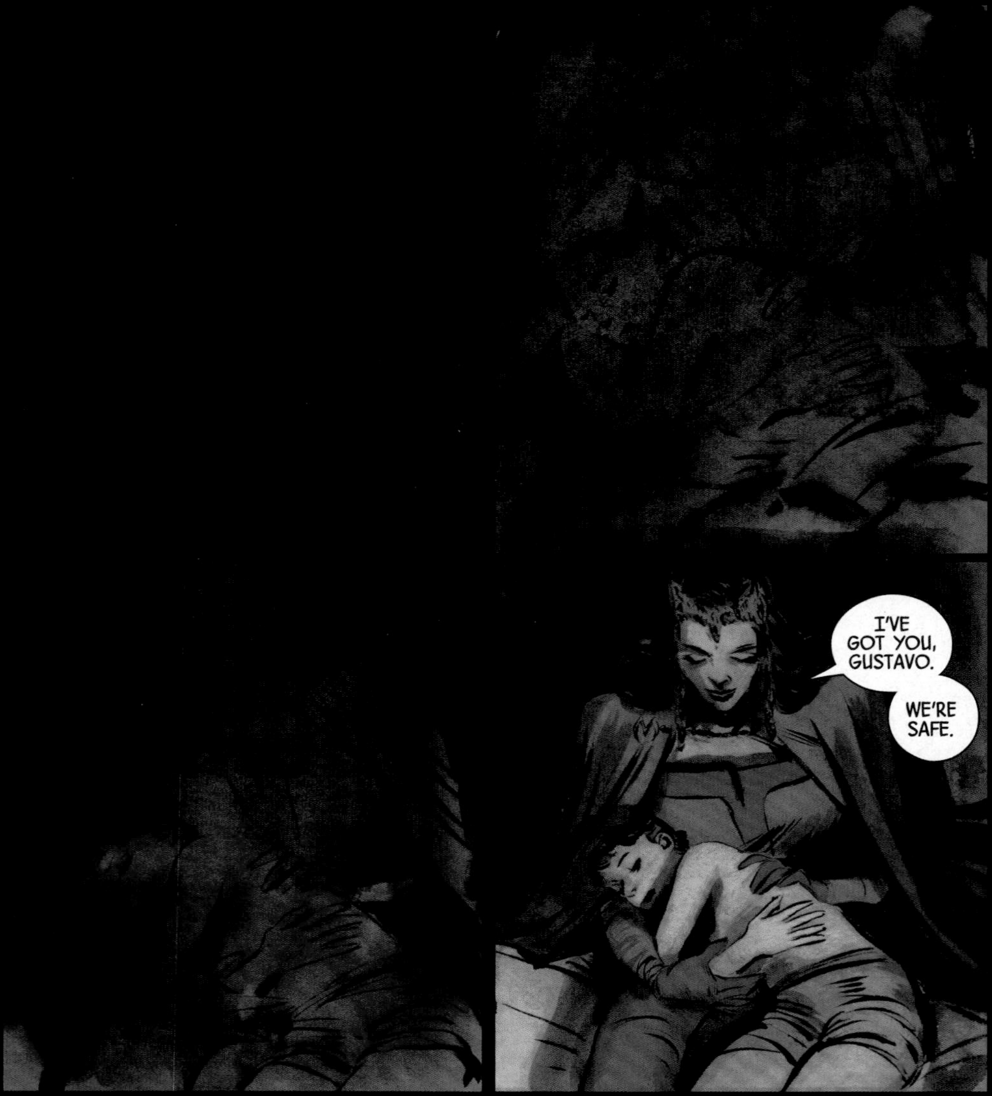
I'VE GOT YOU, GUSTAVO.
WE'RE SAFE.

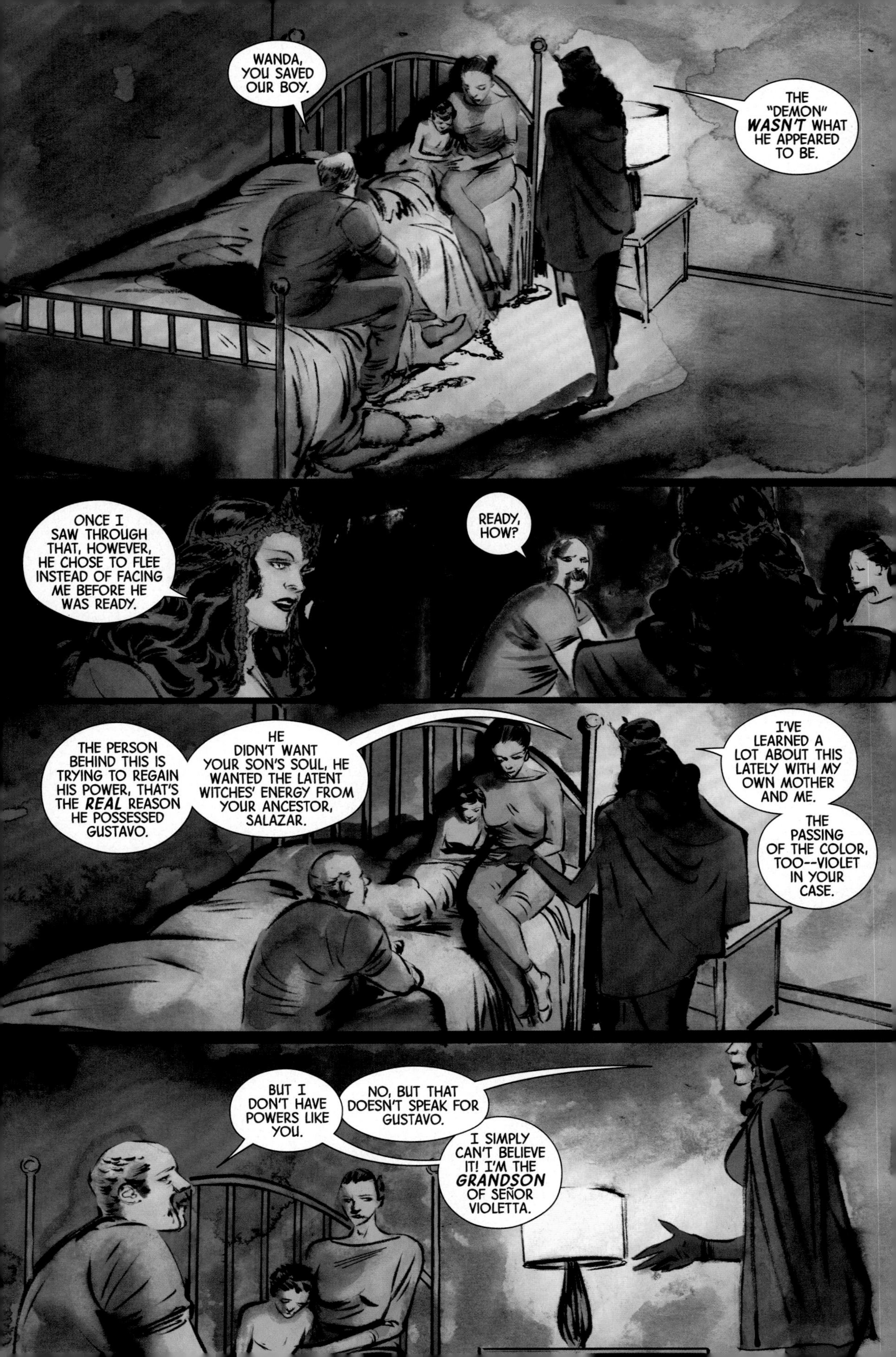
WANDA, YOU SAVED OUR BOY.
THE "DEMON" **WASN'T** WHAT HE APPEARED TO BE.
ONCE I SAW THROUGH THAT, HOWEVER, HE CHOSE TO FLEE INSTEAD OF FACING ME BEFORE HE WAS READY.
READY, HOW?
THE PERSON BEHIND THIS IS TRYING TO REGAIN HIS POWER, THAT'S THE **REAL** REASON HE POSSESSED GUSTAVO.
HE DIDN'T WANT YOUR SON'S SOUL, HE WANTED THE LATENT WITCHES' ENERGY FROM YOUR ANCESTOR, SALAZAR.
I'VE LEARNED A LOT ABOUT THIS LATELY WITH MY OWN MOTHER AND ME.
THE PASSING OF THE COLOR, TOO--VIOLET IN YOUR CASE.
BUT I DON'T HAVE POWERS LIKE YOU.
NO, BUT THAT DOESN'T SPEAK FOR GUSTAVO.
I SIMPLY CAN'T BELIEVE IT! I'M THE **GRANDSON** OF SEÑOR VIOLETTA.

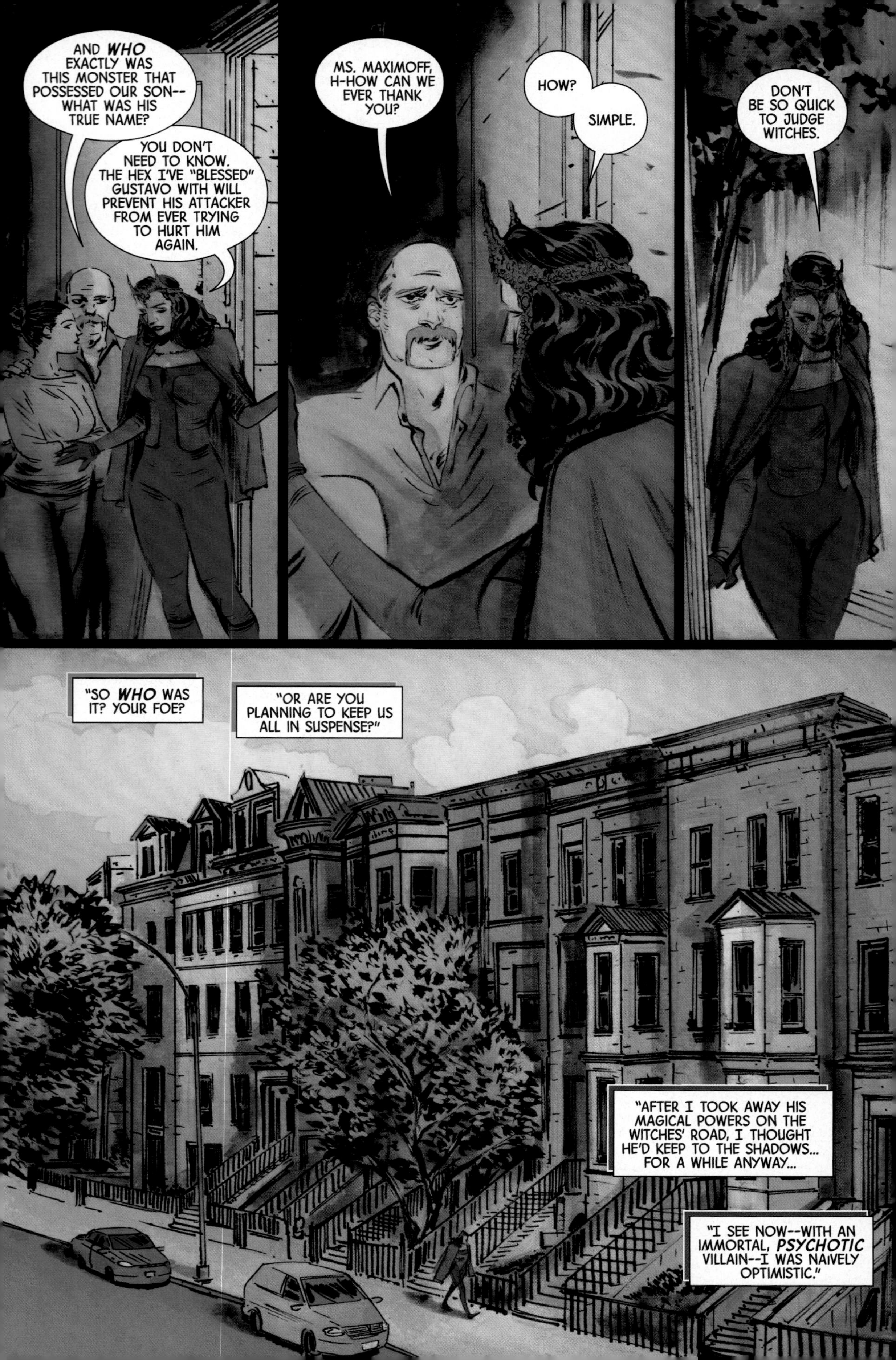
AND WHO EXACTLY WAS THIS MONSTER THAT POSSESSED OUR SON-- WHAT WAS HIS TRUE NAME?
YOU DON'T NEED TO KNOW. THE HEX I'VE "BLESSED" GUSTAVO WITH WILL PREVENT HIS ATTACKER FROM EVER TRYING TO HURT HIM AGAIN.
MS. MAXIMOFF, H-HOW CAN WE EVER THANK YOU?
HOW?
SIMPLE.
DON'T BE SO QUICK TO JUDGE WITCHES.
"SO WHO WAS IT? YOUR FOE?
"OR ARE YOU PLANNING TO KEEP US ALL IN SUSPENSE?"
"AFTER I TOOK AWAY HIS MAGICAL POWERS ON THE WITCHES' ROAD, I THOUGHT HE'D KEEP TO THE SHADOWS... FOR A WHILE ANYWAY...
"I SEE NOW--WITH AN IMMORTAL, PSYCHOTIC VILLAIN--I WAS NAIVELY OPTIMISTIC."

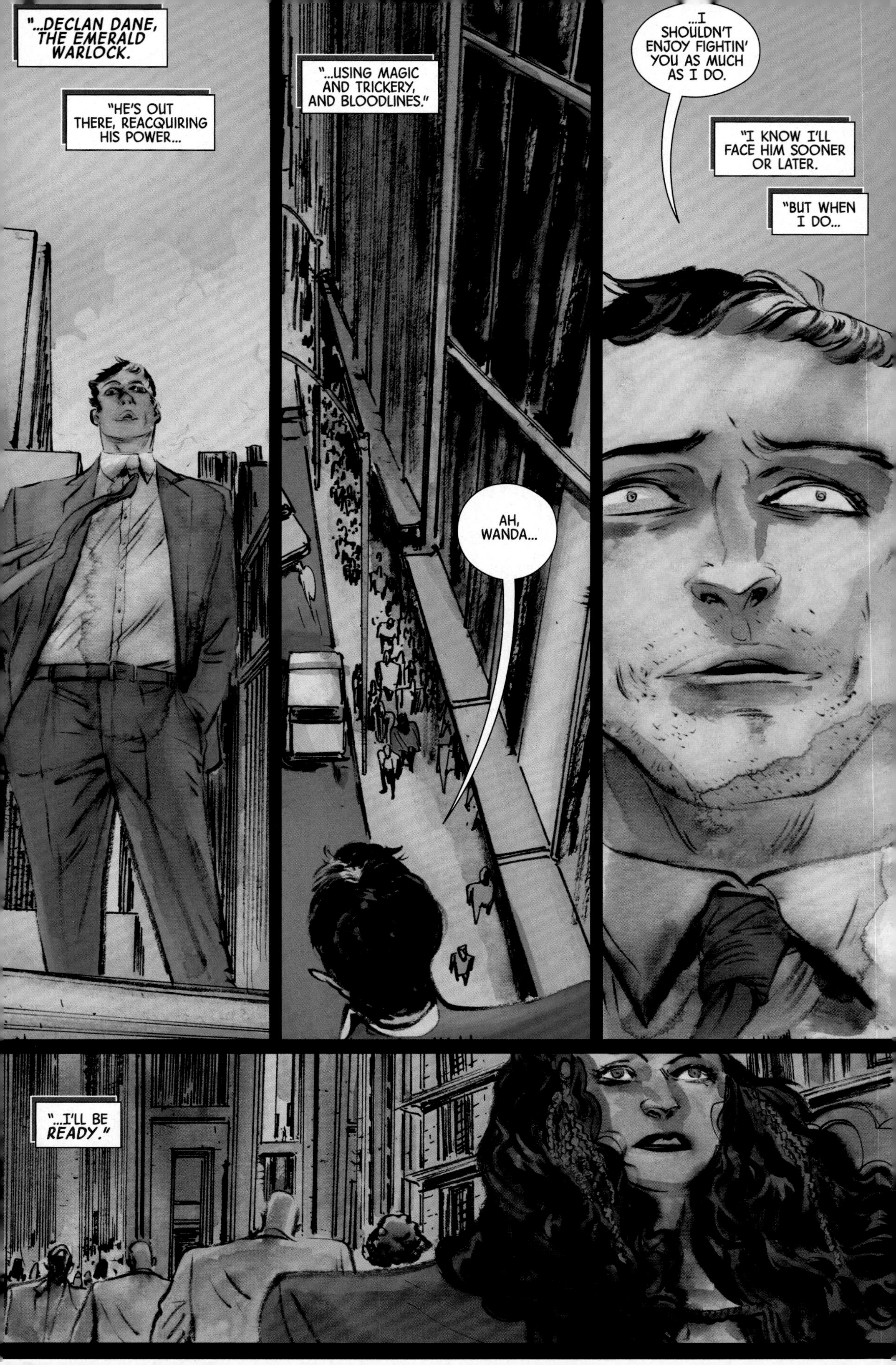
"...DECLAN DANE, THE EMERALD WARLOCK.
"HE'S OUT THERE, REACQUIRING HIS POWER...
"...USING MAGIC AND TRICKERY, AND BLOODLINES."
AH, WANDA...
...I SHOULDN'T ENJOY FIGHTIN' YOU AS MUCH AS I DO.
"I KNOW I'LL FACE HIM SOONER OR LATER.
"BUT WHEN I DO...
"...I'LL BE READY."

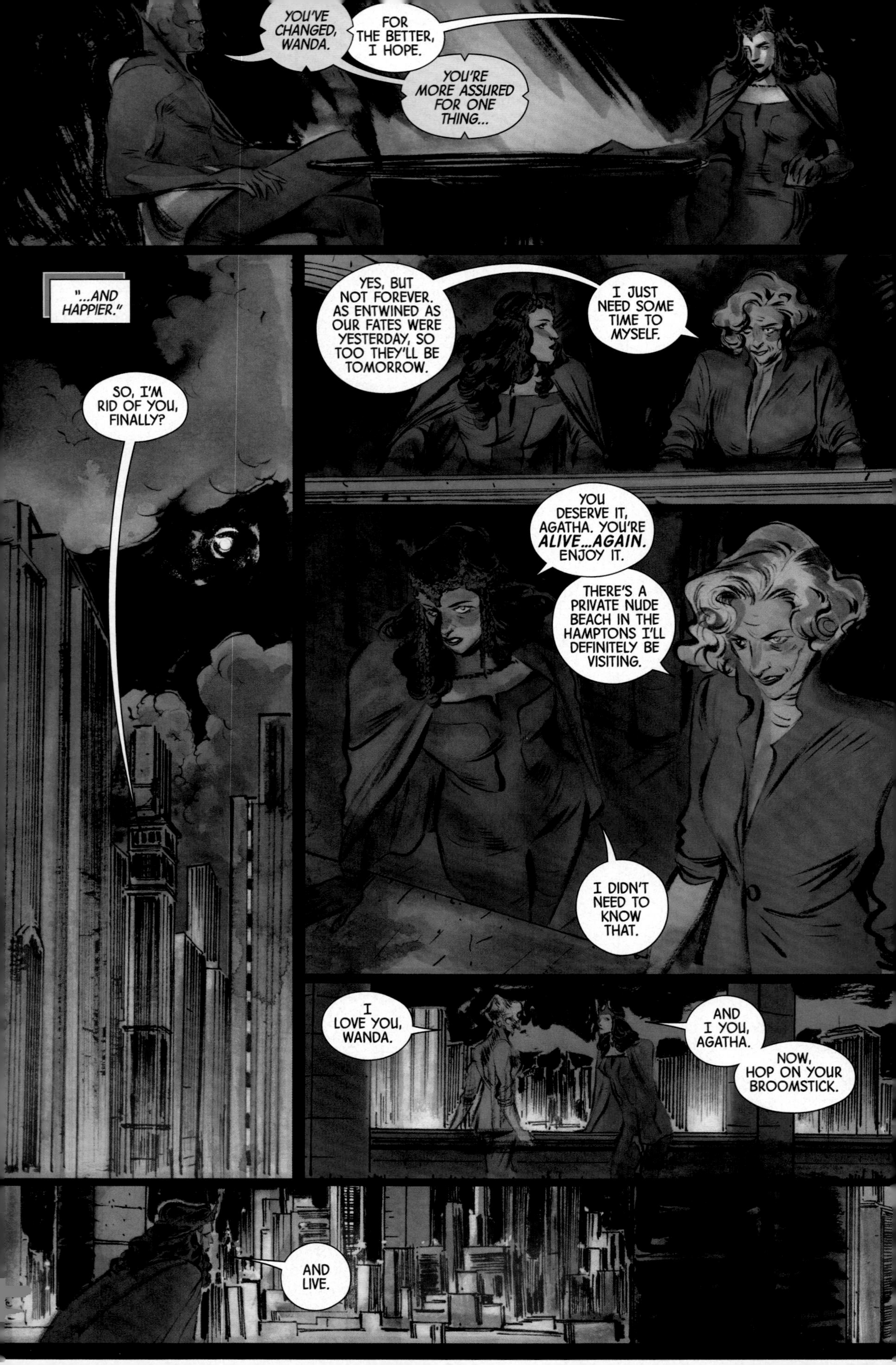
YOU'VE CHANGED, WANDA.
FOR THE BETTER, I HOPE.
YOU'RE MORE ASSURED FOR ONE THING...
"...AND HAPPIER."
SO, I'M RID OF YOU, FINALLY?
YES, BUT NOT FOREVER. AS ENTWINED AS OUR FATES WERE YESTERDAY, SO TOO THEY'LL BE TOMORROW.
I JUST NEED SOME TIME TO MYSELF.
YOU DESERVE IT, AGATHA. YOU'RE *ALIVE...AGAIN.* ENJOY IT.
THERE'S A PRIVATE NUDE BEACH IN THE HAMPTONS I'LL DEFINITELY BE VISITING.
I DIDN'T NEED TO KNOW THAT.
I LOVE YOU, WANDA.
AND I YOU, AGATHA.
NOW, HOP ON YOUR BROOMSTICK.
AND LIVE.

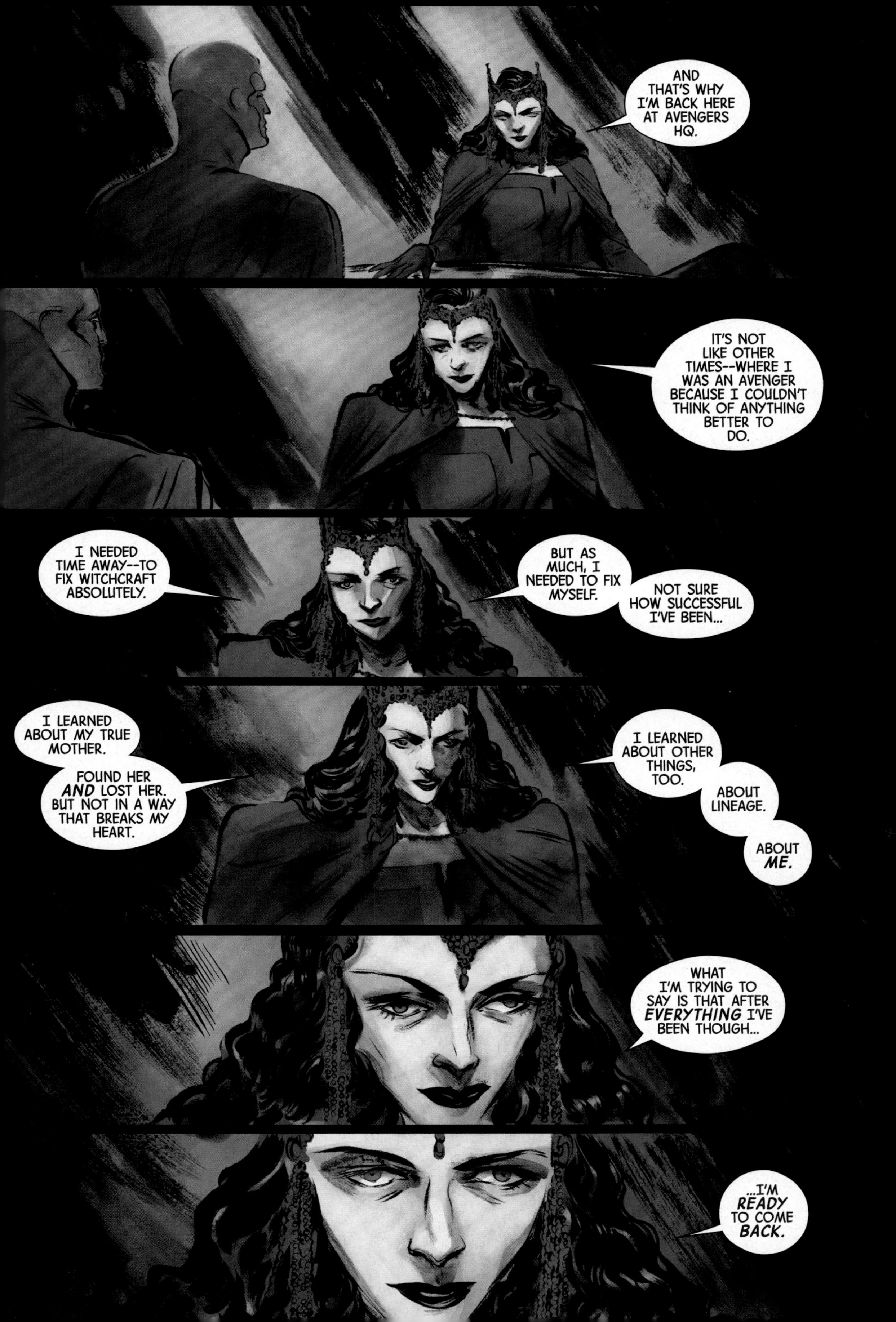
AND THAT'S WHY I'M BACK HERE AT AVENGERS HQ.
IT'S NOT LIKE OTHER TIMES--WHERE I WAS AN AVENGER BECAUSE I COULDN'T THINK OF ANYTHING BETTER TO DO.
I NEEDED TIME AWAY--TO FIX WITCHCRAFT ABSOLUTELY.
BUT AS MUCH, I NEEDED TO FIX MYSELF.
NOT SURE HOW SUCCESSFUL I'VE BEEN...
I LEARNED ABOUT MY TRUE MOTHER.
FOUND HER AND LOST HER. BUT NOT IN A WAY THAT BREAKS MY HEART.
I LEARNED ABOUT OTHER THINGS, TOO.
ABOUT LINEAGE.
ABOUT ME.
WHAT I'M TRYING TO SAY IS THAT AFTER EVERYTHING I'VE BEEN THOUGH...
...I'M READY TO COME BACK.

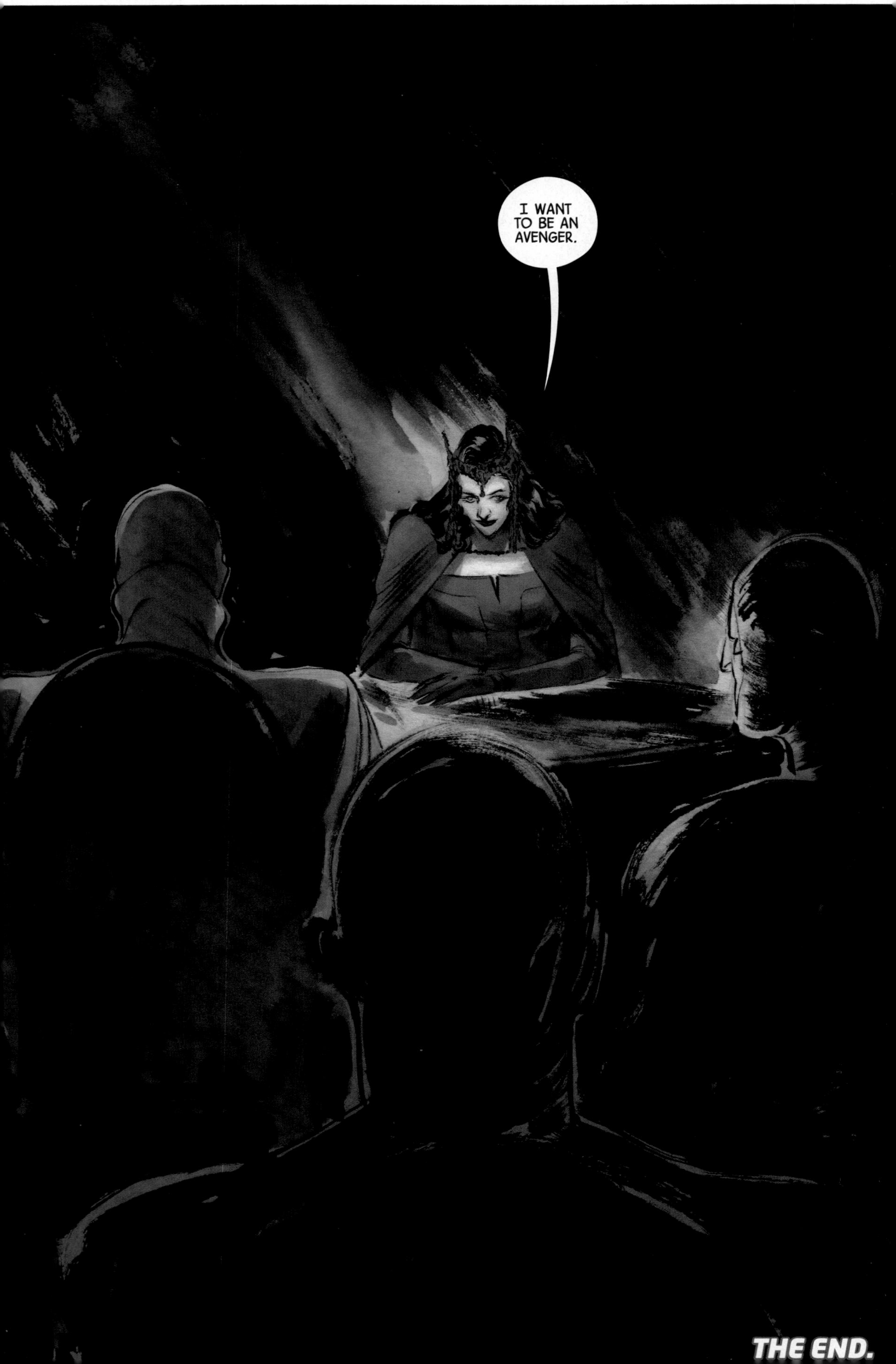
I WANT TO BE AN AVENGER.
THE END.

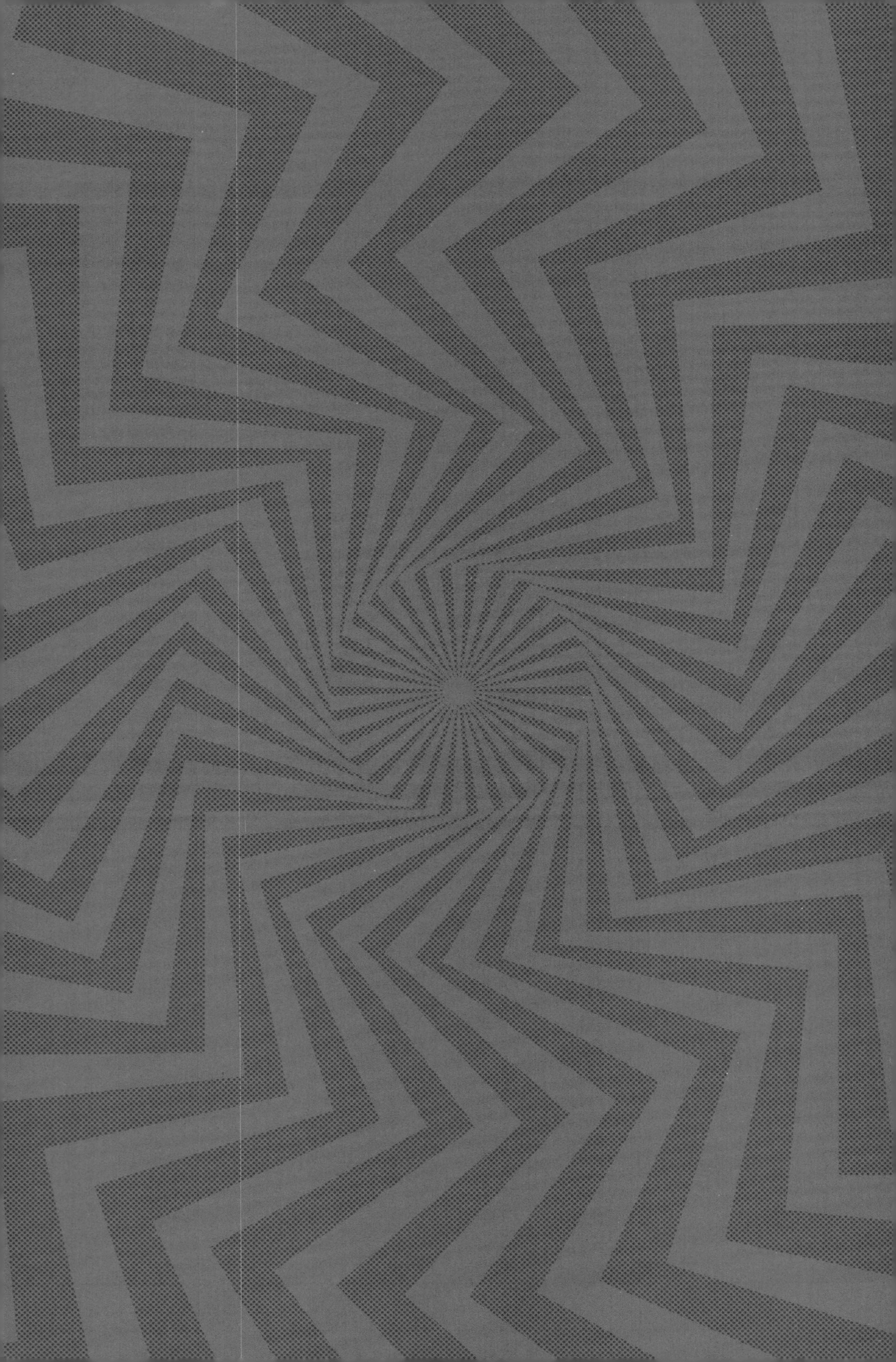